EVERYTHING DOGS EXPECT YOU TO KNOW

EVERYTHING DOGS EXPECT YOU TO KNOW

Karen Bush

NH
NEW
HOLLAND

For Ashley – and, of course, Archie and Angel.

With thanks to Sarah Fisher and Julie Webb,
also to Sarah Wright at *Your Dog* magazine.

This edition first published in 2007 by New Holland
Publishers (UK) Ltd
London • Cape Town • Sydney • Auckland
www.newhollandpublishers.com

Garfield House, 86–88 Edgware Road, London, W2 2EA,
United Kingdom
80 McKenzie Street, Cape Town, 8001, South Africa
Unit 1, 66 Gibbes Street, Chatswood, NSW 2067,
Australia
218 Lake Road, Northcote, Auckland, New Zealand

ISBN 978 1 84537 954 4

Although the publishers have made every effort to ensure
that information contained in this book was meticulously
researched and correct at the time of going to press, they
accept no responsibility for any inaccuracies, loss, injury
or inconvenience sustained by any person using this book
as reference.

Senior Editors: Naomi Waters, Emma Pattison
Cover design: Zoe Mellors
Designer: Zoe Mellors
Production: Hema Gohil, Tammy Knowles

Artworks reproduced with permission from Dover
Publications, Inc., except for pages 6, 24, 56, 76, 91,
115, 122, 128, 169, 180, 182, 192, 197, 205, 249
Copyright © New Holland Publishers (UK) Ltd/Coral Mula

Cover reproduction by Pica Digital PTE Ltd, Singapore
Inside reproduction by New Holland Publishers (UK) Ltd
Printed and bound in India by Replika Press Pvt. Ltd

2 4 6 8 10 9 7 5 3 1

CONTENTS

INTRODUCTION
6

EVERYTHING DOGS EXPECT YOU
TO KNOW
8

INDEX
250

INTRODUCTION

Since joining their destiny to ours, dogs have played a huge part in our lives; without them it's likely that we would have been considerably less successful in our early days – and even now they continue to do many jobs and duties we either can't or won't do ourselves, as well as remaining our steadfast and uncomplaining companions through thick and thin.

There is evidence to suggest that the majority of modern dogs evolved from a mere handful of wolves living in or near China around 15000 years ago, with around 95% of all current dogs descending from just three founding families.

Modern canines are the end product of many thousands of years of selective breeding practices by mankind, but even though their survival no longer depends on them, they nevertheless still retain many behaviours from their wild wolf ancestors. Some of these behaviours we have modified and in some cases even exaggerated to suit our own purposes, enabling the dog to be better able to fulfil a number of valuable working functions as well as to be a sociable and affectionate companion.

The early Romans believed that worms living in dogs' tails caused rabies, and that docking would therefore prevent the disease. Later on, the practice continued as a way of saving money; in some areas dogs which were used for work were not taxed, and docking was a way of indicating that the animal was used for work.

A common feature in many ancient Roman houses was a mosaic located at the threshold of a dog, often accompanied by the words "Cave canem" – beware of the dog. Whether it is the equivalent of our modern day signs warning of danger, or merely an admonition to step carefully so as to avoid injuring small pet dogs is not, however, clear.

I've tried to include a little of everything here to reflect our long and changing partnership over the millennia, ranging from the practical and informative to the trivial and amusing. Inevitably I've had to cherry pick as there is easily enough material to fill a dozen books a dozen times over; hopefully you will enjoy reading what is ultimately a subjective selection as much as I've enjoyed putting it together.

✦ GREYHOUND BIBLE ✦

The greyhound is the only breed of dog mentioned by name in the Bible, appearing in Proverbs 30: 29 –31 (King James version):

'There be three things which go well,
yea, four are comely in going:
a lion, which is strongest among beasts,
and turneth not away for any;
a greyhound; a he-goat also;
and a king, against whom there is no rising up.'

✦ WORTH ITS WEIGHT... ✦

A search and rescue dog is reckoned to be the equivalent of 20 human searchers in good conditions – and more in poor ones.

THE CLASSIC
"My dog's got no nose."
"How does he smell?"
"Terrible..."

✦ LIFESAVING FOR DOGS ✦

If your dog stops breathing or his heart stops beating following an injury, it is essential to get veterinary attention as quickly as possible. In an emergency situation, knowing how to give artificial respiration and heart massage will give you something practical and constructive to do whilst waiting for help or transport to the vet's to arrive – and could save the dog's life.

Make sure it is safe to approach the dog and that there are no hazards which you need to attend to first. Move him to a safer area if necessary.

Check the level of consciousness by calling the dog's name. If there is no response, gently touch the eyelids at the inner corner of the eye; if he is conscious he will automatically blink, but if he is unconscious the eyelids will stay open and still. Pinch either one of the dog's toes, or the web of skin connecting them; if he is conscious, he'll pull his foot back immediately, if lightly unconscious will retract his foot more slowly, while if he is deeply unconscious there will be no movement. If there is little or no response, carry out the same ABC (Airway, Breathing and Circulation) checks that you would for a human casualty.

Airway – place the dog on his side and make sure the airway is clear by straightening the head and neck out. Draw the tongue forward slightly and remove anything which is blocking the airway.

Breathing – place a hand around the dog's muzzle just in case he suddenly recovers consciousness and snaps in fear, and position your head with the side of your face close to his nose and looking back along the line of his ribcage as you do so. Listen for the sound of breathing, feel for breath on your cheek, and look to see if the chest is rising and falling. If you still can't tell, hold a piece of tissue in front of the nostrils.

If he isn't breathing, try stimulating him first by rubbing his sides briskly; if this fails to work after 30 seconds, start artificial respiration. The air which you breathe out isn't composed solely of waste gases, but still contains a useful percentage of oxygen. Making sure the airway is still open, pull the tongue forward slightly and place a hand around the muzzle to hold the mouth closed. Place your mouth around the dog's nose to form a seal,

and blow just hard enough to make the chest rise. If you can't see the chest rising it may be that the airway is not straight enough and the head needs to be stretched out further, keeping it in line with the neck. Give one breath every 3 – 5 seconds, taking your mouth away after each breath to allow the lungs to deflate again.

Circulation – after giving four or five breaths, check for a pulse or heartbeat. If this is still present, but breathing remains absent, continue to give artificial respiration, but check the circulation again every 15 seconds – if someone else is present, they could monitor this for you. Should the dog start breathing again on his own, stop giving artificial respiration.

If the heart either isn't beating, or stops beating, you can try giving compressions combined with artificial respiration, as with a human: this is called cardio-pulmonary resuscitation or CPR. With large dogs, place him on a firm surface so he is lying on his right hand side. Position the heel of one hand at the point on the ribcage where his elbow touches his body, put the other hand on top of it and clasp the fingers together. Use quick, firm downward pumps at a rate of around 60 – 100 times a minute to compress the chest walls and push blood up towards the brain. If the dog is small, grasp the chest between thumb and forefingers just behind the elbows instead, and then squeeze them together to compress the ribcage while you support his body with your other hand on his back. After every 5 compressions, give another breath if a large dog, or after every 3 compressions if a small one; after one minute check for a pulse or heartbeat again. Repeat the process if there is still no circulation.

If the heart starts beating again, stop giving compressions but continue to give artificial respiration until breathing returns.

Never give artificial respiration or heart massage unless the breathing or heart has actually stopped and it is obvious that the dog will die without help. Starting the breathing and heart again can be difficult even in the most ideal conditions, so if your efforts fail, don't feel that it's your fault; you will have done your best and given the dog some chance rather than none at all.

> *Outside of a dog,*
> *a book is probably man's best friend;*
> *and inside of a dog,*
> *it's too dark to read.*
> Groucho Marx

WACKY DOGGY GADGETS 1

In 2003 animal behaviourist Roger Mugford unveiled his invention of a device he christened the 'Wagometer'. Fitted onto a dog's back and with sensors attached to it's tail, the gadget was intended to help determine a dog's mood by noting and measuring details such as speed, direction and arc of wag.

*His very dog at Council Board
Sits grave and wise as any Lord.*
John Wilmot, Lord Rochester

GUIDE DOG FACTS

- It costs £35,000 to train and maintain each guide dog throughout its life; each dog takes around 8 months to train. Almost half of the dogs in training will go to succeed those that have retired.
- Labradors and Golden Retrievers are most commonly used, or crosses between these breeds as they have a very high success rate, and are also least likely to cause apprehension amongst members of the public. There are also German Shepherds, Border Collies and Curly Coated Retrievers.
- Guide dogs need to be in peak physical condition, so their working lives end at around the age of ten years. There are usually plenty of loving homes waiting for retired dogs.
- There are around 4,800 guide dogs currently working with their owners
- Around 800 people are matched with a dog each year
- Approximately 1200 potential guide dog puppies are born every year as part of the Guide Dogs for the Blind Association's breeding programme. Only 2 out of 3 pups makes the grade, but unsuitable dogs often find alternative careers as Hearing dogs, Assistance dogs, or with the police.
- The cost of a guide dog to his new owner is a token 50p to ensure that no-one is prevented from having one by reason of lack of money.
- It costs around £45 million each year to run the Guide Dogs for the Blind Association in the UK, which receives no statutory or government funding, but relies entirely on voluntary donations.
- In 2003, at the age of 90, Marion Rice became the oldest person to receive a guide dog, after losing her sight three years previously.

MOST COMMON HEALTH PROBLEMS IN SENIOR DOGS		
Arthritis	Constipation	Cancer
Incontinence	Dental disease	Obesity
Hearing/ear infections	Kidney disease	
Heart disease	Cataract formation	

✼ ✼ **STUCK ON YOU** ✼ ✼

Inventor George de Mastral enjoyed getting out in the countryside, but found removing burrs from his trousers and his dog's coat afterwards annoying. Wondering just why they stuck so firmly in his pet's hair he looked at one under a microscope, and noticed that it had hundreds of little hooks which grabbed the fur loops. This gave him an idea, and after finding a fabric manufacturer interested in taking on a challenge, the first "hook and loop" tape was created, produced by the Velcro company.

> *I may appear nothing more*
> *than you would call a Pug,*
> *yet within this canine form*
> *an heavenly emanation dwells,*
> *the genius that inspired Hogarth*
> *in all his performances.*
> An anonymous contemporary admirer of Hogarth

❀❀ FROM RUSSIA WITH LOVE ❀❀

Of all the dogs used in the USSR's space programme, it was Laika who was destined to become the most famous – although what was to be claimed as a triumph by the scientists was to be the opposite for her. A three-year-old stray, she was launched into space on Sputnik II on November 3, 1957, becoming the first living creature born on Earth to make it into orbit around the planet. From the start however, it had always been planned as a one-way trip, with no possibility of returning alive for the unfortunate canine cosmonaut; various stories were reported, stating that she had either been painlessly euthanized after several days, by receiving poisoned food rations, or had died due to oxygen starvation. It wasn't until 2002 that the truth was at last revealed; poor Laika had in fact died extremely unpleasantly between five and seven hours into the flight from overheating and stress. Her space 'coffin' orbited the Earth 2,570 times before finally burning up in the Earth's atmosphere on 4 April 1958. Oleg Gazenko, one of the leading members of the team that sent Laika into space commented 41 years later that "The more time passes, the more I'm sorry about it – we did not learn enough from this mission to justify the death of the dog".

❀❀ BLUE PETER 1 ❀❀

In 1962 the children's TV programme 'Blue Peter' had a brainwave – why not have a dog on the show each week, which could be a surrogate pet for all youngsters everywhere, especially those who couldn't have one of their own? Consequently Petra – destined to be the first in a long line of pets on the programme – made her debut a week before Christmas.

❀❀ LEST WE FORGET ❀❀

In 2004, an Animals in War memorial was erected at Park Lane, London, the inscription on which reads: "This monument is dedicated to all the animals that served and died alongside British and Allied forces in wars and campaigns throughout time. They had no choice". After its unveiling, an anonymous man left a wreath of poppies with a touching note attached; "Dear Animals, you have smelt our fear. You have seen our bloodshed. You have heard our cries. Forgive us dear animals that we have asked you to serve in this way in war".

THE OLDEST

The record for the oldest dog is held by Bluey, an Australian Cattle Dog. Born in 1910, he retired from herding cattle after 20 years, and died in 1939 at the grand old age of 29 years and 5 months. Britain's oldest dog was a pedigree Papillon called Fred. He died in 2000 at the age of 29 years old, and just a few months short of Bluey's record.

WHY DO DOGS BARK?

Wolves vocalise to a much lesser extent than dogs – and it's most likely to happen amongst juveniles at play. It's thought that our pets' tendency to bark is partly due to selective breeding during early domestication; this particular characteristic was preserved along with other immature traits that made them safer to have around as companions. Actively breeding to encourage this attribute is also likely to have happened once it was realised that it increased usefulness as a watchdog. Generally, the reasons why dogs bark is as a warning or threat, to demand attention, through excitement, frustration, fear – and very often when left on their own for long periods if they become stressed or bored.

COLD DOGS

In 1984, all the countries involved in Antarctic programmes agreed to begin phasing out the use of dogs, and since 1993 there have been none there at all. The decision to withdraw them was due to evidence of canine distemper spreading to the Antarctic seal population.

> *Ay, in the catalogue ye go for men;*
> *As hounds, and greyhounds, mongrels, spaniels, curs,*
> *Shoughs, water-rugs, and demi-wolves, are 'clept*
> *All by the name of dogs.*
> William Shakespeare

OLYMPIC MASCOT

Waldi, a multicoloured stripy dachshund was the official mascot for the 1972 Olympic Games held in Munich, West Germany.

HOW MANY DOGS DOES IT TAKE TO CHANGE A LIGHTBULB?

Afghan: Lightbulb? What lightbulb?

Australian Shepherd: First I'll put all the lightbulbs in a little circle ...

Border Collie: Just one. And then I'll check and replace any wiring that's not up to scratch.

Boxer: Who cares? I can still play with my squeaky toys in the dark

Chihuahua: Yo quiero Taco Bulb

Dachshund: You know I can't reach that stupid lamp!

Dobermann: While it's dark, I'm going to sleep on the couch.

German Shepherd: I'll change it just as soon as I've led these people from the dark, checked to make sure I haven't missed any, and made one more perimeter patrol to see that no-one has tried to take advantage of the situation.

Golden Retriever: The sun is shining, the day is young, we've got our whole lives ahead of us, and you're worrying about a stupid lightbulb?

Greyhound: It isn't moving, who cares?

Jack Russell Terrier: I'll just pop it in while I'm bouncing off the walls and furniture.

Labrador Retriever: Oh, me, me!!!! Pleeeeeze let me change the lightbulb! Can I? Huh? Huh? Huh? Can I?

Old English Sheepdog: Lightbulb? Lightbulb? That thing I just ate was a lightbulb?

Pointer: I see it, there it is, right there ...

Poodle: I'll just blow in the Border Collie's ear and he'll do it. By the time he's finished rewiring the house my nails will be dry.

Rottweiler: Make me!

Schipperke: It's your lightbulb – change it yourself. Unless ... is there food involved?

Whippet: For goodness sake, just let the Border Collie get on with it. You can pet me while he's busy.

SNUPPY: ONE OF A KIND

On April 24 2005 the birth of an Afghan Hound puppy named Snuppy by caesarean section made history – and some four months later when the news was released – headlines all over the world. No ordinary puppy, this, but the very first ever cloned dog; created by scientists at Seoul National University (SNU) in South Korea, his name is a combination of 'SNU' and 'puppy'.

The attempt to clone dogs began in 1997 when American billionaire John Sperling is reputed to have spent more than $19million trying in vain to clone his dog Missy in a project dubbed 'Missyplicity'. Missy was a much loved pet, a Border Collie and Husky cross who had been adopted from an animal rescue shelter; as she was spayed, cloning was the only way of being able to obtain any offspring. Although two pregnancies were eventually achieved, all that resulted was a still-born clone; Missy herself died in 2002 at the age of 15 years.

The Missyplicity work did, however, lay the foundations for scientists to progress from, as well as revealing the difficulties in cloning dogs in particular. Snuppy was made from a cell taken from the ear of a three-year-old Afghan Hound named Tei; genetic material was removed from this cell and placed within empty egg cells which were then stimulated to start dividing and develop into an embryo. These were then transferred to a surrogate mother – in Snuppy's case a yellow Labrador – but of the 1,095 embryos transplanted into 123 female dogs, only three pregnancies were induced; and of those, one foetus was miscarried, and one clone died of pneumonia after three weeks; only Snuppy survived. On his first birthday, he celebrated with two of his favourite foods – sausages and ice cream.

YOU KNOW YOU'RE A DOG PERSON WHEN...

- You can't see out the window on the passenger side of the car because there are nose prints all over the inside.
- You like people who like your dog. You despise people who don't.
- You are the only idiot out walking in the pouring rain because your dog wants to go out.
- You keep a bowl of water in your bedroom in case your dog gets thirsty in the night.
- You carry pictures of your dog in your wallet instead of parents, siblings, children, significant other, or anyone remotely human.
- You carry a supply of dog treats in your pockets at all times.
- You talk about your dog the way other people talk about their children.

- You've traced your dog's family tree further than your own.
- You sit on the floor because you don't want to disturb your dog on the sofa.
- You meet someone out walking and introduce your dog first.
- Your dog gets more presents at Christmas than you do – but you really, genuinely don't mind.
- You check your dog's horoscope before your own.

(Author unknown)

✣✣ ORIGIN OF BREEDS ✣✣

Although recognisable types appear in pictures dating back to ancient times, most of the modern breeds we are familiar with today have been developed within the last 200 – 300 years for specific purposes. The Kennel Club registers around 200,000 breeds each year, and recognises 203 different breeds. The American Kennel Club registers about 900,000 dogs each year, but officially recognises only 157 breeds. The breeds are placed within different groups, according to their origin; both the British and American Kennel Club have seven 'groups' although some have different names, and some breeds are placed in different groups. Breed 'standards' – the blueprint describing the characteristics of each breed can also very slightly from country to country.

There is sorrow enough in the natural way
From men and women to fill our day;
But when we are certain of sorrow in store
Why do we always arrange for more?
Brothers and sisters I bid you beware
Of giving your heart to a dog to tear.
Rudyard Kipling

✣✣ HOMEWARD BOUND ✣✣

Burglar Stephen Williams made a big mistake when breaking into the home of an elderly couple – he took his dog with him. When the owners returned earlier than he had anticipated, he escaped through a window leaving Roxy, a crossbreed, behind in his haste. Police arriving at the scene put Roxy on a lead, and she obligingly led them 200 yards down the road to Williams' home.

He wa'n't no common dog, he wa'n't no mongrel;
he was a composite. A composite dog is a dog that is
made up of all the valuable qualities that's in the dog
breed – kind of a syndicate; and a mongrel is made up of
all riffraff that's left over.
Mark Twain

TYPES OF COLLAR

FLAT COLLAR:

plain or pretty, this type of collar is suitable for most exercise and training purposes.
Wider collars are preferable for the neck structure of sighthounds,
whilst Staffordshire Bull Terriers traditionally have brass decorations.

COMBI-COLLAR:

also known as a half check, this incorporates a sort section of chain which tightens
around the neck. This action is limited, and can be useful with dog's whose head and
neck shape make it easy to slide out of a conventional flat collar.

ROLLED:

made from rolled leather, to help prevent the lie of the coat of long haired breeds
from being spoilt.

BANDANNA:

purely decorative neckwear.

FLEA/INSECT REPELLING:

impregnated with chemicals to try and help keep bugs at bay.

HI-VIS COLLAR:

with added strips of reflective fabric and/or flashing lights to help make your
pet easier to see at night or when light conditions are poor.

MAGNETIC:

incorporating special magnets, these are alleged to have a beneficial therapeutic effect
on certain health problems, such as arthritis.

VIBRATING COLLARS:

producing a gentle vibrating feeling when triggered by a remote handset,
these can be useful when training dogs which are deaf –
or to gain the attention of a dog whose hearing is failing.

RADIO TELEMETRY DEVICES:

kits which attach to your pets collar, to enable you to keep track of where
he's gone if he disappears out of sight.

MONGREL

The word 'mongrel' comes from the Old English word 'gemong' meaning 'mingling'
which seems appropriate enough. However the added suffix 'rel' gave it a negative
connotation, as for example in wastrel.

Collie and Lhasa Apso:

Collapso, a dog that folds up for easy transport

Spitz and Chow Chow:

Spitzchow, a dog that throws up a lot

Bloodhound and Borzoi:

Bloodybore, a dog that's not much fun

Pointer and Setter:

Pointsetter, a traditional Christmas pet

Kerry Blue Terrier and Skye Terrier:

Blue Skye, a dog for visionaries

Pekingese and Lhasa Apso:

Peekasso, an abstract dog

Labrador Retriever and Curly Coated Retriever:

Lab Coat Retriever, the choice of research scientists

Newfoundland and Basset Hound:

Newfound Asset, a dog for financial advisors

Terrier and Bulldog:

Terribull, a dog that makes awful mistakes

Bloodhound and Labrador:

Blabador, a dog that barks incessantly

Collie and Malamute:

Commute, a dog that travels to work

Deerhound and Terrier:

Derriere, a dog that's true to the end.

WHY DO DOGS WAG THEIR TAILS? 1

Tails are used in several ways – as a rudder whilst swimming, and to help balance when running at speed. It's also one of the ways in which dogs communicate, but don't assume that a wagging tail means that they are in a good mood, or pleased to see you. It's important to look at the way in which the tail is being wagged; submissive animals tend to have a loose, wide wag, and an aggressive one, short stiff movements. Tail carriage also needs to be considered; the higher the tail, the more confident the dog, and the lower it is, the more submissive or fearful. Anxious dogs also often wag their tails frantically fast;

bearing all this in mind, tail signals can often be misinterpreted and many people have been bitten by dogs whose tails were wagging, but not out of happiness. What the tail is doing should always be read in context with the posture of the rest of the body.

> *I suppose I am ungrateful,*
> *but I did want to be given a dachshund.*
> *And I just don't have one.*
> *Perhaps I'll get one next year, or much later,*
> *when it will be more appropriate*
> *for a budding old maid.*
> Eva Braun

❧ CANINE CAT-ASTROPHE ❧

Following his mauling in November 2000 by a cat living in the library at Escondido, California, the owner of Labrador cross Kimba filed a US$1.5 million lawsuit against the city. Assistance dog Kimba suffered scratches to the nose, neck and chest resulting in a veterinary bill of $46.49. Following the rejection of a settlement offer of $1500, the case dragged on before finally being dismissed, four years after the incident, and two years after the offending cat had died.

FRIEND TO THE END 1

Alexander the Great slept beside his mastiff, Peritas, which he'd raised himself since a puppy. When the dog died, Alexander founded a city and named it after him.

BREEDS NAMED AFTER PEOPLE

Jack Russell Terrier – developed by Reverend John Russell (1795-1883), who was often known as 'Parson Jack'. He had an especial interest in terriers and whilst a student in Oxford bought a dog called Trump from a milkman, who became the founder of the breed.

Dobermann Pinscher – named after German tax and debt collector Louis Dobermann (d.1894 who wanted to produce a larger and more aggressive version of the Pinscher to help protect him whilst carrying out his job. Luckily it proved easy to train, and has since been popular with the police, army and as guard dogs.

Alaskan Malamute – so called after the Mahlemut people who settled along the upper western shores of Alaska. Used primarily to pull sleds, they were also used to hunt seals and track polar bears.

Samoyed – gained their name from the nomadic tribesmen of north western Siberia. As well as herding reindeer they pulled sleds, hunted and acted as guard dogs.

King Charles Spaniel – received their name due to the fondness King Charles II had for them; it was said that he could hardly bear to be parted from his little spaniels.

DOGS TO THE STARS

George, Great Dane: Jim Carrey
Karu, mixed breed: Hilary Swank
Petals and Bacci, Italian Greyhounds: Sigourney Weaver
Garcia, Australian cattle dog: Owen Wilson
Frank Sinatra, English bulldog; Coco Chanel,
French Bulldog; Chi Chi Rodriguez, Chihuahua: Reese Witherspoon.
Polly and Willy, both Malteses: Halle Berry
Syd, Pug: Jessica Alba
Rosalita, Wyatt and Daisy, all Labradors: Kevin Costner

RIPPING YARN

So valuable was the collection of teddy bears on display at Wookey Hole Caves in Somerset that the insurers insisted on dogs being used to help keep it safe. The services of Barney the Doberman Pinscher were duly called upon; but after six years of perfect service, something went horribly wrong when his handler let him in to check things out. He promptly went on the rampage, and during the twenty minutes it took for his handler to wrestle him to the ground and then remove him, over one hundred teddies were caught up in a frenzied attack. One of the victims proved to be 'Mabel', a 1909 German made Steiff bear which had once belonged to Elvis Presley and valued at £40,000, who had her head unceremoniously ripped off. Following the incident, in which an estimated £20,000 of damage had been done, dogs are now banned from the teddy bear collection.

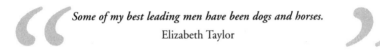

Some of my best leading men have been dogs and horses.
Elizabeth Taylor

FRIEND TO THE END 2

Tsar Peter the Great's Italian Greyhound Lissette famously saved an innocent man's life, albeit indirectly, when Peter's wife Catherine attached a message to the dog's collar pleading for leniency after the man had been wrongly accused. Signed with Lissette's name and pawprint, Peter found it as he was getting ready to go to bed; after reading it whilst his dog sat by his side, he sent immediately for his secretary and had a pardon made out there and then.

PRESIDENTIAL POOCHES 1

Bill Clinton's Labrador continued to demonstrate his unwavering devotion to his owner when the Monica Lewinsky scandal broke in 1998; when no-one else in the family was prepared to talk to him, Buddy remained by his side.

Chosen by wife Hillary, Buddy was named after a favourite uncle of Clinton's who had died that year; when he left the white house in 2000 he settled happily at the family home in Chappaqua. Unfortunately he was killed by a car two years later – a fate that had also befallen the previous family dog Zeke when Clinton was governor of Arkansas.

PET SCHEMES

Although the main objectives of the Kennel Club were originally related only to the interests of purebred dogs and competing with them in showing classes and trials, in recent years it has also become more involved in schemes aimed at pet owners.

These include:

THE CANINE CODE

Published in 1988.

GOOD CITIZEN DOG SCHEME

Set up in 1992

DISCOVER DOGS

A twice yearly show which started in 1996;
showcasing around 180 different breeds it gives prospective owners
the chance to meet dog breeds they are interested in at first hand
and to find out more about them.

COMPANION DOG CLUB

Started in 2001, membership is open to both pedigree and crossbreed pet dogs.

THE KENNEL CLUB CHARITABLE TRUST

Founded in 1985 donates to projects such as rescue and dogs for the disabled,
and supports research into canine diseases.

✻ SPACE DOG FACT 1 ✻

The National Canine Defence League campaigned against the use of Russian space dogs in 1957, and organised a minute's silence in honour of space dog Laika (see page 13).

Her memory lives on – when a monument to fallen space heroes of the Soviet Union was erected at Star City in 1997, the cosmonaut training centre near Moscow, an image of the little dog, ears pricked, was included.

Following a safe return from space after orbiting Earth 18 times in 1960, Strelka, the dog, had six puppies, one of which was named Pushinka and presented to President John F Kennedy. Pushinka in turn had four pups of her own which JFK nicknamed 'pupniks'. Fathered by Charlie, a Welsh Terrier they were called Butterfly, White Tips, Blackie and Streaker. After the death of Strelka and her companion Belka, the pair were stuffed and placed on display.

They (dogs) are better than human beings,
because they know but do not tell.
Emily Dickinson

✻ RECORD WALKS ✻

The record for the world's largest dog walk has been hotly contested for many years between the UK and the US. All previous records were completely smashed in 2007, however, when 10,272 dogs took part in Butcher's Great North Dog Walk in South Shields, UK. The first record attempt took place in 1990, attended by 13 dogs; since then the Tyneside Walkees have claimed the record 12 times, raising thousands of pounds for charity in the process.

✻ ANYONE FOR FLYBALL? ✻

Even if your dog isn't a blue-blooded pedigree, it can still be registered at the Kennel Club, on the Activity Register. This will then allow it to compete in any Obedience, working trials, Agility, Heelwork to Music or Flyball competition licensed by the Kennel Club. Alternatively, he could be signed up with the Kennel Club's Companion Dog Club, when he will automatically be entered on the Companion Dog register.

❧ NOBLE BLOODED ☙

Bloodhound actually means 'noble hound' – the 'blood' part of the name is to do with being of aristocratic breeding rather than bodily fluids.

❧ WHY DOGS ARE BETTER THAN CATS ☙

- Dogs try to understand every word you say. Cats take a nap.
- Cats look silly on a leash.
- When you come home from work, the dog is pleased to see you. The cat is still cross with you for leaving in the first place.
- Dogs will give you unconditional love until the day you die. Cats will make you pay for every mistake you've made since the day you were born.
- Dogs know when you're feeling sad, and will try to comfort you. Cats don't care how you feel as long as you remember where the tin opener is.
- A dog will bring you your slippers. A cat just drops dead mice in your slippers.
- Dogs will come when you call them. Cats will have someone take a message, and get back to you later.
- Dogs will wake you up if the house is on fire. Cats will sneak quietly out the back door.

DESIGNER DOGS

A current trend in dog-ownership is towards so-called 'designer dogs' – intentional crossings between two different purebred breeds to produce a hybrid hopefully possessed of the best qualities of both parents, and generally with an amusing name. Devotees claim that such crosses have benefits, such as hybrid vigour whilst critics (who have coined their own name, 'Frankendoodles') point out that unless careful breeding is practised, offspring can just as easily inherit health problems from both parents. Certainly the process of breeding can often be unpredictable, with characteristics varying quite considerably between individuals, even within the same litter.

In some cases breeders are actually trying to bring about the creation of a new breed, but others merely see it as an opportunity to make a quick profit. Such is the popularity of these dogs that there are waiting lists for some crosses and puppies may change hands for thousands of pounds; it is possible to pay more for a Labradoodle than a pedigree Labrador or Poodle.

WHAT'S THE DIFFERENCE

- A purebred pedigree dog must have parents both of the same breed, as must all their ancestors, traceable back to the establishment of the breed.
- A crossbreed is the offspring of parents of two different purebred breeds.
- A mongrel is the offspring of parents, one or both of which are of mixed ancestry.

Regardless of ancestry, most owners of non-purebred dogs prefer to call them cross- or mixed breed rather than mongrels.

Purebred pedigree breeds may be more expensive to purchase than a crossbreed or mongrel, but they all incur similar running costs and expenses.

> *The great pleasure of a dog*
> *is that you may make a fool of yourself with him*
> *and not only will he not scold you,*
> *but he will make a fool of himself too.*
> Samuel Butler

COMPANION DOG SHOWS

Pedigree dogs aren't the only dogs which can be shown – there are many 'companion' dog shows held each year at which cross- and mixed breeds can compete. As they obviously can't be judged on breed standards, these shows have novelty classes instead such as 'waggiest tail', 'prettiest bitch' and 'best six legs'; conformation is not a consideration although good behaviour, health and condition are taken into account. The most prestigious of all these shows is the annual Scruffts show hosted by the Kennel Club, with heats held all around the country and a grand final taking place each November at the Discover Dogs exhibition at Earls Court in London.

Every dog must have his day
Jonathan Swift

LARGEST LITTER

For some time three dogs shared the world record: Lena, an American Foxhound gave birth to 23 puppies in 1944, as did a St.Bernard in 1975 and a Great Dane in 1987. Then in November 2004, Neapolitan mastiff Tia produced 24 puppies, much to the surprise of owners Anne Kellegher and Damien Ward, who following an earlier scan, had only been expecting ten. Just before the birth, Tia was so heavily pregnant that she was unable to stand up and had to be rushed to the vets where she had a Caesarean section. One puppy didn't survive the birth, and three more died later. With so many mouths to feed, Tia was unable to cope by herself, and four hourly bottle-feeds became the order of the day, necessitating in Ward having to give up his job in order to help out.

SURF'S UP

The world's first ever canine surfing championships took place in August 2006 at Coronado Dog Beach in California, with over fifty dogs taking part. Judging was by a panel of professional surf instructors who scored each dog according to confidence level, length of ride and overall surfing abilities. The team of Scott Chandler with his seven-year-old daughter Tyler standing on his shoulders while Jack Russell terrier Zoey balanced on the nose of the board cruised off with first prize after the trio rode three waves to the beach in perfect form.

During the human Surf World Championships in the same year, all eyes were on the dog sharing a board with his owner during intervals. Police were eventually called in to remove the pair because they were attracting more attention than the competitors.

❀❊ LEADING THE WAY 1 ❊❀

Dogs have been helping visually impaired people for thousands of years; a 1st century AD mural discovered in the buried ruins of Herculaneum show a blind man being led by a dog, and a wooden plaque from the Middle Ages also exists, showing a similar image. In 1788, a blind sieve-maker from Vienna called Josef Riesinger trained a Spitz so well that people often doubted that he was blind, whilst in 1847 Jakob Birrer from Switzerland wrote about his experiences of being guided by a dog which he had specially trained himself. An organised approach to guide dog training didn't really happen until 1916 in Germany though, when dogs were trained at the first guide dog school for the blind at Oldenburg to help soldiers who had lost their sight during the First World War; as the school grew and new branches opened, 600 dogs were being produced each year. The venture shut down in 1926, to be superseded by another even more successful training centre at Potsdam, near Berlin; 12 fully trained dogs could be provided each month, and in its first 18 years over 2,500 dogs were trained.

WHY DOGS DON'T USE COMPUTERS
You can't stick your head out of Windows XP
Fetch command not available on all platforms
Too messy to 'mark' every website you visit
Can't help attacking the screen when you see 'You've got mail'
Involuntary tail wagging is a dead giveaway that you're browsing
the '100 ways to catch a cat' site instead of working
Three words: Carpal Paw Syndrome
Saliva coated floppy disks refuse to work
Sit and Stay were hard enough,
Delete and Save are out of the question
TrO{gO HyAqR4tDc TgrOo TgYPmE WeljTyH P;AzWqS
(Too hard to type with paws)

❧ BEST IN SHOW ❧

The highlight of Crufts is the judging and award of the prestigious 'Best in Show' title, which was first presented in 1928; the most successful breeds have been the Cocker Spaniel with 7 titles, followed by the Irish Setter and Welsh Terrier with 4. The English Setter, German Shepherd, Greyhound, Labrador Retriever, Standard Poodle and Wire Fox Terrier have all won 3 times, while the Afghan Hound, Airedale Terrier, Kerry Blue Terrier, Lakeland Terrier, Pointer, Toy Poodle, West Highland White Terrier and Whippet have won twice.

The following breeds have all won once: Australian Shepherd, Basenji, Bearded Collie, Bulldog, Bull Terrier, Chow Chow, Cavalier King Charles Spaniel, Clumber Spaniel, Dalmatian, Flat Coated Retriever, Great Dane, Lhasa Apso, Keeshond, Irish Wolfhound, Norfolk Terrier, Pekingese, Pyrenean Mountain Dog, Scottish Terrier, St. Bernard, Tibetan Terrier, Yorkshire Terrier.

❧ WHY DO DOGS LIKE TO ROLL IN SMELLY THINGS? ❧

To be honest, nobody really knows for sure, but there are plenty of theories about it. One is that it's an inherited characteristic from when he had to hunt for his food; rolling in something strong smelling such as a rotting carcass or animal faeces helped to disguise his smell, making it easier for him to get close to prey. Another is that it's a way of 'advertising' what he's found to other members of the pack, letting them know of intruders or quarry in the area. Most humans wonder why, with such a powerful sense of smell, dogs seem to be so fascinated by things which smell terrible to us – but this question is answered by one of the other theories; that to dogs, smell is a sense which we can only barely begin to comprehend with our own limited olfactory abilities. In the same way that a partially sighted person could perceive a painting, but not be able to comprehend it's complexities and beauty, it's possible that scent works in a similar way for our pets. For him, he may feel that he's discovered the doggy equivalent of an Old Master, and would rather like to keep it!

To get rid of particularly strong and hard to eradicate smells, such as from fox urine or faeces, try rubbing tomato ketchup into the coat, and then bathing and shampooing as normal.

❋❊ SKY'S THE LIMIT ❊❋

Brutus the dachshund holds the record for the world's highest skydiving dog, jumping (with his owner) from a height of 15,000ft (4,572m)

Wherever friendship consecrates a loving heart,
Wherever Nature lights the flame of love,
There God will not snuff out his divine spark
Not in the splendour of a night star's blaze
Nor in a humble spaniel's loving gaze.
Alphonse de Lamartine

❊❊ URBAN MYTH 1 – DOG YEARS ❊❊

It's traditionally said that each human year is roughly equivalent to seven 'dog years', but this doesn't always produce a good comparison since the rate at which dogs age varies according to size. Smaller dogs generally live longer than larger ones; some giant breeds have an average life expectancy of just 8 – 10 years. Compared to humans, dogs also mature much faster during the early part of their life, whilst small breeds also tend to mature more quickly than their bigger canine relatives.

At 1 year old
- a small dog will be approximately equivalent to a 15-year-old human
- a medium sized dog to a 13-year-old human
- a giant breed to a 12-year-old human

At 2 years old
- a small dog will be approximately equivalent to a 24-year-old human
- a medium one to a 21-year-old human
- a giant breed to a 19-year-old human

From this age onwards, add either 4, 5 or 7 'dog years' respectively for each human year that passes, according to whether he is small, medium or giant sized.

❊❊ THE STRONGEST ❊❊

The world's strongest dog is Lobo, an Alaskan Malamute. Weighing just 165 lb himself, he is reputed to have pulled a 10,000 lb truck a distance of twenty feet.

Tuck regularly comes when I am writing,
and lays her head on the desk,
rooting up my hand with her long nose
until I consent to stop and notice her.
George Armstrong Custer

❧ TOP OF THE PUPS ❧

When researchers tried playing music to canine residents at a Dogs Trust centre, they selected different styles in order to compare the effects each had on the listeners. A pop compilation, including tracks by Britney Spears, Robbie Williams and Bob Marley made little appreciable difference to behaviour, whilst playing Metallica resulted in an increase in the noise the dogs made. Recordings of classical music including Grieg, Vivaldi and Beethoven on the other hand, calmed and relaxed them, encouraging them to rest more and bark less; ironically Bach seemed to be the composer which soothed them most.

❧ HOW TO MAKE YOUR WALKS MORE INTERESTING ❧

- When time allows, venture further afield to explore new areas.
- Vary regular routes by walking them in reverse – starting at your usual finishing point – or even begin in the middle and turn it into a figure of eight route instead.
- Take a different toy each day and stop every now and then to have an exciting game with your dog.

UK DOG LAWS	
Animal Welfare Act 2006	Guard Dogs Act 1975
Control of Dogs Order 1992	Dangerous Dogs Act 1991
Dogs Act 1871	Dogs (Protection of Livestock) Act 1953
Animals Act 1971	Wildlife and Countryside Act 1981
Road Traffic Act 1988	Town Police Clauses Act 1947 (outside
Clean Neighbourhoods and	London) and Metropolitan Police Act 1839
Environment Act 2005	(inside London)

- Introduce a few training exercises in between periods of free running and games. You could include recalls, sits, stays, downs, send aways, heel work and retrieves.
- When walking on the leash, vary your speed from slow to brisk and back again; try stopping and starting; turn and then retrace your footsteps a short way then head back in your original direction again.
- In open areas where you don't need to stick to a path, keep your dog guessing where you're going by zigzagging back and forth instead of heading in straight lines.
- Introduce a few hide and seek games along the way: hide yourself, a walking companion, a toy or a cache of food treats.
- Invite a dog-owning friend to join you both.

 Our dog chases people on a bike.
We've had to take it off him.
Winston Churchill

∵ LEADING THE WAY 2 ∵

In 1927 American dog trainer Dorothy Eustis heard about the first guide dog for the blind centre at Oldenburg in Germany, and intrigued, spent several months studying there. A blind American, Morris Frank, heard about an article she had written about it and contacted Dorothy asking if she could train a dog for him. Taking up the challenge she found and trained a dog, Buddy, for him, which was to become America's first guide dog and led to her setting up training schools of her own in Switzerland and the US. She named them The Seeing Eye, from 'the hearing ear and the seeing eye' in the Old Testament of the Bible. In 1930 two British women, Muriel Crooke and Rosamund Bond contacted Dorothy after hearing about the programme, and she sent over one of her trainers. By 1931 the first four British Guide dogs completed their training: the partnerships or 'units' as they were called were Allen Caldwell and Flash, G W Lamb and Meta, Musgrave Frankland and Judy, and Thomas ap Rhys and Folly. Three years later The Guide Dogs for the Blind Association was founded, training from a lock-up garage in Wallasey, Cheshire, until the first training centre was built at Leamington spa in 1940, and since when centres have opened across the whole of the UK.

✺ TOYS YOU SHOULD NEVER GIVE A DOG ✺

- Children's toys – or anything with small pieces which might come apart and be swallowed, or rough or sharp edges. Any paint should be pet safe and not flaking.
- Stones – these can damage teeth and may be swallowed.
- Plastic bottles or yoghurt cartons – they can splinter in the mouth if chewed or bitten on hard.
- Sticks – may leave splinters in the mouth and throat, sharp ends can pierce the throat, and fragments may penetrate the intestines.
- Balls that are small enough to be swallowed or become wedged in the throat; or which can be compressed to a swallowable size.

✺ WACKY DOGGY GADGETS 2 ✺

A doorbell for dogs allows pets outside in the garden to let their owner know when they want to come back inside again without having to scratch at the door or annoy the neighbours by barking.

QUESTION
Why do dogs bury bones in the ground?
ANSWER
Because you can't bury them in trees!

SMARTEST DOG

One of the smartest dogs of all time must be Chanda-Leah, a toy poodle from Canada who achieved the Guinness World Record for most tricks performed by a dog at the age of five years, and who went on to be able to respond to over 1000 hand and verbal signals. Chanda-Leah had a repertoire of 469 tricks, including playing the piano, fetching a tissue when someone sneezed, riding a skateboard and counting and spelling.

BATTERSEA DOGS AND CATS HOME

Battersea has been rescuing dogs since 1860, when the 'Temporary Home for Lost and Starving Dogs' was established by Mary Tealby at Holloway, London. Moving to Battersea in 1871 it became known as Battersea Dogs Home – and in 1883 began rescuing cats as well, although the charity didn't change it's name to reflect this until 2005.

Dedicated to caring for lost and abandoned dogs, Battersea has a fascinating history: in 1862 Charles Dickens wrote an article about it, whilst Queen Victoria became the first of many royal patrons in 1885, making a £10 donation. Her son Prince Leopold adopted a terrier called Skippy to be a companion for his daughter Princess Alice, and one hundred sled dogs were lodged at the Home's country site in Hackbridge in preparation for Ernest Shackleton's second Antarctic expedition. In 1917, Battersea also became a temporary home to 27,253 dogs and 2,608 cats – the pets of soldiers posted abroad during the First World War. In 1982, the two and a half millionth dog to come into Battersea's care arrived, and was duly named Lucky. The Home also piloted the micro chipping scheme, and currently cares for up to 600 dogs at any one time; there are also two other sites at Old Windsor and Brands Hatch.

The dog was created specially for children.
He is the god of frolic.
Henry Ward Beecher

SKIPPER

In 1998, an eight-year-old Russian wolfhound named Olive Oyl managed 63 jump rope skips to set a new canine record.

EXERCISE TIPS

Every breed has its own exercise requirements, which can differ considerably. Working breeds such as collies and many terriers enjoy lots of exercise, but others may be less demanding, such as Cavalier King Charles Spaniels and Bulldogs. The breed of dog you have will also influence the type as well as duration of exercise. Other points to remember are:

- Don't suddenly increase exercise – build it up gradually or your dog may feel uncomfortable later in the day. If you're planning on taking your dog on holiday with you, he'll probably get more exercise than usual, so try to prepare him by getting him a little fitter beforehand.

- Beware of over-exercising younger dogs, especially larger breeds (anything from Labrador size upwards) and particularly during the first 6 – 12 months whilst they are still growing rapidly. Damage can be caused to immature joints which may not be apparent immediately, but may cause problems later in life.

- Exercise can go hand-in-hand with dieting if you have a portly pet, but does need to be very slowly and carefully increased; consult your vet for advice on how much to do with him.

- Just as human athletes do, allow your dog to warm up gently before he launches himself into strenuous activities; pop him on the leash if it's necessary to curb his enthusiasm, and begin by walking steadily and then gradually pick up the pace and striding out more briskly.

- If you'd like to take your dog jogging with you – and he's of a breed which will be able to cope with it – try to run on softer going such as grass verges where possible to avoid problems such as sore pads from running on roads and pavements.

- Pay attention to your dog and let him tell you when he's had enough; if he starts lagging behind or is panting excessively for example. Enthusiastic dogs who love to please may try and keep going even when they are tired, so be observant. If you notice him having difficulty walking, getting to his feet, showing marked breathlessness or lameness after exercise, ask your veterinary surgeon to check him over.

- Remember to take a poop scoop on your outings, plus a small pocket first aid kit, and water for your pet on longer outings.

- Don't exercise your dog just before, or until 2 hours after a meal.

- Never exercise your dog during the hottest part of the day in summer; go out early in the morning or wait until later in the evening when it's cooler.

MAJOR
Born a dog
Died a Gentleman
Epitaph on a dog's gravestone in Maryland, USA

BATTERSEA FACTS

- Around 10,000 dogs pass through Battersea's centres each year.
- Around 5,000 dogs are rehomed annually.
- Up to 1,000 calls a day are received from the public.
- 45 per cent of the strays received by Battersea are reunited with their owners.
- The average length of stay for a dog is 23 days.
- It costs an average of £900 to take in and care for each animal.
- The Behaviour Hotline receives over 300 calls a month, 40 per cent of which come from owners of non-Battersea dogs.

DOGGY DEFINITIONS

LEASH:
A strap which, when attached to your collar,
allows you to lead your human wherever you want him or her to go.

DOG BED:
Any soft clean surface, such as the white bedspread in the guestroom,
or the recently re-upholstered sofa in the living room.

DROOL:
What you do when humans have food, but you don't. To do this properly, you must sit as
close as you can and look really sad, whilst letting the drool fall to the floor – or better
still, on their laps.

DEAFNESS:
This is an affliction which affects dogs at times when their human wants them in,
but they want to stay out. Symptoms include staring blankly at the human,
then running in the opposite direction.

THUNDER:
This is a signal that the world is coming to an end. Humans remain amazingly calm
during thunderstorms, so it is necessary to warn them of the danger by trembling
uncontrollably, panting, rolling your eyes wildly, and following at their heels.

WASTEBASKET:
This is a dog toy filled with paper, envelopes and old sweet wrappers.
If you get bored, tip the basket over and artfully arrange the contents
all around the house until your human comes home to admire your efforts.

SOFAS:
The dog equivalent of human napkins. After eating it is entirely appropriate to run up to
the sofa and wipe your whiskers clean on it.

BATH:
An activity during which humans soak the walls, floors and themselves as thoroughly as
possible. You can assist by shaking vigorously and frequently.

NUDGE:
The perfect way to get your owner's attention when they are busy drinking a cup of tea
instead of paying attention to you.

LOVE:
A feeling of intense affection, given freely and unconditionally.
If you're lucky, your human will love you in return.

✸ WEIRD RECORDS ✸

Some records are odd ...... and some are downright weird. The world record for manually opening a car window is held by a Border Collie from Canada called Striker, who succeeded in a time of 11.34 seconds. The record for the most tennis balls held in a dog's mouth at one time goes to a Golden Retriever from Texas called Augie who managed to fit in five.

✸ PRESIDENTIAL POOCHES 2 ✸

President Richard Nixon's black and white spotted spaniel Checkers is often credited with having saved his career in 1952 while he was campaigning for office. After being accused of setting up a secret slush fund with donations from political cronies he appeared on TV to say that the only gift he had received was a little puppy called Checkers, who he had no intention of returning because his children loved it so much. Sympathy was stirred up for Nixon, and the pet-loving American public voted him in as Vice-President. Checkers died in 1964 at the ripe old age of 18 years.

Dogs are obsessed with being happy.
James Thurber

✸ FRISBEE FUN ✸

As is so often the case, what starts off as a bit of fun with the dog becomes a craze, which in turn develops into a new canine sport – and this is exactly what happened with Frisbees.

In the early 1970s Frisbees had become popular and it was a common sight to see people flipping them to each other in parks and on beaches; college student Alex Stein in turn introduced them to his whippet Ashley, who demonstrated both an amazingly acrobatic talent plus huge enthusiasm for the whole idea. Thinking that this was a gift that Hollywood might be interested in, Stein contacted agencies, telling them that his dog could run at 35 mph and then leap high in the air and catch a Frisbee. Finding that little interest was forthcoming, he found a different way to gain some publicity – clutching Ashley, he leapt over the fence during a nationally broadcast baseball game and proceeded to entertain an astonished audience with several minutes of canine Frisbee.

Disaster nearly followed when Stein left the field. He was arrested for trespassing, and subsequently had to pay a $250 fine – but worse still, in all the confusion, he became separated from Ashley, and the dog went missing. Luckily, three days later he was returned by a teenager who had taken Ashley home and then read about the incident in a newspaper, and shortly after that, the pair were invited to make appearances at such events as the World Frisbee Championships (at that time, a humans-only event) and on TV guest spots. Other owners became inspired to teach their dogs the same skills, and the first 'Catch & Fetch' competition was introduced in 1975; the object of the competition was to complete as many throws as possible within two minutes, each of which covered a minimum distance of 15 yards, with extra points being awarded if all four paws were off the ground during a catch. After three years as reigning champion, Ashley retired from competition but continued to tour the country demonstrating his Frisbee-catching skills; he frolicked with Amy Carter's dog Grits on the lawn of the White House, made numerous TV and public appearances, had a biography written about him, starred in an award winning documentary, became a 'spokesdog' for a dog food company and fathered a family of 60 sons and daughters. Widely considered to be the greatest Frisbee dog ever, by the time he died in the arms of his owner at the age of fourteen, the national Catch & Fetch competition had been officially renamed the Ashley Whippet Invitational in his honour, with the event attracting over 15,000 dogs.

DATING DOGS

A dating agency in Germany had the bright idea of using dogs to help the selection process along; owners post a picture of their pet alongside a description of themselves – and can decide whether they want to get in touch, and arrange to walk their dogs together. No dog? No problem – dogs are available for hire.

9/11 DOGS

When the 2001 attack on the World Trade Center took place, more than 300 search and rescue dog and handler teams from all over America joined the New York Police Department's dogs in searching for survivors. Over 70 different organizations were involved, and NYPD dog Apollo was chosen to receive the PDSA Dickin Medal on behalf of all his canine colleagues.

MAKING A SPLASH

Dock jumping is another recent canine sport to take off in the US; introduced in 2000, handlers use toys such as balls to encourage their dogs to race after them along a 40 ft dock sitting 2 ft above the water, and to go airborne in pursuit on reaching the end. Leaps into the water are measured with similar equipment to that used in the Olympics; average distances in competitions are between 6 – 18 ft, with previous record holders including a Labrador and a greyhound cross reaching distances in excess of 28 ft. Dock jumping is expected to make its official debut in the UK under the name of 'Jetty Dogs' in 2007.

EXTREME DOGS

The record for canine extreme sports is held by Part-Ex the Jack Russell who has so far joined his owner surfing, kayaking, rock jumping, wind surfing and coasteering. He is currently planning to cross the Irish Sea in a kayak and to make his first parachute jump.

CHEW ON THIS

One of the most popular and successful dog toys must be the Kong, a favourite with both dogs and owners. It can be thrown like a ball, when it's curved conical shape produces an unpredictable erratic bounce as it hits the ground, or stuffed with food and treats to help keep dogs from becoming bored – as much fun to chew at as a bone, and much safer.

It was invented by Joe Markham, whose German Shepherd ex-police dog Fritz was hooked on chewing rocks and stones – a damaging habit that wore his teeth down and which both worried and irritated his owner.

Whilst working on a van one day, Fritz was lying nearby, once again chewing as was his custom, on some rocks. Joe threw him a piece of radiator hose to see if that might distract him ... Fritz wasn't interested in the slightest ... until a suspension part was tossed in his direction. He pounced on it gleefully, giving Joe the inspiration for what was to become – after some shape modification and the development of a super strong rubber formula – the Kong, which went into production in 1976.

The idea of stuffing the hollow interior with food was dreamt up by trainer Dr Ian Dunbar. They can be filled with any foods which dogs enjoy, whether pieces of biscuit, kibble, cheese, meat, or combinations of these; if the small hole at the end is stopped up with a dab of cream cheese or peanut butter, the interior can even be filled with cooled chicken or beef broth and frozen to make a chilled treat during hot weather.

When introducing it to your dog, fill it loosely with food at first so it's easy to get out; as he becomes more expert, pack the food in more tightly to make it more challenging and keep him occupied for longer. If giving several Kongs during the day, reduce the amount of food given in meals accordingly so your dog doesn't become overweight.

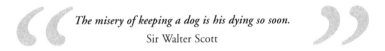

The misery of keeping a dog is his dying so soon.
Sir Walter Scott

LABRADOODLE

The first 'designer dog' was the 'Labradoodle' which appeared in Australia in 1989 when the Royal Guide Dog Association of Australia in Victoria produced a litter of puppies from a mating between a Standard Poodle and a Labrador Retriever. The idea was to try and create a dog which could be used by vision-impaired people who suffered from allergies and consequently had difficulty working with the usual guide dog breeds. One of the offspring of this experiment was a dog named Sultan, who had all the right qualities: an allergy friendly coat, an even temperament and trainability to do the job, and eventually he went on to work for ten years as a companion to a lady in Hawaii.

RIGHT WAVELENGTH

Leaving a radio on can help to provide company of sorts for your pet while you are out, but the director of a dog grooming school in Thailand has taken the idea to a whole new level. Noticing how music seemed to improve the mood of the dogs he groomed, he launched an internet radio station especially for canines; enlisting the services of his staff as DJ's, a Thai pop music mix is played, interspersed with chat directly addressed to the dogs.

MUSIC FOR DOGS

Yuri Knanin: *Symphony of dogs*
Erik Satie: *Genuinely Flabby Preludes for a Dog*

✿✿ WE WUS ROBBED... ✿✿

Amateur footballer Alistair Bone thought he was on target for a goal after being awarded a penalty kick – but a black collie ran onto the pitch, deflected the ball over the bar and then ran off. The referee refused to allow a re-take, but in the event Bone's team still won.

QUESTION
Why did the poor dog chase his own tail?
ANSWER
He was trying to make both ends meet!

✿✿ DOGS AT WAR ✿✿

Dogs have been used in warfare from the earliest of times right up to the modern day; ancient civilizations including the Assyrians, Egyptians, Greeks and Romans all used huge mastiff-type dogs which were trained to fight in battle, often wearing large protective metal collars with spikes and body armour. According to report, dogs have been present at any number of famous military encounters, such as the Battle of Marathon in 490 BC; and when the Carthaginian general Hannibal made his epic march across the Alps, his infantry, cavalry and elephants were also accompanied by battalions of war dogs. In 1298 Marco Polo wrote of the 5,000 war dogs kept by Kubla Khan, and similar mastiffs were also employed in similar roles – as attack dogs - by English armies, up to and including during Henry VIII's reign. Greatly prized as gifts amongst the nobility, Henry even sent 400 over to Charles V of Spain as a present.

✿✿ CANINE CAMEOS ✿✿

David Duchovny's Border Collie cross 'Blue' appeared with him in an episode of the cult TV series 'X Files' entitled 'Hollywood AD'.

Butkus Stallone appears in the films 'Rocky' and 'Rocky II', although he is only credited in the first. Both he and owner Sylvester Stallone lived out their own real life rags-to-riches Hollywood success story when the idea for 'Rocky' occurred to Stallone, who then sat down and hammered out the script in just three days. He had acquired the dog, a 140 lb Bullmastiff when he was just 6 weeks old, naming him after ferocious football player Dick Butkus when he ate his security blanket instead of snuggling up with it. After two years of struggling along together, Stallone found himself in such severe financial straits that he was forced to rehome Butkus; but as soon as he received the news that Rocky was definitely going ahead, he knew he had to try and get his dog back. After owning Butkus for six months, the other family weren't thrilled, but eventually Stallone's pleading won the day and the pair were reunited. In the original script, Rocky owns a scruffy 'fleabag' but when it came to casting, he was astounded by the expense of an animal actor, trained for films and available for hire – and the budget didn't allow 'even for a feeble hamster, much less a trained dog'. The producers enquired whether he perhaps had a dog of his own which could be used instead - although Butkus nearly missed his screen debut when a few days beforehand he lay down on a wet carpet which coloured one side of his body red. The film was a massive success, nominated for 10 Academy Awards and setting Stallone on the road to fame and fortune.

> *It is fatal to let any dog know*
> *that he is funny,*
> *for he immediately loses his head*
> *and starts hamming it up.*
> PG Wodehouse

FAMOUS OWNERS OF RESCUE DOGS 1

Julian Clary – Julian first met Fanny the Wonder Dog at Battersea Cats and Dogs Home, where she begged him so eloquently with her eyes to take her home that he was unable to refuse. She is often largely credited with helping to get Julian's career off the ground, after accompanying him in his stage act. She appeared with him during his first TV appearance in 1988 and promptly shot to stardom. A showbiz natural she soon developed her own fan base, had her own production company (Wonderdog Productions) and graciously accepted cameo roles on a number of shows. Following her death at the age of 19 in 1999, Julian acquired another crossbreed rescue dog described as 'a whippetty affair' and called Valerie. Less smitten by silver screens small or large, and spurning the smell of greasepaint, Julian has perhaps a little ungenerously been reported as saying that she has 'no talent' - despite the fact that she overcame nerves to turn in a creditable performance on TV's 'Celebrity Dog School', plus some remarkably accurate impressions which succeeded in winning the hearts of viewers and putting her in top position following a phone poll.

FIRST EXPORT

A large type of mastiff was present in Britain when the Romans landed, whose size, large jaws and ferocity in battle so impressed the invaders that numbers of them were sent back to Rome, with a special officer placed in charge of their export.

A descendant of one of these fearsome mastiffs accompanied knight Sir Piers Legh to France to fight at the battle of Agincourt in 1415. Although the English won, Sir Piers was severely wounded and unable to fall back to a place of safety. His dog stood guard over him until his comrades were able to carry him away. When the knight later died of his wounds in Paris, his body was returned to England, still accompanied by his faithful hound – plus a litter of puppies which she had given birth to in the meantime.

> *Cry 'Havoc' and let slip the dogs of war.*
> William Shakespeare

DISC DOGS, UK

Although Disc Dog (Frisbee) classes have been around in the US for over thirty years now, it's something of a newcomer in the UK, with the first Disc Dog event being held in 2006.

❧ UK BREED GROUPS ❧

HOUND:

This group contains breeds originally used for hunting either by scent or sight; although often having significant exercise requirements they can make dignified and trustworthy companions. Examples of scent hounds are the Beagle, Basset and Bloodhound, whilst sighthounds include breeds such as the Saluki, Whippet and Greyhound.

WORKING:

Over the centuries, these dogs were bred for very specific jobs such as draughting, guarding and search and rescue. Some of the most heroic canines are in this group, specialists in their field and aiding humans in all walks of life. Breeds include the St. Bernard, Newfoundland, Great Dane, Dobermann and Siberian Husky.

TERRIER:

Tough, brave and hardy terrier types have been around since ancient times, used for hunting vermin both above and below ground – the name is derived from the Latin word 'terra' meaning 'earth'. The British Isles is believed to be the origin of most of them. This group includes the Airedale, Cairn, Fox Terrier, Manchester Terrier and Staffordshire Bull Terrier.

GUNDOG:

These dogs were trained to find live game and/or to retrieve game which had been shot or wounded. Intelligent, active and requiring plenty of attention many of the breeds in this group make good companions, having the sort of temperament which equally suits them to being family as well as working dogs. Examples of breeds in this group include the English Setter, Labrador retriever, Golden Retriever, Cocker Spaniel, English Springer Spaniel and Hungarian Viszla.

PASTORAL:

This group contains herding dogs associated with working cattle, sheep, reindeer and other cloven footed animals. They usually have weatherproof double coats to help protect them when working in severe weather conditions. Within this group are breeds such as the Old English Sheepdog, Samoyed, German Shepherd, Lancashire Heeler, Pyrenean Mountain Dog and Welsh Corgi.

UTILITY:

The breeds in this category are a mixed and varied bunch which have in the past been bred to fulfil a specific function not included in the sporting or working groups. Some of the breeds which come under this heading include the Lhasa Apso, Shih Tzu, Bulldog, Dalmatian, Japanese Akita and Poodle.

MOST COMMON BEHAVIOURAL PROBLEMS		
Aggression to people	House training	Inappropriate chase
Aggression to other dogs	Attention seeking behaviours	behaviour
Separation anxiety	Car travel	Training problems
Fears and phobias		

TOY:

Attention loving and with friendly personalities, many of these were bred purely to be companion dogs, although some have been placed in this group due to their size. Bright and faithful, breeds in this category include the Cavalier King Charles Spaniel, Chihuahua, Pug, Yorkshire Terrier, Pekingese and Pomeranian.

KENNEL CLUB ORIGINS

The first organised dog show held in England was in 1859, at Newcastle-on-Tyne; there were 60 entries, all pointers and setters. By 1870 the popularity of shows had increased sufficiently that it was felt that a controlling body was needed, and to this end a Mr S E Shirley called together a meeting which resulted in the founding of the Kennel Club in April of 1873.

One of the organisations earliest undertakings was to compile a Stud Book, and by 1880 it had also introduced a system of registration. At the time this was purely to try and avoid duplication and confusion – the pedigree was of little importance. Nowadays the Kennel Club receives around 280,000 registrations each year, and the computer database now contains over 6 million dog names. In the late 1940s, the Kennel Club took over the world's most famous dog show, Crufts, which has been a huge success with the public as well as exhibitors.

*You who pass by, if you do mark this monument,
do not laugh, I beg you, though it is a dog's grave.
Tears fell for me, and the earth was heaped
above me by a master's hand, who likewise
engraved these words on my tomb.*
Ancient Greek epitaph

TOP DOGS

The biggest and most famous dog show in the world is Crufts; held each year at the National Exhibition Centre, Birmingham it attracts in excess of 140,000 visitors and over 22,000 entries which include around 1000 overseas exhibitors from 32 countries and about 178 different breeds.

It's origins were a little more humble, dating back to 1876 when Charles Cruft decided to opt out of the family jewellery business, taking up a job selling 'dog cakes' for James Spratt instead. Travelling round Europe in the course of his duties he was invited by French dog breeders to organise the promotion of the canine section of the Paris Exhibition, and on returning to England took up the management of the Allied Terrier Club show in 1886. The first show which carried his name was 'Cruft's Greatest Dog Show' held in 1891; it was also the first in which all breeds were able to compete, rather than being a specialised affair, and 2,000 dogs attended.

From then on the show continued to grow; when Charles Cruft died in 1938 his widow ran the 1939 show, but feeling that the responsibility for running it was too great and wishing it to continue, sold it to the Kennel Club. The first show run under their auspices was held in 1948 at Olympia, but with the number of entries increasing every year, it relocated to Earls Court in 1979, running over three days in 1982, and over four days in 1987 in order to accommodate both dogs and spectators. Even this didn't prove to be spacious enough, and in 1991, the show was held for the first time at the NEC.

10 THINGS TO CHECK AFTER WALKING

Fleas – these can be acquired from wildlife as well as other pets your dog may meet during the course of a walk.

Ticks – these can transmit a variety of diseases, including Lyme Disease in the UK and other parts of the world, and which can affect humans as well as dogs. Swab with surgical spirit, spray with a suitable acaricide or cover with Vaseline (petroleum jelly) to smother it, and then remove a few hours later with a suitable tick removing tool. Check that the mouthparts have not been left behind, and dab with antiseptic.

Grass seeds –these can be easy to miss so look carefully; pick out any present, using tweezers to carefully draw out any which have penetrated the skin. If one has tracked right up under the skin and you can't reach it, ask your vet to deal with it. Seeds can also fall into the ears causing extreme irritation shown as headshaking and scratching at the affected ear; this is also another job for the vet.

Burrs – locate these by running your fingers through the fur, and use fingers to tease them out. If the hair is very matted around them it may be necessary to cut them out. Check carefully behind the ears and between toes and pads where the coat may be more woolly and dense and they can be harder to spot.

Harvest mites – in the Autumn months, harvest mites may attach to the skin, most often between the toes, but also around the mouth and ears where they then feed on blood and lymph. They may just be visible to the naked eye as tiny orange dots, and cause inflammation and itchiness leading to biting and scratching. Take your dog to the vet for diagnosis and treatment.

Cuts and grazes – check from head to toe, and either treat yourself or seek veterinary advice as appropriate.

Sore paws and torn or damaged nails – treat yourself if minor, or obtain veterinary assistance.

Ice and snow balls – can pack tightly between pads, as can clumps of mud and small stones, causing discomfort.

Breathing – any signs of distress, coughing, wheezing, gasping, rapid, shallow or laboured breathing, or unusual noises or other departures from the normal should be a matter for concern and veterinary help sought as soon as possible.

Mobility – dog shouldn't appear uncomfortable, stiff or reluctant to either move or rise from a lying position following exercise. Consult your vet if discomfort or difficulty is evident.

> *This soldier, I realised,*
> *must have had friends at home and in his regiment;*
> *yet he lay there deserted by all except his dog.*
> *I looked on, unmoved,*
> *at battles which decided the future of nations.*
> *Tearless, I had given orders which*
> *brought death to thousands.*
> *Yet here I was, stirred, profoundly stirred,*
> *stirred to tears. And by what?*
> *By the grief of one dog.*
> Napoleon Bonaparte,
> on finding a dog beside the body of his dead master, licking
> his face and howling, on a moonlit field after a battle.

✤ A DOG'S LIFE DURING THE WAR ✤

On the outbreak of World War II the National Canine Defence League (now Dogs Trust) issued instructions on constructing gas proof kennels and gas masks for dogs. They also produced leaflets offering advice on anticipated emergencies which would affect dogs such as air-raid precautions and war time pet food, and paid for over 12,500 dog licences for families whose main breadwinner was away. A more bizarre example of the organisation's war work was the collection of combings from pet fur to be knitted into clothing for the troops.

As food rationing was introduced, dog owners would queue patiently outside pet food shops, often accompanied by their dogs. Meat for them was scarce, especially since horsemeat which was intended for animal consumption was frequently misappropriated for human use instead.

✤ FACING EXTINCTION ✤

Some breeds remain constant favourites throughout the years, but others fall in and out of favour with owners according to the fashions and lifestyle of the times. Based on the premise that a birth rate of 300 puppies born each year is necessary to guarantee a large gene pool and ensure a long term healthy population, the Kennel Club has published a list of endangered breeds native to the UK and Ireland. The lowest number of registrations in 2006 was the Glen of Imaal Terrier with just 41 puppies, and the Otterhound with 51. Others on the endangered list are: Bloodhound, Deerhound, Greyhound, Gordon Setter, Irish Red and White Setter, Curly Coated Retriever, Clumber Spaniel, Field Spaniel, Irish Water Spaniel, Sussex Spaniel, Dandie Dinmont Terrier, Smooth Fox Terrier, Irish Terrier, Kerry Blue Terrier, Lakeland Terrier, Manchester Terrier, Norwich Terrier, Sealyham Terrier, Skye Terrier, Soft-Coated Wheaten Terrier, Welsh Terrier, Smooth Collie, Lancashire Heeler, Cardigan Welsh Corgi, English Toy Terrier (Black and Tan), King Charles Spaniel.

He is your friend, your partner, your defender, your dog.
You are his life, his love, his leader.
He will be yours, faithful and true,
to the last beat of his heart.
You owe it to him to be worthy of such devotion.
Anonymous

✹✿ MERCY DOGS ✿✹

One of the jobs which dogs were used for in the Great War was as mercy dogs, seeking out wounded soldiers and leading stretcher bearers to the casualties, and a powerfully built Irish Wolfhound named Bally Shannon was one such of these. Having saved ten men by dragging them out of No-Man's land, a shell burst nearby and both Bally and his master were wounded. On their way home together on a hospital ship, disaster struck again when they were torpedoed by a German submarine and the ship went down with nearly all on board. Only three men survived, one of them Bally's master, plus the huge dog; somehow the men managed to pull themselves onto a piece of wreckage, but there was no room for Bally as well. Forced to order him to keep off for fear that otherwise they would all perish, Bally obeyed as always, swimming round the makeshift raft despite his injuries and only resting his chin on it when he was almost at the end of his strength. In the morning they were rescued by another ship, and this time reached safety; Bally's wounds were treated and despite the ordeal he made a full recovery.

LONGEST EARS

The longest ears in the world belong to Tigger, a Bloodhound from Illinois, USA, measuring in at 34.9 cm (13.75 in) and 34.2 cm (13.5 in) for the right and left ears respectively.

WHY DO DOGS COCK THEIR LEGS?

For male dogs, urinating isn't just about relieving themselves – it's also about leaving the equivalent of a calling card, letting other dogs know of their presence. By cocking a leg, urine marks are left at the nose-level of other passing dogs; the scent also lasts longer than if left on the ground. Dogs can mark up to 80 times in an hour and never seem to run out, even if they can only produce a few drops. Females generally scent mark less frequently, although this my increase when they are coming into season, as a way of letting any potential suitors know.

TOY RULES

- Buy toys specifically made for dogs, and suitable for the size and strength of each individual.
- Replace toys which begin to show signs of wear and tear before they fall apart.
- Supervise play with toys which may be more easily destroyed, such as those made from latex or fleece.
- If you have another dog, don't leave them alone together with activity type toys which contain food in case it leads to disputes over possession.
- Teach your dog to surrender toys to you on command.
- Don't use toys as a substitute for your company and attention.

BREED NAMES

- The name 'Corgi' comes from the Welsh phrase meaning 'dwarf dog'.
- One theory as to how pugs gained their name is that it's derived from the Latin word 'pugnus' meaning 'fist', because that's what their faces are supposed to resemble.
- The word 'beagle' supposedly originates from an old French word meaning 'open throat', referring to the distinctive baying noise this breed makes when on the scent of their quarry.

Looking like the wings of a butterfly, the distinctive large fringed ears of the Papillon are responsible for giving the breed it's name. There is also a drop-eared variety called the Phalene, the French for 'moth'.

PRESIDENTIAL POOCHES 3

'Grits' was the crossbreed puppy given to Jimmy Carter's daughter Amy by her teacher Verona Meeder when she moved into the White House, and named after her father's 'Grits and Fritz' campaign slogan. He apparently happily spent his first night sleeping on a pink rug in Amy's bedroom, together with her Siamese cat 'Misty Malarkey Ying Yang' before being moved to the kennel. Observers noted that Amy 'sure loves that dog' – yet two and a half years later Grits was returned to Verona Meeder. The official line was that his mother had died, leaving Meeder dog-less, but leaks alleged that the real reason was that not only didn't he get on with the cat, but still wasn't housetrained and was in the habit of soiling on the White House carpets

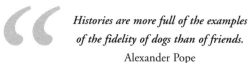

Histories are more full of the examples of the fidelity of dogs than of friends.
Alexander Pope

FRIEND TO THE END 3

After the dashing nephew of Charles I, Prince Rupert of the Rhine (1619 – 1682) was taken prisoner at the Battle of Lemgo in 1638, he was confined at Lintz until 1641. To keep him company during his captivity, Lord Arundell gave him a white Poodle, Boye, who was to remain his constant companion until the dog's death. Rupert taught him many tricks, such as to jump with joy on hearing the name Charles; one commentator observed that "It is curious to observe this daring and restless man amusing himself by teaching a dog that discipline he could never learn himself". Boye enjoyed many privileges; he shared Rupert's bed and had more haircuts than his master, sat in the King's chair, played with his children and Charles I himself fed him choice morsels of roast beef and capon from his own plate at dinner. Before long, Boye became the subject of a smear campaign by the Parliamentarians; in an age when witchcraft was widely believed in and feared, he was accused of possessing demonic powers and being the familiar of Rupert.

Sadly, Boye met his end in 1644 at the hands of a Roundhead soldier during the Battle of Marston Moor.

The dog, to gain his private ends,
Went mad and bit the man.
The man recovered of the bite,
The dog it was that died.
Oliver Goldsmith

⁕⁎ ARGOS ⁎⁕

Considering how long dogs have been our faithful companions, it's not surprising that they crop up frequently in folklore and legends, although less so in superstition. One of the most famous tales dates back to antiquity, and concerns Argos, a dog which belonged to the Greek warrior and king of Ithaca, Odysseus. Following an absence of twenty years whilst fighting at Troy and then voyaging home, the faithful hound had grown old and feeble waiting for his master's return. Neglected, covered with fleas and lying on a dung heap, he was the first to recognise the disguised Odysseus; pricking up his ears, he did his best to wag his tail and tried to wriggle towards him, dying with a final whimper of pleasure at finally being reunited.

QUESTION
What do you get if you cross a sheepdog with a rose?
ANSWER
A collie-flower!

⁕⁎ DEAD LOSS ⁎⁕

In the first twelve months following England's declaration of war on Germany in 1939, over 200,000 dogs were put to sleep; with food rationing introduced, many felt it was unpatriotic to keep pet animals which didn't contribute in any way to the war effort, yet actively drained precious resources.

As a result, when it was decided to begin training dogs again for the military and the

Army War Dog School was set up in 1942, so many had been destroyed that there was a shortage of appropriate candidates. Of the 10,000 initially offered, only 3,500 were found to be acceptable.

LICK IT BETTER

In old days, the lick of a dog was thought to encourage the recovery of human patients; and if a dog licked a newborn baby, it would be a quick healer throughout its life.

Like a dog, he hunts in dreams.
Lord Alfred Tennyson

PERSIAN POWER

In Persia, dogs were held to have special powers and were led to the side of a dying person to ward off evil spirits.

HOW TO POP PILLS

If you need to give your dog worm pills or medications, the easiest way is generally to disguise it with food. Inserting pills into a piece of cheese or sausage usually does the trick, especially if you give an 'undoctored' piece first. Watch carefully just to check that the pill doesn't reappear again, as some dogs have an amazing talent for separating tablets from food and spitting it out again.

If the medication comes in granule or powder form, adding it to food may do the trick, as long as you know he'll clear the bowl. Otherwise, mixing them with a dollop of honey or peanut butter and making into a small sandwich may convince your pet that he's getting a treat rather than some medicine.

Before giving a medicine, always check first as to the recommended method of administration; some may need to be given with food, or within a certain period before or after eating. Some may need to be taken whole whilst others can be crushed into a powder if it's easier to give them that way, or made smaller with a pill splitter.

If tablets can't be given with food, or if your dog isn't fooled by camouflaging it in a tasty morsel, you will need to pop it down his throat instead. Sit him down by your left hand side, then place your left hand over the top of his muzzle, fingers on one side and thumb on the other, just behind the canine teeth. Hold his head tilted upwards, and with the tablet in your right hand, use one or two fingers to open his mouth and draw the lower jaw downwards. As his mouth opens, drop the tablet as far back in the mouth as possible, beyond the point where you can see the tongue rise upwards. Keeping his head tilted up, close his mouth again and hold both jaws shut with one hand whilst you gently massage his throat with the other to encourage him to swallow. Some dogs are very good at working a tablet back up to the front of the mouth if it wasn't placed far enough back, so keep an eye out in case he drops it back out on the floor when you release him.

With a dog which is very wriggly, it may be easier to position him so he is between your legs instead, with your knees just behind his shoulders so he can't scoot backwards or sideways. If he is a very small dog, kneel instead of standing, or ask someone else to hold him.

When giving a liquid medication, open the mouth in the same way as when giving a tablet, but keep the head level instead of tilting it upwards. Squirt it into the side of the mouth, but don't blast it forcefully into the back of the throat as it may go down the

wrong way, into the lungs rather than the stomach. Close the mouth, gently rub the throat until he swallows, and praise.

With dogs which are very resistant to the idea of taking medications, or which are likely to bite, don't persevere; ask your vet for advice instead, as there may be a way of providing the treatment in a different form, such as an injection given by him.

But thinks, admitted to that equal sky,
His faithful dog shall bear him company.
Alexander Pope

❄❄ SAVED BY A NOSE ❄❄

According to legend, the Ark on which Noah, his family and all the animals who had been saved from the Flood were living, suddenly sprang a leak. The dog pushed his warm, dry nose into the hole until repairs could be made – and still has a cold, wet nose to this day.

❄❄ HEAL, FIDO... ❄❄

Healing goddesses in ancient Mesopotamia were frequently associated with dogs; one of the most important of these, Gula is usually shown sitting on a throne with her holy dog by her side. There were many temples dedicated to Gula, including three at Babylon, but the main cult centre was at Nin-Isina, which had a sacred dog kennel where the occupants lived a life of luxury, although very possibly some ended up as sacrifices . Many votive offerings with images of dogs have been discovered along with canine figurines, one of which carried an inscription reading 'Don't stop to think – bite!'

All knowledge,
the totality of all questions and all answers
is contained in the dog.
Franz Kafka

TOP 10 BRAINIEST BREEDS		
Border Collie	Dobermann Pinscher	Rottweiler
Poodle	Shetland Sheepdog	Australian Cattle Dog
German Shepherd Dog	Labrador Retriever	
Golden Retriever	Papillon	

GONE BUT NOT FORGOTTEN

'Bad, mad and dangerous to know' poet Lord Byron was passionate about animals; when he discovered that dogs were not allowed at Cambridge University he is said to have taken a bear instead. He was especially fond of his Newfoundland, Boatswain who he nursed devotedly when he contracted rabies, showing no fear of being bitten and infected himself. When Boatswain died, Byron erected a monument to him on the grounds of his country seat in Newstead Abbey, on which is inscribed a poem, plus what has probably become one of the most famous canine epitaphs.

"Near this spot are deposited the remains of one who possessed Beauty without Vanity, Strength without Insolence, Courage without Ferocity, and all the Virtues of Man without his Vices. This praise, which would be unmeaning Flattery, if inscribed over human ashes, is but a just Tribute to the Memory of BOATSWAIN, a dog."

Byron said more than once that he would like to be buried next to his dog, but in the event, circumstances conspired against it and he was laid to rest in the family vault in Nottinghamshire.

THE HOWLING DOG

A common superstitious belief is that dogs have the ability to see apparitions and sense if death is imminent. To hear a dog howling has often been considered to be an omen of death, especially if it howls by an open door. A barking dog on the other hand, is merely a sign of impending misfortune if heard first thing in the morning.

President Warren Harding had a close bond with his large Airedale, Laddie Boy. The dog would bring back golf balls for him from the White House lawn, greeted official delegations from the front steps and even had his own hand carved chair to sit on at Cabinet meetings. When Harding died in office after becoming ill on a trip to Alaska, it is said that sensing something was wrong, Laddie howled for three days before his master passed away.

Two weeks after Howard Carter opened the burial chamber of the ancient Egyptian pharaoh Tutankhamen in 1922, Lord Carnarvon, who had sponsored the excavation was bitten by a mosquito. The bite became infected after he cut it whilst shaving, and he fell ill and subsequently developed pneumonia, dying five weeks later. At the precise moment that Carnarvon died, his dog Susie, back home in Britain is said to have howled and then died herself.

DOG OATHS

Ancient Egyptians would swear 'by the Dog' when making oaths that they would not break.

QUESTION
Why do dogs wag their tails?
ANSWER
"Because no one else will do it for them!"

WAR DOG SCHOOL

At the start of the First World War, the Germans had at least 6,000 dogs trained to undertake all sorts of different roles - as messengers, guards, sentries and tracker dogs. Britain had none, and it was not until 1917 that the British War Dog School was set up. Recruited dogs were put through a three month training course which included mock battles complete with explosions, gun fire, smoke, barbed wire and other hazards.

BLACK DOGS

There are many traditional tales of canine phantoms and hauntings, often malevolent and frequently involving black dogs known by a variety of different names including Black Shuck, Skriker, Gytrash, Cappel, Padfoot, Moddey Dhoo and Bargest. In 1577 for example, a large black hound with flaming yellow eyes the size of saucers ran up the aisle of the church at Blytheburgh, killed two of the congregation as it passed, caused the church tower to collapse through the roof, and left the imprint of scorched claw marks on the doors as it departed.

Countless other stories are told around Britain, but are by no means unknown in other parts of the world: in the US, Route 666 is a lonely, deserted stretch of road which has a long history of accidents and apparitions – one of which is of a pack of black dogs with yellow eyes and sharp teeth which shred the tyres of passing motorists at night.

Some phantom black dogs are benevolent, such as the Gurt Dog of Somerset, which watches over and protects children playing on the Quantock Hills, but generally their appearance is often considered to be a harbinger of ill fortune. US President William McKinley never owned a dog; but just a few hours before he was assassinated, he was photographed at Niagara Falls, accompanied by a mysterious black dog. In West Peak, Connecticut, tales are told of a small, sad looking dog who barks silently and leaves no pawprints; seeing him the first time brings good luck, but the second time brings misfortune and the third time, death.

HOW MUCH CAN YOU EAT?

A Dog's stomach can hold a surprising amount – around 100-250 ml (4-10 fl.oz) per kg (2.2 lb) of it's bodyweight. A Labrador therefore has a capacity of up to 8 litres (14 pints). The intestines measure approximately three times the length of the dog.

IT'S IN THE STARS

Aries *(Mar 21 – Apr 20)*

Intrepid and daring, his feelings can run deep and he likes to be with his owner.

Taurus *(Apr 21 – May 21)*

Brave and affectionate, but can be stubborn. Easygoing unless pushed too far.

Gemini *(May 22 – June 21)*

Loves to spend time at play. Intelligent and quick to learn tricks.

Cancer *(June 22 – July 23)*

A sweet and sensitive nature, often enjoys the company of children.

Leo *(July 24 – Aug 23)*

Outgoing and gregarious, loves outings and likes to be the centre of attention.

Virgo *(Aug 24 – Sep 23)*

Responsive and bright, likes to please his owner.

Libra *(Sep 24 – Oct 23)*

Easy company to have around; he enjoys attention, but doesn't constantly demand it.

Scorpio *(Oct 24 – Nov 2)*

Astute, very loyal, and expecting loyalty in return.

Sagittarius *(Nov 23 – Dec 21)*

Faithful companion, courageous and smart, and who loves to amuse.

Capricorn *(Dec 22 – Jan 20)*

Constant and dependable, enjoys home comforts and eats pretty well anything.

Aquarius *(Jan 21 – Feb 19)*

Can be a one-man dog who doesn't enjoy sharing his owner with others.

Pisces *(Feb 20 – Mar 20)*

Loves to be fussed and petted; highly sensitive to his owner's emotional state.

WHERE THE DOG RAN

A Cherokee legend tells of a dog who stole corn meal at night while everyone was asleep. Next morning, his footprints were spotted nearby, and a small group of people lay in wait for him in case he returned again that evening. Sure enough, as soon as the dog thought everyone was asleep, he went over to the corn meal and started eating, whereupon the watchers jumped out from their hiding place and started beating him. The dog ran off howling, dropping meal from his mouth as he did so, and leaving behind a white trail where we now see the Milky Way.

DOG BRIDE

In 2003, a nine-year-old Indian girl was married to a dog; according to the beliefs of her tribe, this would ward off an evil spell. The bride said that she was fond of the dog, 'Bacchan' which was a local stray, and promised to take good care of him. Tribal elders said that she would be free to marry again later, and wouldn't need to divorce Bacchan first.

For he was speechless, ghastly, wan
Like him of whom the story ran
Who spoke the spectre hound in Man.
Sir Walter Scott

DOGGEDLY DEVOTED

When four-year-old German Shepherd Chyna's best friend Coco the Cavalier King Charles Spaniel went missing, she wasn't prepared to sit back and wait for him to turn up. Instead she set off, following his scent until she found him stuck in mud on a riverbank four miles away. For the next three days she stayed by his side until finally her barking alerted farmer Graham Prosser, who in turn called the RSPCA to aid in the rescue. The riverbank was so deep that a human chain had to be formed to reach Coco, who by this time had sunk so deep that only her ears and nose were still poking out of the mud. Minutes from death, she was unceremoniously plucked out of the mire by her ears, shooting out 'like a cork from a bottle'. Covered in mud and suffering from exhaustion, thirteen-year-old Coco made a good recovery following a meal and a good sleep, much to the relief of owner Kathy Seaborn who had been sick with worry when both dogs disappeared.

FIRST OF MANY

Many dogs were presented to Queen Victoria during her reign, but one of the first to hold a special place in her affections was her Cavalier King Charles Spaniel Dash – her diary for the day of her coronation reads that she returned home afterwards to give him a bath. A portrait of him by Edwin Landseer was commissioned as a 17th birthday present from her mother, starting a fashion for similar portraits of animals.

In the beginning, God and his dog created the world

......

Kato Indian creation story

IN HONOUR OF DOGS...

Following World War I, a public memorial building was erected at Kilburn Park in London to honour all the British animals which were killed. Part of the inscription reads: "This building is dedicated as a memorial to the countless thousands of God's humble creatures who suffered and perished in the Great War of 1914-1918 knowing nothing of the cause but looking forward to final victory. Filled with only love, faith and loyalty, they endured much and died for us".

CUCHALAINN

The great Irish hero Cuchulainn gained his name when he was still a child; summoned to a feast at the house of the blacksmith Culann he promised to attend as soon as he'd finished his game of hurley with some other boys. Once at the feast, it slipped everyone's mind that he hadn't yet arrived, and the smith's fierce watchdog was set loose outside. Suddenly a tremendous commotion was heard, and realising that they were still awaiting their last guest, the revellers rushed to the doors. To their amazement and relief, the dog was dead, killed with nothing more than the boy's hurley stick and bare hands; Culann however, was upset by the loss of his dog. In recompense, the boy offered himself in the hound's place until such time as another could be found and trained. In this way he gained the name of Cuchulainn, or 'the Hound of Culann'.

BLUE PETER 2

Petra, the original Blue Peter dog, unfortunately contracted distemper and died soon after her debut, but rather than confessing what had happened, a frantic search for a look-alike was conducted, and Petra II was eventually discovered in a pet shop in Lewisham. She continued to make weekly appearances on the show until ill health forced her to retire; when her death was announced on TV and in the national press in 1977, a generation who had grown up with her went into mourning, and a bronze statue of her was erected in the Blue Peter garden as a memorial.

✿ IMPERIAL DOGS ✿

Originating in Imperial China, only emperors, relatives and courtiers were allowed to own a Pekingese. Considered sacred, anyone who attempted to steal one was sentenced to death by stoning.

When Allied troopers looted the Summer Palace in Peking, five of the little dogs were found guarding the body of one of the Emperor's aunts, who had taken her own life rather than face defeat by enemies. They were taken back to England where they created something of a stir since this was the first time they had ever been seen outside China. One was presented to Queen Victoria who rather appropriately named him 'Looty';

✿ ROYAL NIPPERS 1 ✿

During their courtship, Empress Josephine's dog Fortune had been instrumental in carrying romantic messages between her and Napoleon; but on their wedding night, matters took an unexpected turn. Thinking that his mistress was being attacked, the dog felt the need to step in and protect her, doing his best by nipping Napoleon on the leg.

QUESTION

What did the cowboy say when the bear ate Lassie?

ANSWER

"Well, doggone!"

✿ AGILITY ✿

First seen in public in 1978 at Crufts, Agility proved an instant hit and since then has gone on to become the fastest growing canine sport in the UK, Western Europe and North America. Whilst thousands enjoy competing with their pets, just as many join a class simply to have fun with their dog; it's an excellent way of improving the level of communication, and encourages dogs to use their brains as well as their bodies.

Not entirely dissimilar to equestrian show jumping, in addition to good communication, agility also combines elements of trust, obedience, confidence, and quick thinking. A variety of obstacles are used; some to be jumped over, and others to move through, including pipe and collapsible tunnels, hurdles, long jump, tyre, weave poles, wall, well, brush and water fences. Other pieces of equipment include an A frame, Dog

walk, See saw and Crossover; these are termed 'contact' obstacles as certain areas must be touched by the dogs paws, otherwise penalty points are incurred. Similarly, in competition, penalty points are also incurred for other errors such as knocking a fence down, with the fastest 'clear' round (no penalties gained) being deemed the winner. Competitions are generally timed over a course of 16 – 20 obstacles which have to be tackled in the correct order and within a set time limit; there are classes to suit all, with Level 1 being suitable for beginners and progressing up to Level 7 at the top end. Classes are further divided into small, medium and large categories so that little dogs don't compete at a disadvantage against big ones. As well as agility competitions, there are jumping classes, which are the same but excluding the contact obstacles, and a number of novelty classes such as Helter-skelter, Knockout and Pairs. All dogs are welcome to take part, of any shape or size, pedigree or crossbreed, although in order to avoid overstressing young joints and muscles it is best to wait until they are 12 months old before introducing it, and if you wish to compete they must be a minimum of 18 months. Even if just done for fun, it can be a demanding sport, so dogs should be reasonably fit and not overweight; they should also already have some basic obedience training to ensure control and safety.

Age is no barrier for people; young or old can all take part, and although a reasonable degree of fitness and mobility is an asset, even that is not necessarily a bar - some owners have been known to continue into their seventies, and there have even been successful disabled competitors. The cost is generally minimal too, making it a relatively inexpensive as well as fun way of interacting with your dog, deepening the bond between you, and enabling you to meet and make friends with other owners.

If you have never done agility before, it's best to start off by joining a club which runs classes. The wellbeing of your dog is paramount, and a club should be able to provide properly constructed obstacles and to teach you and your pet how to negotiate them safely. Later on, when you have learnt how to build, position and approach each obstacle, you can build or buy your own set of equipment for use at home if the bug really bites you both. Progress can sometimes feel slow initially, but it is important not to hurry your dog in the early stages or to encourage him to go too fast too soon. Gradually, as your control increases and our dog learns to interpret the hand signals and verbal commands used to direct him, the thrill and satisfaction of working as a team together will be experienced.

❧ DOG IN A MILLION ❧

In 1999, Allen Parton had plenty to look forward to, with a wife and two children at home and a promising career ahead of him in the Royal Navy. Then his life was turned upside down when a road accident wiped out his memories and left him unable to speak, walk, talk, or do any of the everyday things most of us take for granted. Allen spent the next five years in hospital, becoming increasingly more introverted and so depressed that he tried to commit suicide. In the meantime his relationship with his wife, who he couldn't remember marrying, and with his children whose births he couldn't recall, grew very strained.

Then Allen was partnered with yellow Labrador Endal by Canine Partners for Independence and gradually Allen's outlook on life became brighter as his four legged assistant helped rebuild his confidence and restore a degree of independence. Endal has learnt to respond to sign language, knows 100 commands and also shows an ability to problem solve – one day when Allen was struggling to reach a cashpoint machine, Endal reached up, took the money and gave it to his owner, and then retrieved the card as well. This ability also helped save Allen's life on one occasion when he was knocked out of his wheelchair in a car park by a driver who failed to spot him and was left lying unconscious on the ground. Endal calmly moved Allen into a recovery position, covered him with a blanket from the wheelchair, brought the mobile phone over, and only moved from his side to summon help from the hotel staff once Allen began to show signs of consciousness.

This remarkable dog's talents and devotion to duty have been recognised many times over, having amongst other awards been voted 'Dog of the Millennium', won the Golden Bonio Award 2002, received a gold Blue Peter badge, and a unique 'lifetime achievement' award normally only given to humans, the PDSA Gold Medal, and in 2001, 2002 and 2003 was voted Assistance Dog of the Year.

QUESTION
Why didn't the dog speak to his foot?
ANSWER
Because it's not polite to talk back to your paw!

✤✤ NO ROOM IN THE JAG ✤✤

In 2005, the Queen famously rejected the offer of a new Jaguar car – because she was concerned that there wouldn't be enough room for all the Corgis.

Ethereal essences may roam Elysian Fields beyond the grave,
But we, my dog, will saunter home,
to all we love and all we crave.
Ada Cambridge

✤✤ ON THE TRAIL 1 ✤✤

In 1888, in response to a request from Sir Charles Warren, Commissioner of the Metropolitan Police, two bloodhounds Burgho and Barnaby were taken by Edwin Brough from Scarborough to London to help track down the brutal serial killer known as Jack the Ripper. The reputation for excellence of Brough's team of dogs was legendary, yet the London press expressed doubt about the whole idea. Trials carried out in Hyde Park in October were extremely successful, with the two hounds able to stay on the trail of a young man who had been given a head start; further trials were carried out in the dark at night to prepare them for the streets of Whitechapel. These also went well, and after Sir Charles himself twice volunteered to be tracked and was impressed with their performance, Brough felt it safe to return home, leaving the dogs with a London breeder.

When the body of Mary Jane Kelly was discovered in Whitechapel on November 9th things didn't go quite as hoped for, as a delay in getting the dogs to the scene of the crime meant that the trail was not only cold, but the scent blurred by the presence of others in the crowded streets. Despite not being able to prove their worth on this occasion, Sir Charles and his idea of using bloodhounds is nowadays credited with helping to pave the way for the use of police dogs today.

Other jobs in which dogs excel are in fire investigation (when they search sites for signs of arson), hunting out truffles, locating avalanche victims, and in search and rescue.

✤✤ PROVERBIAL DOGS ✤✤

A dog owns nothing, yet is seldom dissatisfied
(Irish proverb)

GHOST OF BATTERSEA

The ghost of founder Mary Tealby is said to haunt Battersea Cats and Dogs Home, welcoming the new arrivals.

ROYAL NIPPERS 2

The British royal family's dogs have acquired something of a reputation over the years following a series of unfortunate and sometimes tragic incidents. Susan is said to have nipped the ankle of the royal clockmaker, a grenadier guardsman, various servants, a detective and a policeman. Other Corgis since then have torn the seat out of the trousers of a Guards officer, nipped Princess Diana, and allegedly knocked royal butler Paul Burrell out cold after they pulled him across icy steps causing him to fall over.

In 1991 the Queen needed three stitches after being bitten on a hand breaking up a fight that had broken out between six of the Corgis.

In 2006 it was noticed that she was sporting a plaster on her hand, having once again been bitten when interceding during another squabble.

Princess Anne was convicted in 2002 after Dotty, one of her three English Bull Terriers bit two children. In 2003 the dogs were in the headlines again just before Christmas, when Florence attacked one of the Queen's Corgis, Pharos, injuring him so badly that he had to be put to sleep. This wasn't the first time that one of the Queen's pets had been a victim; in 1989 her dorgi Chipper was killed by the Queen Mother's Corgi Ranger.

Not long after Christmas, Florence was in trouble once more, this time for biting the knee of a maid at Sandringham.

WHO TO CONTACT IF YOUR DOG IS STOLEN	
Police	The Kennel Club if he's a pedigree
Local dog warden	Internet 'lost and found' websites
All animal rescue centres in the area	Local media – newspapers, TV and radio
Local veterinary practices	stations – to increase publicity and make it
Your insurance company, if your dog	harder for your dog to be passed on
is insured	

STRANGE DIET

It seems that some dogs will try and eat just about anything. Some of the most peculiar items retrieved by vets include a two foot length of chain, an entire sweatshirt, a £10,000 brooch, a glass eye, false teeth, a vibrator, sunglasses, fishhooks and a jar of peanut butter. Even more heroic efforts include 14 golf balls found in the stomach of a Labrador, 427 pebbles weighing over 1kg (a Springer Spaniel), a 15 in bread knife (a crossbreed puppy measuring only 18 in long) and a positive hoard of 8 assorted batteries, a plastic raccoon, 7 rocks, a marble, 2 broken light bulbs, machine parts and a variety of staples, all scoffed down by a Samoyed.

But the accolade of greediest dog must surely go to the Bull Terrier who swallowed a bottle cap, cling film, a toy car and some wire. He underwent an operation to remove the objects, was put on a drip … and ate the drip.

 My little dog … a heartbeat at my feet.
Edith Wharton

WHY DO DOGS PANT?

There are many reasons why dogs pant – it may be through pain, fear, stress, anxiety, excitement or after strenuous exercise. Panting is also a way in which they regulate body temperature, although it isn't very efficient; cool air is breathed in and warm air from inside breathed out. Heat is also lost through evaporation, with the tongue providing a large surface area to assist with this.

Dogs also possess a structure called a rete mirabile in the carotid sinus at the base of the neck. This is a complex network of intermingled small arteries and veins which act as a heat exchanger to thermally isolate the head, which contains the brain, the most temperature sensitive organ, from the muscles of the body where most of the heat is generated

- Dogs are more susceptible to heatstroke than humans so care should be taken on warm days.
- Exercise in the cool of the day – early morning and late evening.
- Don't allow your dog to toast himself in the sun for too long if he enjoys sunbathing.
- Never leave him in a car for even the shortest of periods; leaving windows cracked open isn't sufficient to prevent the interior from reaching intolerable temperatures. Every year many dogs die from owners doing exactly this.
- Dogs will drink more in warm weather, so ensure that a supply of fresh water is always available.

Dog Haiku
I lift my leg and
Wiz on each bush. Hello, Spot –
Sniff at this and weep.
Anon

❧❧ FLEA CHECK ❧❧

Unless your dog is very heavily infested, it's not always easy to spot if he has fleas, although you may have noticed him scratching more than usual, and perhaps found a few tell-tale bite marks in areas where his coat is thin. Check for problems by combing through the coat and collecting any debris on a piece of wet white paper. If any of the specks which fall on the surface dissolve into reddish brown stains, it's a sign that flea dirts – and therefore fleas – are around.

❧❧ THE BIGGEST ❧❧

The Irish Wolfhound is the tallest breed, standing a minimum 28" – 31" (71 cm – 79 cm) at the shoulder, depending on whether it is a bitch or a dog, and with 32 in – 34 in (81 cm – 86 cm) being the ideal. Great Danes come in a close second, standing a minimum 28 in – 30 in (71 cm – 76 cm).

❧❧ WATER MUSIC ❧❧

When Sir Edward Elgar wrote the Enigma Variations, each was dedicated to a friend – except for the 11th variation which was allegedly inspired by a dog. Whilst out walking with Hereford Cathedral organist George Sinclair, his friend's bulldog Dan suddenly fell into the river, paddled upstream and then emerged again further along, and the music is supposed to represent this incident. Elgar was also fond of wordplay, and the manuscript for The Dream of Gerontius has the word DAN written at the top – probably the composer amusing himself with a private pun on the initial letters of the composition – 'DoG'

❧❧ DOG KING ❧❧

An old Scandinavian tradition tells of how King Eysteinn conquered Trondheim and left his son behind to rule over the people in his stead; but as soon as Eysteinn left, the people promptly rose up in rebellion and killed the son. Eysteinn returned and having once more subdued the kingdom this time offered the people the choice of either his slave or his dog Saurr to be king over them. They chose the dog, which was given all the trappings appropriate to his royal status – a gold collar, courtiers, a throne, and a palace. Royal decrees were signed with a paw print, and everyone seemed satisfied with the arrangement until one day a wolf broke into the palace and tore Saurr to pieces.

❧ CARRIED AWAY ❧

The Bichon Frise first became a great favourite at court in France during the reign of Francis I (1515-1547), and the popularity of the breed continued to grow. Henry III was said to be so smitten that he fashioned a special tray-like basket which he hung round his neck to carry his Bichon around in.

Dogs are not our whole lives,
but they make our lives whole.
Roger Caras

❧ PRESIDENTIAL POOCHES 4 ❧

Another short-lived tenant at the White House was Heidi, one of two dogs which Dwight Eisenhower brought with him to the White House. The Weimaraner soiled a rug in the Diplomatic Room and was promptly sent off to the farm.

❧ WAGNER'S DOGS ❧

The composer Wagner had a firm appreciation of dogs; almost penniless, he set sail for England with his first wife Minna and Newfoundland, Robber. All three were miserably seasick and nearly shipwrecked, but on arrival things were to get worse when Robber managed to get lost in London somewhere along Oxford Street. Although he was able on this occasion to find his way to the family's lodgings in Soho, he got lost for good when they travelled on to Paris. Later, his dog Peps sat behind him in the same chair while he worked, and after dying in his arms Wagner wrote "I cried incessantly, and since then have felt bitter pain and sorrow for the dear friend of the past 13 years who has walked and worked with me". When he died himself, the composer was buried in the garden of his villa, alongside his dog Russ.

In 2004, artist Ottmar Hohrl decided to create a large scale installation entitled 'Wagner's Dog' to coincide with the Bayreuth Festival dedicated to Wagner's works. Seventy black plastic dogs representing Russ were placed all around the town, but although popular with visitors, the official art commissioner didn't approve and banned them – many also became victims of theft.

IN A HOLE

One sunny day in September of 1940, four boys walked to the top of Lascaux Hill in France, a favourite place to play. With them was a dog called Robot, belonging to one of the boys; but when he suddenly disappeared and failed to answer Simon's whistle they grew worried. Searching for him they found that he had fallen down a hole in the ground, inadvertently discovering some of the most beautiful, important and famous prehistoric cave paintings in the world.

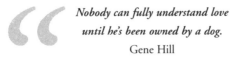

Nobody can fully understand love until he's been owned by a dog.
Gene Hill

MUSIC HALL FAVOURITE

'Daddy wouldn't buy me a Bow-wow' was written by Joseph Tabrar in 1892 after he overheard a singer asking his agent to find her a 'really good song'. Whilst they were talking about it, he sat down in a corner and wrote the song which went on to become a huge music hall favourite; but when he offered it to the singer she turned it down on the grounds that anything written that quickly was unlikely to be any good. Several years later in 1895, Toulouse-Lautrec painted Mary Belfort singing the song.

THE DOG STAYS

In 1573, Veronese was summoned to appear in front of the Inquisition, who took exception to an image of the Last Supper he had been commissioned to paint, and in which he had included animals, cavorting dwarfs and drunkards. After being asked to explain the painting, he was sent away with explicit instructions to remove the dog which takes a prominent central position and to replace it with the Magdalene ...... he ignored the orders, and simply changed the name of the painting instead to Feast in the House of Levi.

FOOD FACTS 1

Dogs are the biggest consumers of commercially made pet treats in the UK, munching their way through £120 million of snacks and goodies every year.

❋ WHY DO DOGS LICK? ❋

Affection: grooming and licking can be a bonding behaviour

Submissiveness: licking another dog on its muzzle can indicate there is no threat; it mimics a puppy's food begging action of an adult.

Irritation: trying to relieve discomfort from an itch or an injury

Taste: salty human hands and feet can taste nice to a dog

Stress: licking can be a way of self-calming

Compulsive disorder: may have its roots in medical or anxiety related problems

❋ CANINE MUSE ❋

When Lump the Dachshund met Picasso it was love at first sight for both of them; the little dog shared his bed, ate from a plate decorated with his own picture by the artist, and generally took over the house. Later on Lump became a model; when Picasso started work on his series of variations of the Velazquez painting Les Meninas, the dachshund replaced the mastiff of the original.

❧ DECORATIVE DOGS ❧

Staffordshire pottery dogs are as popular now as collectibles as they once were as cheaply made and modestly priced decorative pieces to adorn the mantelpieces of less well-off homes. Dating back to the late 18th century, many different breeds were produced, including spaniels, Dalmatians, poodles, pugs, pointers, foxhounds, sheepdogs and greyhounds.

❧ FLEA FACTS ❧

Apart from the fact that they can make your dog's life a misery and trigger skin allergies, flea control is important as they can carry tapeworm which can infect your pet. Fleas are also involved in transmission of a bacteria called Bartonella henselae which can cause mild flu-like symptoms in people, and can carry Rickettsia species, a bacteria causing fever and a skin rash in humans.

- Most flea infestations are with cat fleas; human fleas are also sometimes found on dogs. There is a dog specific flea Ctenocephalides canis, but it is actually quite rare!
- Adult fleas can live for several weeks on a dog, biting and sucking blood up to 10 times a day, and laying as many as 300 eggs a week.
- For every flea you spot, there can be another 99 lurking in the environment, waiting to re-infest your dog.

NAME THAT PUP		
An recent survey found that the favourite dog names were		
Molly	Buster	Charlie
Jack	Lucy	Sam
Holly	Jake	Toby
Max	Barney	

- Adult fleas are just the tip of the iceberg – a mere 5% of the whole infestation. The other 95% consists of flea eggs, larvae and pupae spread around your home, and ready to develop into new adult fleas within weeks – which is why it's important to treat the environment and bedding as well as the dog.

URBAN MYTH 2 – HYPOALLERGENIC DOGS

There is no such thing as a completely hypoallergenic dog – one which won't cause an allergic reaction in a sufferer. However, dogs who shed minimally are less likely to cause problems, such as wire haired and curly coated breeds whose hair has a long growth cycle, plus of course hairless breeds such as the Chinese Crested. It is also a myth that it is the hair itself which is the cause of allergies; they are actually due to the dander (dried skin flakes) and saliva, and allergens can also be found in the urine.

A dog teaches a boy fidelity,
perseverance, and to turn around
three times before lying down.
Robert Benchley

SNAP TIMING

Dogs only make connections between events that happen within one or two seconds of each other. If they are to be effective as a way of motivating your dog, rewards therefore need to happen as quickly as possible after a desired action has been offered. This is also the reason why there is no point in telling your dog off for being naughty – unless you actually catch him in the act, he'll have no idea why you are cross.

STAR QUALITY

The role of 'Eddie' in the popular TV comedy series 'Frasier' was played by a Jack Russell called Moose; at the height of his fame he received more fan mail than any of his human co-stars, and was reputed to have earned $10,000 an episode. As a puppy Moose was always in trouble of some kind; constantly escaping, chewing things up and running off tried his owners patience to the limit, and it finally ran out altogether after he killed a neighbours cat and chased some horses. He was saved from the pound by his trainer who spotted some hidden star quality; after appearing in 192 episodes he retired from show business at the age of 10 and for the last two seasons his role was taken over by his look-alike son Enzo who had already appeared as his stunt double. He died in 2006 at the age of 16.

FINDING A GOOD TRAINER OR CLASS

The Association of Pet Dog Trainers was founded in 1995 by John Fisher to offer pet dog owners a guarantee of quality when trying to find a puppy or dog class or trainer in their area. All APDT members are assessed according to a strict code of practice, and agree to abide by kind and fair principles of training – coercive and punitive techniques are not used. A list of trainers can be obtained by contacting the APDT either by post, telephone, or via their website.

SIGNING OFF

According to a survey conducted by the American Hospital association, 70 per cent of owners sign their pets' names on greetings cards

A VISIT FROM CHRIS

Playwright and novelist John Galsworthy was devoted to his black spaniel Chris and convinced that he came back to visit after his death, describing the event in the essay 'Memories' in which he recounts the dog's life. Chris' dark shadowy form appeared to Galsworthy's wife Ada one night when she was feeling sad, passing around the table to take up his accustomed place at her feet. Ada not only saw him clearly, but heard the tapping of his nails as he walked across the floor, and felt the warmth of his body pressing against her legs. Just as she thought he would settle down, something disturbed him and he moved off, gradually fading from view.

✧ WALK OF FAME ✧

Only three dogs have been awarded a star on the Hollywood Walk of Fame – Lassie, Rin Tin Tin and Strongheart. Few people nowdays know who Strongheart was, but in his day the German Shepherd was as famous as the other two, and helped pave the way for the success of Rin Tin Tin.

QUESTION
What is the dogs favourite city?
ANSWER·
New Yorkie!

✧ BOYS WILL BE GIRLS ✧

Lassie has been going strong for over 60 years now, appearing in films, radio and TV shows and having been played by a succession of Rough Collies who are always male, as they tend to be larger and apparently have more screen presence than the females.

The first film, based on a novel by Eric Knight, appeared in 1943 with Elizabeth Taylor and Roddy McDowell acting alongside Pal the dog in his first starring role as Lassie. He very nearly wasn't chosen; trainer Rudd Weatherwax was convinced that he had what it took to make the part his own, but the studio bosses thought otherwise and selected a more glamorous looking show dog instead. Pal was retained only as a stunt dog; but his services were called upon almost immediately when the original dog refused to go near a river he was supposed to swim across. Pal not only jumped into the river, but after swimming across and reaching the other side proceeded to do such a good acting job that he was hired on the spot as the new leading 'lady'. Since then, nice generations of "Lassie" descendants have appeared in the films and TV series.

✧ .... AND GIRLS WILL BE BOYS ✧

Toto, the Cairn Terrier was played by a female called Terry in the 1939 film The Wizard of Oz. Five-year-old Terry was paid a weekly wage of $125, which was considerably more than many of the human actors earned.

FIVE MINUTE HEALTHCHECK

Get into the habit of giving your dog a five minute health check every day; the earlier a potential problem is detected, the more successful any needed treatment is likely to be, as well as less costly – plus of course, your pet may be saved unnecessary suffering. Whilst grooming, or after a walk can be good times to carry out your inspection; or any time when your dog is ready to rest quietly so you can look him over thoroughly.

Ears: Looking inside, they should appear clean and pale pink in colour, not sore and inflamed looking, smelly or with waxy or pus like discharges.

Eyes: Bright and clear, without cloudiness of the cornea, the whites completely white, not red, inflamed or with a yellowish tinge. Both eyelids should be fully open, not half closed or blinking rapidly; neither should there be any watery or pus like discharge or tear staining.

Nose: Clean, without crusty deposits or clear or pus like discharge or bleeding.

Mouth: The gums should be salmon pink; they may change colour if he is unwell – paleness may be due to anaemia or dehydration, a blue tinge could indicate a circulatory problem, and yellowness, jaundice. If the gums are pigmented, check the membranes of the eyes instead for a healthy colour. Pressing the gums with the tip of a finger should cause it to briefly go pale, with normal gum colour returning within two to three seconds.

Teeth: Take a good look at the teeth at the back of the mouth as well as those at the front, if you are able. They should be clean, whitish yellow in colour and free of build ups of tartar. The gums at the base shouldn't appear reddened, sore or bleeding; the breath shouldn't smell offensive, and there shouldn't be any sign of excessive salivation or panting.

Feet: Toenails in good order, not split, torn nor overlong, which can put strain on tendons and ligaments; the pads should feel supple and not be sore, cut or cracking.

Body: Standing behind your dog, run both hands along the sides of his body; his ribs should just be discernible beneath a thin layer of fat.

Coat: Whether short, long, glossy or harsh textured, the coat should look and feel healthy, and be free of matting, soiling or bald patches.

Skin: Parting the coat and looking at the skin, it should move easily over the underlying tissue, feel warm to the touch, not hot, cold or clammy, and shouldn't be scurfy or flaky, or showing any itchy, sore or reddened areas.

Genitals: Should be clean and free of soiling, without offensive smell or discharges.

Lumps and bumps: Make a note of any lumps and bumps which occur, and monitor any existing ones for signs of change or feel.

General: Try to spend time observing your dog at other times as well – working, playing, sleeping, eating, drinking and relieving himself so that you become familiar with what is normal for him and sensitive to any departures from this which might indicate the onset of a problem. Behavioural changes are also important to note as they can be symptomatic of physical problems.

❦ EXERT FROM A DOG'S DIARY ❦

8.00 am: Dog Food! My favourite!

9.30 am: A car ride! My favourite!

9.40 am: A walk in the park! My favourite!

10.30 am: Got rubbed and petted! My favourite!

12.00 pm: Lunch! My favourite!

1.00 pm: Played in the garden! My favourite!

1.30 pm: Oh-oh. Bath. Bummer.

3.00 pm: Wagged my tail! My favourite!

5.00 pm: Milk bones! My favourite!

7.00 pm: Played ball! My favourite!

8.00 pm: Wow! Watched TV with my people! My favourite!

11.00 pm: Sleeping on the bed! My favourite!

(Author unknown)

I want to compose a piece for dogs,
and I already have my décor.
The curtain rises on a bone.
Erik Satie

CALL OF THE WILD

In 1897 Jack London joined the Klondike Gold Rush and experienced at first hand the hardships of life which faced both men and dogs, and which he portrayed in his gritty and uncompromising novels. Buck in Call of the Wild was based on a real dog he was loaned while in Dawson City.

FAMOUS OWNERS OF RESCUE DOGS 2

Sandra Bullock – Poppy, a three legged Chihuahua/Pomeranian mix was adopted from a shelter in South California in 2005 following her marriage to Jesse James. The couple went on to celebrate their first wedding anniversary by adopting another dog from the same shelter – this time a one eyed Chihuahua called Bebe.

MEMORABLE MUTTS

There are many books in which dogs are the co-stars or have only small supporting roles, rather than being the primary characters; yet very often, like so many real dogs they are utter scene stealers, and linger on in the memory long after the two legged heroes and heroines of the piece have become little more than faded recollections. A small selection of examples include

Timmy: the mongrel with a long wavy tail and loving brown eyes, loyal, intelligent and beloved companion of tomboy George in the Famous Five books by Enid Blyton.

Montmorency: a fox terrier whose angelic demeanour belies the fact that he enjoys a good scrap with other dogs and who generally leaves a trail of devastation in his wake in Jerome K. Jerome's classic Three Men in a Boat (to say nothing of the Dog)

The Disreputable Dog: a mysterious being created by magic, who takes the shape of a mixed breed dog with pointy ears and accompanies Lirael in Garth Nix's fantasy adventures Lirael and Abhorsen.

Jim: the narrow dog of the title in Narrowdog to Carcassonne, he is described by author

Terry Darlington as a 'cowardly, thieving and disrespectful' whippet who 'loathes boating'.

Sorrow: pet Labrador in John Irving's Hotel New Hampshire; afflicted by chronic flatulence in life, after being put to sleep he is stuffed and literally frightens a grandfather to death when he falls out of a closet

Nana: the Newfoundland engaged by Mr and Mrs Darling as nursemaid to the children in Peter Pan by JM Barrie; prim but perfect she is much resented by other two legged nursemaids whose sloppiness she shows up.

Cafall: a sheepdog who is white all over save for one small black patch and with distinctive silver eyes that can 'see the wind' and who plays a vital, if small role in Susan Cooper's The Grey King, part of the Dark is Rising sequence.

Bullseye: who could fail to shed a tear at the brutal treatment meted out to the loyal dog by villain Bill Sikes, or at his tragic end, faithful to the last in Charles Dickens' Oliver Twist?

Fluffy: the three headed dog who can be lulled into peaceful sleep with the right sort of lullaby in JK Rowling's Harry Potter and the Philosopher's Stone

Fang: Another Rowling creation, Fang belongs to Hogwarts' gamekeeper Hagrid; inclined to slobberiness he is less fierce than he looks.

Wiggins: despite being vain, self-centred and food obsessed the Cavalier King Charles who is Maria Merryweather's companion still manages to be endearing in The Little White Horse by Elizabeth Goudge.

Laddie: blonde and utterly gorgeous, every inch a film star in looks but sadly lacking in the brains department, Laddie is crucial to the sublime Lassie sub-plot in Terry Pratchett's Moving Pictures.

Gaspode: a small scruffy terrier type mongrel blessed with a vast number of diseases, human intelligence and the ability to speak, plus a sharp line in sarcasm, he first appears in Terry Pratchett's Moving Pictures and goes on to pop up again in six further volumes.

THE SMALLEST

The Chihuahua is the smallest breed – sizes can vary as the breed standard specifies weight rather than height. Up to 6 lbs (2.7 kg) is acceptable, but 2 – 4 lbs (1 – 1.8 kg) is preferred. The Yorkshire Terrier comes close, and is another breed where weight, rather than dimensions are the criteria; up to 7 lbs (3.2 kg) in weight is permitted for showing purposes.

NAMESAKE

Victorian artist Sir Edwin Landseer was acclaimed for his depictions of animals, in particular dogs, horses and stags; the black and white variant of the Newfoundland was named the 'Landseer' after him, due to the highly popular paintings he made showing dogs of this colour rescuing children from drowning.

> *It's my dog's birthday and I write*
> *a little piece for him every year.*
> Rossini

✿ DRUG BUSTER ✿

The greatest number of drug seizures by dogs was 969 in 1988 – the canine team of 'Rocky' and 'Barco' who patrolled the Texas/Mexico border were so good at their job that drug lords set a price of $30,000 on their heads.

✿ IT'S A BUST! ✿

The most successful solo narcotics sniffer dog was a US Customs Labrador called 'Snag', who was responsible for 118 drug seizures worth a record $810million.

QUESTION
Who is the dogs favorite comedian?
ANSWER
Growlcho Marx!

✿ SPLASHING OUT ✿

- Fresh water should always be available for your dog; he maybe able to survive weeks without food, but survival may be reduced to a matter of days if he's deprived of liquids.
- Around 60 – 70 per cent of a dog's body is made up of water
- A 10% fluid loss can lead to serious illness unless it is replaced
- Approximately 45 – 50 ml of water per kilogramme of bodyweight per day is required; so a Labrador weighing 30 kg for example, will need around one and a half litres.
- Water intake may vary slightly depending on factors such as weather, exercise and diet: dogs may drink more in warm weather or after strenuous exercise, or if on a dry diet. Bitches feeding puppies will also be likely to drink more as a lot of water will be lost through their milk.
- Water bowls should be washed out daily to prevent scumminess from building up, and the water changed completely twice daily rather than just being topped up when it gets low.
- Never let your dog drink from puddles, ponds, rivers or from the toilet. Don't offer milk to drink instead of water, as adult dogs cannot digest the lactose and may suffer from diarrhoea as a result.

- Note any changes in drinking habits as it could indicate the onset of health problems. Excessive drinking can be linked to more than 65 different ailments, including diabetes, liver and kidney disease and hormonal disorders.

I would rather see the portrait of a dog that I know, than all the allegorical paintings they can show me in the world.
Samuel Johnson

❋ UNLIKELY TITLE ❋

It's strange but true; there really is a book entitled 'Teach Your Dog to Read'. What started out as a matter of light hearted curiosity for top trainer Bonnie Bergin developed into a more serious project on discovering that many dogs could be taught to recognise and distinguish between different printed words. It's not exactly reading as such; pets are unlikely to be found reading novels, or relaxing with the weekend papers – at least in the immediate future – but does have a useful function, in enabling guide dogs, for example, to identify signs such as exits and toilets.

... dogs are generally not interested in art.
David Hockney

❋ DOG'S LIFE ❋

The romantic poet Elizabeth Barrett Browning suffered from ill health for many years, and during this time when she was frequently confined to bed, her constant companion was a Cocker Spaniel, Flush. The dog was given to her as a gift by a friend who thought that he would help cheer and comfort her, and the ploy certainly did the trick of raising her spirits: "Flush amuses me sometimes when I am inclined to be amused by nothing else" she told one of her brothers.

Elizabeth doted on the dog, indulging all his whims; although she wrote 'Voices to the north and south cry 'Flush is spoilt!'' freely acknowledging the fact that she pampered him to a ridiculous extent, it did nothing to prevent her from continuing to cosset him. Convinced that Flush was exceptionally intelligent, Elizabeth took it upon herself to teach him arithmetic and to read; he never succeeded in getting past learning the letters A, B and C, but she dismissed this failure as simply being due solely to the fact that 'he has no very pronounced love for literature'.

When Flush was dognapped, she was distraught. This happened three times, each time with a higher ransom being asked for his safe return; on the third occasion, the sum asked was more than Elizabeth's father was prepared to pay, or that she could raise herself from her own resources. Desperate with anxiety, unable to eat, sleep, or think about anything other than 'poor, darling Flush' she personally negotiated for his return for a smaller amount of money.

When she eloped with poet Robert Browning, she took with her just two bags of luggage – and, naturally, Flush, who had been unable to scupper the romance by biting Browning twice. Although Robert tolerated him for the sake of his mistress, he complained that the dog was noisy, arrogant, overbearing and tyrannical with him, considering that he existed only for the purpose of serving him. Italy's climate didn't suit Flush as well as that of England, and he was to lose his fur to mange; the date of his death is unknown, although he supposedly buried in the cellars of the house where the Brownings lived, Casa Guidi. Whatever his end, he will forever be remembered for the poem which Elizabeth dedicated to him 'To Flush, my dog'. He was immortalised in *Flush: A Biography,* published in 1933, written by Virginia Woolf's. It traces the life of Elizabeth Barrett Browning's spaniel Flush from his carefree existence in the country to his adoption by Elizabeth, and his days in Italy, although Woolf does also take the opportunity to include some pointed social comment.

❊❅ BLUE PETER 3 ❊❅

The third Blue Peter dog was 'Patch', one of Petra's puppies born in 1965; three of his littermates went to children's homes, two to be sheepdogs on farms, one to an old people's home, and one became a regimental mascot. Teamed up with presenter John Noakes, he died suddenly in 1971, to be replaced by Border Collie 'Shep'; the pair became a hugely popular double act creating the catchphrase 'Get down Shep!' which was parodied in a song by the Barron Nights, and being immortalised in wax at Madame Tussauds in 1977. When Noakes left the programme, Shep went too, dying in 1987.

❊❊ WEATHER WARNING ❊❊

The phrase 'raining cats and dogs' dates back to 17th century England, when many dogs and cats drowned during heavy downpours. When rivers burst their banks, their bodies would be seen floating in the torrents which raced through the streets, giving the appearance that it had, literally, rained cats and dogs.

SIGNS OF AGEING

grey hairs round muzzle	stiffer, less flexible joints;	wear and tear on teeth
skin and coat becoming	decreased mobility	sleeping longer, and often
drier and sometimes smellier	deafness	more deeply
more sedate	deteriorating eyesight	incontinence
less inclined to play	weight changes	senility

❊❊ SPACE DOG FACT 2 ❊❊

When Veterok and Ugolyok were launched on February 22 1966 on Cosmos 110, they spent 22 days in space – a record for spaceflight longevity which wasn't broken by humans until 1974.

❊❊ VOTES FOR DOGS ❊❊

When Toby Russell Rhodes sent off an application to New Zealand election authorities, giving his occupation as 'rodent exterminator' no-one seemed to guess that he was no ordinary voter – even though his form was signed with a paw print. Jack Russell terrier Toby was duly sent a voters' card.

My hand will miss the insinuated nose,
Mine eyes that tail
that wagged contempt at Fate.
Sir William Watson

❊❊ INNER NASTIES ❊❊

Worms in dogs fall into two main categories – roundworms and tapeworms. In the UK there are 12 different species of roundworm that can infect your pet: the commonest is Toxocara canis which looks like threads or strands of spaghetti and can reach up to 18 cm in length. Tapeworms are made up of strings of segments: the most common is Dipylidium caninem and can reach up to 70 cm in length.

Even very young puppies may have worms; they can be born infected with worms, or may have them passed on from the mother in the milk, whilst adult dogs most commonly acquire them from coming into contact with other dogs, scavenging, or picking up eggs from walking on contaminated ground and ingesting the eggs during grooming. Even though all trace of dog faeces may have long disappeared, worm eggs can remain infective in the soil or grass for two or more years.

✣✣ DEAR DEPARTED DOGS ✣✣

Loss of a beloved dog can affect owners as deeply as that of a friend, relative or partner, so it is understandable that many should wish to provide a last, final demonstration of affection by arranging a fitting end for the deceased pet's remains. It's not a new concept by any means; the ancient Egyptians loved their dogs too, and they were mummified and buried in family tombs. Imperial Chinese dynasties maintained a dog cemetery in Peking with tombstones made of marble, ivory, gold and silver; and in recent years, an archaeological excavation discovered a thousand-year-old dog cemetery with 43 pets in separate plots, with treats, blankets and food buried with them by owners.

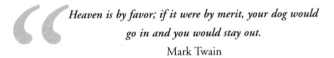
Heaven is by favor; if it were by merit, your dog would go in and you would stay out.
Mark Twain

✣✣ OLDEST CEMETERY ✣✣

The oldest pet cemetery in the world, and one which is still in use, is Hartsdale Pet Cemetery in New York. It all began in 1896, when vet Dr Samuel Johnson offered his apple orchard to a bereaved friend to bury his dog in; following this act of compassion, Johnson was flooded with requests from other owners. Today it is the resting place of nearly 70,000 pets.

✣✣ WINTER PERILS ✣✣

Dogs are attracted to the smell and taste of antifreeze, but it can be highly poisonous if spillages from car radiators and screen washer reservoirs are lapped up. Even the tiniest amounts can be fatal, so clear up any spillages of your own, store coolants well out of reach and keep your dog away from puddles where cars have been parked. Propylene glycol based products are less toxic than the traditional ethylene glycol type, but no antifreeze is entirely safe, and it's best to keep your pet away from both. If your dog does ingest coolant, contact the vet immediately as treatment is only effective if administered early.

Some dogs will try eating anything, to their peril: other seasonal hazards, particularly over the festive period include tinsel and decorative tree baubles, mistletoe and holly berries, poinsettia, gift wrapping and ribbon, and the Christmas tree water.

❉ VACCINATION ❉

Vaccination is a common procedure much taken for granted these days, and one which has saved many lives, but is nevertheless still a relatively recent innovation. In 1928, 23 years after the distemper virus was first identified, a commercial vaccine became available, followed shortly after by a leptospirosis vaccine.

The beggar's dog and widow's cat,
Feed them and thou wilt grow fat.
William Blake

❉ UNFAIR DISMISSAL ❉

In 2004, the Royal Mail lost an employment tribunal hearing against an employee who claimed unfair dismissal over taking time off work in order to mourn the death of his pet dog.

WHY DO DOGS SOMETIMES SLIDE THEIR BOTTOMS ALONG THE GROUND?

This can be due to the presence of tapeworms, when scooting the bottom along is resorted to in an effort to relieve the irritation caused by the small white eggs which look like small grains of rice clinging around the anus. It may also commonly be caused by impaction, or other problems affecting the anal sacs. These are situated on either side of the anus and contain a smelly fluid, a few drops of which are squeezed out onto the stool each time a dog defecates. This is what interests dogs and makes them want to stop and sniff the 'offerings' left by others. You should contact your vet to diagnose the cause and prescribe treatment.

THE RACE TO THE POLE

When Arctic explorer Roald Amundsen led the first successful expedition to reach the South Pole, his achievement was largely down to the teams of dogs who pulled the sledges containing food and equipment. The dogs enabled the explorers to move faster than if they had hauled the sledges themselves – as Scott's ill-fated expedition ended up doing – and at less physical cost to the human members, but the price paid by the dogs was appalling.

Amundsen had spent time learning from the Inuit, and was convinced that dogs were vital to success; consequently the ship that set off from Norway, bound for the Bay of Whales in Antarctica carried 97 Greenland dogs. The first six weeks at sea were a miserable time for them, chained on the decks until confidence in them was such that they were finally allowed their freedom to roam around the boat, although they were still kept muzzled. By the time they arrived, five months later, the number had increased to 116 dogs, due to the birth of 23 puppies along the way; four had been lost – two washed overboard during storms, one dying giving birth, and one the victim of an unknown disease.

After a first, unsuccessful start, Amundsen selected the strongest of those in his party, and on 19th October 1911 set out again with four other men, four sledges and 52 dogs. By the end of the first day he had to cut five of the dogs loose because of injury or poor condition; on October 29th the first dog was shot when it was unable to continue any further. Although Amundsen had tremendous admiration and respect for the dogs and their abilities, it didn't prevent him from driving them on with ruthless determination to the point of exhaustion and collapse. Neither did it prevent him from leaving caches of the bodies behind to provide food supplies for both men and surviving dogs on the way back; it had already been planned from the outset to slaughter half along the route in order to conserve supplies. In comparison, Scott, his rival in the race to the Pole took just 33 dogs and 19 ponies, preferring to rely instead on 3 motorized sledges – which quickly broke down – and the 'man hauling' to which his team ultimately resorted. When the ponies inevitably weakened he was unable to shoot them himself, having to leave the job to others, and he was relieved when finally the dogs were sent back to base, still 360 miles short of his goal. Scott and his men perished in their attempt, whilst Amundsen's team all survived – thanks to their dogs, only eleven of whom returned.

> *I have sometimes thought of the final cause*
> *of dogs having such short lives, and I am quite satisfied it*
> *is in compassion to the human race;*
> *for if we suffer so much in losing a dog after an*
> *acquaintance of ten or twelve years, what would it be if*
> *they were to live double that time?*
> Sir Walter Scott

SIGNS OF WORM RELATED DISEASE

- weight loss
- increased appetite
- scurfy skin
- dull coat
- diarrhoea
- vomiting
- worms seen in faeces or vomit

Other signs include skin disease, constipation, lethargy and signs of heart disease, increased susceptibility to infections, coughing and breathing difficulties.

How often a worming treatment is given depends on the product and age of the dog; generally, puppies are usually wormed every 2-3 weeks until 3 months old, and then monthly until 6 months old, after which treatment is as for adult dogs, every 3 months. Wormers remove worms already present, but don't stop re-infection, so a year-round programme needs to be implemented.

THE FRENCH WAY

Le Cimetiere des Chiens, at Asnieres on the outskirts of Paris is the oldest European pet cemetery. In 1898 a law was passed banning owners from disposing of the bodies of dead pets with household rubbish, or by dumping them in the Seine – 3,000 had been retrieved from the river by sanitation workers the year previously. As a result, George Harmois and Marguerite Durand had the idea of setting up a pet cemetery, and which duly opened in 1899; since then, over 40,000 animals have been buried there. A special monument was erected to the 40,000th animal to lie within it's walls, a stray dog run over near the gates in 1958.

MISSING IN ACTION

Prince Charles had a Labrador called Harvey, who had become an old dog by the time he married Princess Diana; she allegedly wouldn't allow him in the house because of his incontinence, and the Prince reluctantly had to give him away. Harvey was eventually succeeded by Jack Russell Terriers Tigger and Pooh; whilst out walking with them one day, he was faced with every owner's worst nightmare when Pooh ran off and disappeared. The missing terrier was never found, despite a cash reward being offered and it was surmised that she had most likely become trapped in a rabbit hole somewhere.

Animals have these advantages over man:
They have no theologians to instruct them,
their funerals cost them nothing,
and no-one starts lawsuits over their wills.
Voltaire

CANINE AUTHORS

Most dogs are more likely to chew or tear up books than to write one, but with a little help from their owners a few have set paw to paper and produced their own memoirs.

Millie's Book: as dictated to Barbara Bush offers Springer Spaniel Millie's personal insights into life at the White House. As to be expected, her main concerns are with exploits such as digging up tulip beds, chasing squirrels, sitting on antique furniture and raising a family of her own than with matters of state; and she also remains admirably discreet about any Bush family secrets or scandals. Despite this, the book easily outsold that of her master, remaining on the 'non-fiction' bestseller list for 29 weeks.

Copper: A Dog's Life by Annabel Goldsmith relates arrogant mongrel Copper's story as he looks down from Heaven; originally a present for daughter Jemima he becomes the favoured pet of Annabel and gleefully recounts his escapades from solo trips to the pub on the bus, to a visit to Brighton accompanied by one of his many offspring. Following an incident when he bites a child, his opportunities for adventure become more curtailed until finally at the very end, his luck runs out when he is knocked down by a passing car.

Buster's Diaries: as told to Roy Hattersley achieved a notable literary first in that Buster was nominated for an Author of the Year Award. After his courageous act of self-defence against a goose in St James' Park was misreported by the press, Buster, a German Shepherd/Staffordshire Bull Terrier decided to put the record straight. The book charts his meteoric rise from street pup to streetwise sophisticate after being adopted by Labour politician Roy Hattersley in 1995, as well as revealing the truth about what really happened during the infamous goose incident. He has since followed up his earlier success with a further volume, Buster's Secret Diaries (as discovered by Roy Hattersley)

The Tinkerbell Hilton Diaries: My life tailing Paris Hilton by Tinkerbell Hilton (as told to D. Resin) in which Tinkerbell the Chihuahua mercilessly lampoons her owner is a cynical look at the celebrity lifestyle through a dog's eyes; unsurprisingly, it's not an officially authorized account.

COST OF DYING

A Direct Line Pet Insurance survey found that 20 per cent of all owners spend more than £100 after their dog has passed away, with 29 per cent opting for cremation and scattering the ashes somewhere special and 1% for having it stuffed.

HEALTH RISK

Worms aren't just a risk to your dog's health: they can affect humans too. Following the accidental ingestion of Toxocara canis eggs, the larvae travel around the body and may settle in the eye causing impairment of vision or even blindness in young children. For this reason, it's important to always scoop poop, provide a 'no-dog' play area for children, discourage face licking by pets, and to wash hands after playing, handling or petting your dog.

SPOT ON

The inspiration for Dodie Smith's classic book 'The 101 Dalmatians' came when a guest remarked that her own Dalmatian Pongo would make a nice fur coat. The book was made into an animated Disney film in 1961, with a live action remake in 1996 in which 217 Dalmatians were used. A sequel, 102 Dalmatians followed in 2001.

WHERE'S THERE'S A WILL

It's important to ensure that should the unthinkable happen and you pre-decease your pet, you have made adequate provision for him in your will; almost a quarter of Americans include animals in their wills, making an average bequest of around $25,000. In the UK, approximately a fifth of owners leave pets half of their estate, with an estimated 8 per cent of pets being left more in wills than friends and family of the deceased.

American heiress Ella Wendal is generally credited with having started the trend in 1931, when she left her Standard Poodle 'Toby' a sum which nowadays would be equivalent to $75 million. Since then, many dogs have profited handsomely from owners' bequests; Christina Foyle left £20,000 to her cherished dog Bobby, a 14-year-old collie cross and a Chihuahua called Frankie lives in luxury in a £10 million San Diego mansion (although the downside is that he has to share with two cats) while his carer lives in a small flat.

✷❀ WORMS ❀✷

Worming treatments first became available in the 1930s.

✷❀ TRUST FUND ❀✷

If planning to leave your dog a little something in your will, it's worth bearing in mind that as a pet is regarded in law as property, you can't leave it cash; you'll need to set up a trust instead if you want to be able to guarantee his future wellbeing in the event of your demise being in advance of his.

Be comforted, little dog, thou too in the Resurrection shall have a little golden tail.
Martin Luther

✷❀ SIDE BY SIDE ❀✷

The Rosa Bonheur Memorial Park, Maryland USA made headlines in 1979 as the first pet cemetery in the world to allow humans to be buried alongside their pets.

✷❀ EAR PROBLEMS ❀✷

Dogs with floppy ears are more prone to ear problems as the shape keeps the insides warm and damp, encouraging the growth of yeasts, mites and bacteria.

✷❀ GREYFRIARS BOBBY ❀✷

There are many tales of dogs who have refused to desert their owners, even after death. Probably the most famous of these was Greyfriars Bobby, a Skye Terrier who belonged to police constable John Gray, accompanying him wherever he went. When Gray died from tuberculosis in 1858, Bobby waited until the gates of the graveyard were unlocked when the police did their rounds each night, and then slipped in to lie on his master's grave. When Gray's widow and son moved away from the area, they were unable to persuade Bobby to go with them; he remained at the graveyard, leaving only to eat the meals provided for him by an obliging coffee shop owner. As word of Bobby began to spread, he became something of a celebrity, yet with his owner dead, he was in effect now a stray dog and in danger of being collected along with the others and destroyed. Happily, William Chambers, the Lord Provost and director of the Scottish Society for the Prevention of Cruelty to Animals, stepped forward and offered to pay Bobby's licence for life, presenting him with a collar bearing a brass plate on which was inscribed: 'Greyfriars Bobby from the Lord Provost 1867, licensed'. As a consequence of this act of kindness, Bobby became even more famous, and artists and photographers visited to capture his image for posterity. When Bobby died, he was buried just inside the gate, not far from John Gray's final resting place; a headstone marking the spot reads 'Greyfriars Bobby. Died14th January 1872, Aged 16 years. Let his loyalty and devotion be a lesson to us all'. A water fountain and drinking bowl with a small statue of Bobby on top stands in front of a pub of the same name, just in front of the graveyard, and his story has been handed on down in books, the most popular if not particularly accurate versions of which were written by Eleanor Atkinson and Lavinia Derwent. He was also immortalised on the screen in 1961 and again more recently in 2006, in 'Greyfriars Bobby'.

QUESTION

What happened when the dog went to the flea circus?

ANSWER

He stole the show!

❀ PRESIDENTIAL POOCHES 5 ❀

In 1944 Franklin D Roosevelt came under attack from political enemies who asserted that he had dispatched a destroyer, at huge expense, to collect his pet dog. He countered with what became known as the 'Fala speech', saying 'These Republican leaders have not been content with attacks on me, or my wife, or on my sons ......They now include my little dog Fala ...... I don't resent attacks, and my family doesn't resent attacks. But Fala does resent them. You know, Fala is Scotch, and being a Scottie, as soon as he learned that the Republican faction writers in Congress had concocted a story that I had left him behind on the Aleutian Islands and had sent a destroyer back to find him – at cost to taxpayers of two or three, or eight, or twenty million dollars - his Scotch soul was furious. He has never been the same dog since. I am accustomed to hearing falsehoods about myself ...... but I think I have a right to resent, to object to libellous statements about my dog."

Together with Winston Churchill's poodle Rufus, Fala was present at the historic signing of the Atlantic Charter; he was inseparable from FDR, accompanying him everywhere, and appears to have been every bit as cherished – and pampered – as Churchill's pets. Investigation of a series of tummy upsets revealed that the White House staff weren't immune to Fala's charms either and had been overfeeding him titbits in between his breakfast bone (served from his master's breakfast tray) and dinner. FDR was prompted to order that 'not even one crumb will be fed to Fala except by the President', after which the digestive disturbances cleared up.

Fala survived the president by seven years; after attending his funeral, although he adapted to life with Roosevelt's widow Eleanor, he missed his master. When he died in 1952 he was buried alongside him, and is commemorated by a statue at the Franklin Delano Roosevelt Memorial in Washington DC showing him sitting at his master's feet.

LIGHTING UP TIME

In 1993, an Internet chat room group were comparing notes as to what they did when one of their pets died. One of the group, Lisa Sayer, mentioned that each Monday evening she lit a candle for 'Bridge babies' and offered to add the names of other pets to her list. A few others said they'd like to light their own candles too; a time was set, a format worked out for a brief ceremony to commemorate those pets who had passed on, and the first 'Bridge List' was posted on March 15th 1993. Within two weeks the ceremony had become an international event, and continues today, with owners joining in all around the world.

Not the least hard thing to bear when they go from us, these quiet friends, is that they carry away with them so many years of our own lives.
John Galsworthy

UNLUCKIEST DOG

The title of 'Britain's Unluckiest Dog' was bestowed on Zeus, an English Bull Terrier by insurance company PetPlan in 2006 after cataloguing all his woes. The five-year-old dog's problems started when he was just a few months old, when he developed an allergy to dust mites – since then he has had 189 visits to the vet, 12 operations, received £15,000 of treatment and made over 50 claims on his pet insurance.

ORIGIN OF BREEDS 1

After examining the genes from 85 different breeds, scientists not only found that each was genetically distinct from the others, but that they could all be placed into one of four different bred clusters. Three were modern and probably dated back to when breeds officially became formalised in the 19th century - but the fourth was ancient, with the Sharpei, Pekingese, and Shih Tzu all unexpectedly standing alongside the Siberian Husky in this group which shows the closest genetic relationship to their wolf ancestor. Surprisingly, breeds commonly thought to have been very old, such as the Pharaoh Hound and Greyhound shown on tomb walls turned out not to be of ancient origin after all. The scientists concluded that they were more modern recreations rather than the 'real thing'

EAR, EAR

Eighteen or more muscles are used to move the ears to enable dogs to pinpoint the location of a sound. They can identify where noises are coming from in six hundredths of a second, and can hear sounds four times further away than we are able to. Their range of hearing is far superior to ours as well; they are able to hear sounds in a frequency range as low as 16 – 20 Hz (compared to humans at 20 – 70 Hz) and as high as 70,000 – 100,000 Hz (20,000 for humans). Obviously, more natural, upright ear shapes are better at detecting sounds than floppy ears which tend to muffle them; but regardless of ear shape, most dogs are very good at hearing even the quietest of sounds elsewhere which might indicate that food could be on offer.

DOG SHOOTS MAN

There have been numerous reports over the years of dogs shooting their owners – generally accidents occurring during hunting expeditions. One case might have been considered as just retribution, or at least self defence, when a Florida man decided to shoot his seven German Shepherd crossbreed puppies because he couldn't find them a home. He was holding two of the puppies when one of them wiggled and put it's paw on the trigger of the .38 calibre revolver, causing him to shoot himself in the wrist.

 You think dogs will not be in heaven? I tell you, they will be there long before any of us.
Robert Louis Stevenson

WHAT A MOUTHFUL

Like humans, dogs have two sets of teeth during their lifetime. The first 'milk' teeth are very small, white and sharp, and begin to erupt when the puppy is 2-4 weeks old. Puppies have fewer milk than adult teeth; as they don't need to chew their food very much, they don't have any molars.

At around 4 months old the baby teeth begin to fall out, making room for them to be replaced with a permanent adult set. The roots are dissolved and reabsorbed into the jaws, which frees the teeth from the gums so they become loose and drop out, often being swallowed. The first teeth to be shed are the incisors, with the molars the last to erupt.

DOG LITTER

At the ovulation stage of the sexual cycle, between 2 and 10 eggs are released in small breeds, and between 5 and 20 eggs in larger breeds – which is why bigger dogs tend to have bigger litters than small dogs. The normal length of pregnancy in dogs is 59 – 66 days. Although fertility decreases with age, female dogs do not have a menopause.

WHY DO DOGS EAT GRASS?

There are several theories about this; that it's due to a lack of fibre in the diet, lack of certain nutrients which they are trying to top up, that they have an upset stomach and are trying to make themselves vomit, or that they instinctively know what foliage to eat and are trying to self medicate. Many just seem to enjoy it. If your dog appears healthy a little occasional grazing is probably nothing to worry about, although care should be taken that he doesn't nibble at foliage which has been treated with fertilisers, pesticides or herbicides, and in gardens, toxic plants should not be planted.

WINTER LOSS

More dogs are lost during the winter months than at any other time of year.

TITANIC SURVIVORS

When the supposedly unsinkable liner Titanic went down in icy waters in April of 1912, there was a huge loss of human life; of the 2,223 people on board only 706 survived. Amazingly, three dogs also lived to tell the tale: a Pekingese called 'Sun Yat Sen' owned by Henry Sleeper Harper, a Pomeranian named 'Lady' owned by Miss Margaret Hays of New York, and another Pomeranian belonging to Elizabeth Barrett Rothschild. Carried in the arms of their owners, the lifeboats they entered were so empty and the dogs so small anyway, that no-one appears to have objected to them.

An eye witness account by one of the stewards on the SS Carpathia, the first rescue ship to reach the scene of the tragedy stated: 'One of the earlier boats to arrive was seen to contain a woman tenderly clasping a pet Pomeranian. When assisted to the rope ladder and while the rope was being fastened around her she emphatically refused to give up for a second dog which was evidently so much to her.' The steward further added that one of the survivors told him that one woman declined to leave the Titanic because they would not take off a pet dog belonging to her. This may possibly have been the same woman spotted two days after the sinking by a passenger on the German liner 'Bremen'; she was floating in her lifejacket with her arms tightly wrapped around a large dog.

There is no record as to what befell Sun Yat Sen following his lucky escape, and some dispute as to what happened to the Pomeranian belonging to Mrs Rothschild, the passenger who had refused to let go of her pet during their rescue by the Carpathia. One report states that it was killed by another dog soon afterwards while staying at her summerhouse, and another that it was run over by a streetcar. Miss Hays' pet was more fortunate; after the rescue they were inseparable, with Lady even accompanying her mistress to the New York opera, comfortably ensconced in a bag in which she was not only small enough to fit but evidently well enough behaved to go unnoticed. Lady died in 1921, and was cremated and interred in a pet cemetery in New York.

MOST ACCIDENT PRONE DOGS

German Shepherds and Labradors are most likely to need a trip to the vets as a result of an accident, and Poodles and Shih Tzus are the least likely.

✾✾ URBAN MYTH 3 – DOG NOSE ✾✾

A wet nose isn't always a sign of good health, or a dry one a sign of illness.

✾✾ HOW OLD? ✾✾

If trying to guess the age of a dog whose history is unknown, checking to see how many baby teeth are present can provide a clue. Once over a year old it becomes a matter of making an educated guess based on the amount of wear and tear and tartar present on the teeth, together with taking into account the general physical appearance.

 Dogs are such fine creatures that rare is the man who desireth not one for this purpose or for that......
Gaston Febus de Foix-Bearn

✾✾ DOGNAPPING ✾✾

The Dogs Trust estimates that around 50,000 dogs are stolen in the UK every year. Some are stolen to order, or for resale, breeding, illegal coursing or fighting – and many are held for ransom. A survey by the Missing Pets Bureau also revealed that:

- Dognapping rose by 141 per cent in 2005
- One third of all dogs stolen are crossbreeds
- Dogs are five times more likely to be stolen than cats

Dogs most at risk of theft:

- Labrador Retriever
- English Springer Spaniels
- Jack Russell and other terriers
- Bull Terriers
- Lurchers
- Yorkshire Terriers

✾✾ WEIRD USA DOG LAWS ✾✾

- Assaulting a dog in Maryland, earns a felony crime charge; assault of a police officer on the other hand only attracts a lesser charge of a misdemeanour.

- In Normal, Oklahoma, you can be sent to prison for 'making an ugly face' at a dog.
- In Venture County, California, cats and dogs are not allowed to have sex without a permit.
- In Hartford, Connecticut, it is illegal to educate a dog.
- In Sheridan, Wyoming, a policeman can bite a barking dog in order to quiet him.
- In Northbrook, Illinois it is illegal for dogs to bark for more than 15 minutes.
- In Zion, Illinois it is illegal to give a lighted cigar to a dog.
- Some areas of North Carolina prohibit fights between cats and dogs.
- In Michigan it is illegal to kill a dog using a decompression chamber
- In Fort Thomas, Kentucky, dogs may not molest cars.
- In Anchorage, Alaska, you are not allowed to tie a dog to the roof of a car.
- In Illinois it is illegal to give a dog whiskey.
- In Chicago you are not allowed to take a French poodle to the opera.
- In International Falls, Minnesota, owners can be fined for allowing a dog to chase a cat up a telegraph pole.
- In Arkansas you can be fined and your dog impounded if he barks after 6pm.

QUESTION
How can you tell if you have a stupid dog?
ANSWER
It chases parked cars!

❧❧ ALTERNATIVE TREATMENTS FOR DOGS ❧❧

Acupuncture: Long, fine, flexible needles are inserted at specific points to help rebalance energy flow within the body and stimulate the immune system, making it possible for healing to take place. It can also be very effective in providing pain relief. Other forms include laser therapy, and the application of a thermal stimulus using Moxa. Only vets are allowed to perform acupuncture.

Aromatherapy: Use of aromatic, highly concentrated oils extracted from different flower and tree parts which are inhaled or absorbed. Oils are not imposed on animals: a method of 'self-selection' is used whereby a patient's preferences and dislikes are noted.

Bach Flower Essences: Diluted flower preparations added to drinking water or placed directly on the tongue, of which Rescue Remedy is probably one of the best known. Most frequently used to treat emotional and psychological states rather than physical illness, although they can influence the latter. As well as Bach Flower remedies, other essences have been developed such as Australian Bush Flower Remedies, but all are prepared and used in the same way.

Canine Bowen technique: A 'light touch' gentle hands-on technique which promotes healing, pain relief and body/energy rebalancing. Based on the human principles of Bowen technique, fingers and thumbs are placed on specific points and gentle rolling movements are applied over soft tissues.

Crystals: Various crystals and gemstones are thought to possess an electrical charge or vibration which can help balance and restore the body's natural energy flow if it has been disrupted by injury or disease and elicit a healing response. Certain crystals have an affinity for certain body systems or symptoms, and can also be used for emotional and psychological problems as well as physical ones.

Herbalism: Parts of plants mixed with food or used in a liquid tincture form. Each plant has unique properties; different herbs can also be mixed together to produce a balanced effect best suited to the individual patient. Not all herbs are compatible with others, whilst some are not suitable for long term use, so it is essential to consult an experienced veterinary practitioner.

Homoeopathy: Highly diluted remedies derived from plants, animal products or minerals and produced in different forms, including tablets, pillules, powders, lotions, sprays and tinctures. Paradoxically, the more dilute the remedy, the greater its potency. Based on the principle of 'like cures like' the remedies are selected by picking the one which, in a healthy body, most closely reproduces the symptoms exhibited by the patient.

Hydrotherapy: Swimming, especially in a purpose built heated pool, can be a good form of non weight-bearing physical therapy; it also improves circulation and can have a positive psychological effect.

Magnets: Used in collars and bedding; said to have calming properties and to help relieve aches and pains and accelerate healing. Although generally considered safe, they should not be used with certain conditions, so consult with your vet first.

Massage: Purposeful manipulation of muscles, ligaments and joints to help develop elasticity, improve range of movement within tissues and promote circulation. Can also have a beneficial psychological, calming and relaxing effect.

McTimoney Chiropractic: Aims to restore and maintain the musculo-skeletal system through manipulation of the spinal column, pelvis and other joints of the body. A very gentle form of manipulation, it employs a type of technique which makes it particularly suitable for use on dogs and small animals.

Physiotherapy: Chartered physiotherapists are trained to assess and treat problems relating to muscles, joints and soft tissues. Techniques such as massage, stretches and specific mobilisation of the limbs and spine are used; they are also trained in the correct use of electrotherapy such as laser and ultrasound.

Reiki: Energy based technique; practitioners use their hands to channel healing energy through chakras (energy centres) dotted along the spine to help relieve pain, promote healing, increase life-force and reassure dogs which are emotionally upset.

Shiatsu: A combination of Japanese massage and traditional Chinese medicine; finger pressure is applied to different points. It is said to heal and promote health by influencing and improving energy within the body.

Spiritual healing: Spiritual healers act as a conduit for transfer of healing energy by placing their hands on the body. Healing touch has a spiritual aspect, but is not a religious practice and does not require any particular belief by either giver or recipient.

TTEAM: Devised by Linda-Tellington Jones, and based on Feldenkrais technique, touch and various groundwork exercises are used to move the body in a variety of non-habitual ways. Although classified as a teaching technique it has also proved to have therapeutic effects and is beneficial in rehabilitation and pain relief following injury or surgery.

A dog starved at his master's gate
Predicts the ruin of the state.
William Blake

FRIEND TO THE END 4

As a dog owner, Hitler is probably best remembered for his association with Blondi a German Shepherd given to him by his private secretary Martin Bormann in 1941. He kept Blondi by his side, allowing her to sleep with him when he retreated to the Führerbunker during the Fall of Berlin, and where she became a favourite playmate for the Goebbels children. In April of 1945 Blondi gave birth to a litter of five puppies, one of which Hitler named Wolf – a nickname he particularly liked. When it became apparent that defeat was imminent, he ordered his physician to give Blondi and the pup cyanide capsules to ensure that they worked; it was later said by one of the bunker staff that the death of Blondi affected them more than the subsequent suicide of Hitler's mistress Eva Braun. The Soviets later found the bodies of Blondi and one pup, presumably Wolf; it's not known what happened to the other five youngsters.

DOG ASBO

In 1992, a judge in Los Ogos, California ordered the owners of three basset hounds to restrict the dogs' barking to once an hour, and then for no more than two minutes at a time.

His friends he loved. His fellest earthly foes –
Cats – I believe he did but feign to hate.
Sir William Watson

INSURANCE FACTS

• Only around 12 per cent of dogs are insured.
• One in three insurance claims turn into ongoing claims lasting longer than a year.
• Pedigree pets are the most likely to be insured – even though treating a crossbreed costs just as much.

MAN BITES DOG

When a robbery suspect found himself cornered by a German Shepherd police dog in New Zealand, he attacked 'Edge' by biting him. The dog bit him back – many would agree with justification since he had already required life-saving surgery the previous year after being stabbed in a frenzied attack by another armed robber.

BLUE PETER 4

Goldie, a Golden Retriever and the fourth Blue Peter dog made her first screen appearance at the age of 7 weeks, her rather imaginative name being chosen by viewers in what was by now a well established tradition. Like Petra before her, she also had a litter of puppies; born in 1981 one (Prince) was chosen for guide dog training, and his progress was followed until he qualified. When Goldie had a second litter in 1986, six of the puppies became guide dogs, with the seventh, Bonnie joining the show in the same year, whilst her mother bowed out to retire at presenter Simon Groom's farm.

 You always sympathize with the underdog, except when the other dog is yours.
Anonymous

GOTCHA!

In 2003, the Sun newspaper printed a story about a scuba-diving Westie called Hamish as an April Fool's day joke. In fact a scuba-diving dog genuinely does exist; called Shadow he is a rescued crossbreed dog who joins his owner on thirteen foot dives in Florida, USA. His special canine diving gear, including a special helmet, respirator and harness, plus an intercom system have already been patented.

Other April Fool's day hoaxes in which canines have played a key part include:
• an Old English sheepdog which could drive a car, and was featured in an edition of 'That's Life!' a TV programme which often featured talented pets
• a press release issued by Labour MP Dan Norris in 1998 announcing the formation of an All Party Parliamentary Group, one of the aims of which would be to re-ignite interest in sheepdog trials. It was promised that at the launch of the new party, a surprise Sheepdog Trial would be held in the Commons Chamber itself.

- a claim in 2005 that the reintroduction of wolves ten years before had proved so successful that in Wyoming, USA the Endangered Species Act had been declared no longer in force and that the state now considered the wolf as a "'feral dog, unworthy of protection".

THE SHAME OF 'NAM

One of the most shameful episodes in the history of canine warfare must surely be the treatment the war dogs received at the end of the Vietnam war. During the course of the conflict, they had to contend with appalling conditions, substandard food rations and virtually non-existent preventive healthcare, but after all of this, there were to be no happy endings for the majority, despite desperate pleas from many handlers on discovering what their fate was to be.

In Vietnam, 5,000 dogs served with US troops. Just 150 ever returned home – not because all the others had been killed in action, but because they were abandoned and left to fend for themselves.

 Fox terriers are born with about four times as much original sin in them as other dogs.
Jerome K Jerome

FIDO GM

There is a PDSA Gold Medal, which is the animal equivalent of the George Medal, and awarded in recognition of any animal whose bravery and dedication is instrumental in the saving of human or animal life when its own life is in danger, or through exceptional devotion to duty; it has been awarded a total of ten times to date. The PDSA also awards a Certificate for Animal Bravery and Commendation for Animal Bravery for other acts of bravery deserving of recognition.

QUESTION
What is a dog's favorite sport?
ANSWER
Formula 1 drooling!

IN EXILE

Japan's Emperor Ichigo (986-1011) once exiled a dog and imprisoned the owner because the dog chased his favourite cat.

FILM FIRST

The first ever canine movie star was a collie called Blair; having made his debut in the 1903 version of 'Alice Through the Looking Glass' he went on to star in the British film 'Rescued by Rover'. Shot on a tight budget of seven pounds, thirteen shillings and sixpence (£7.65 1/2p) the cast – including 'Rover' – was largely drawn from director Cecil Hepworth's own family. In the film, a baby is kidnapped by an old beggar woman, but the faithful hound 'Rover' comes to the rescue - and incidentally prompting a surge in popularity for the name amongst family pets around the country. The film was so hugely successful with over 400 copies ordered that when the first two negatives wore out two shot-by-shot remakes had to be made. Blair went on to follow up his success in several further films including 'Dumb Sagacity' where he shared top billing with a horse.

LITTLE DOG LOST

Charles II made no secret of his fondness for his spaniels, leading to them periodically being stolen and held to ransom. Item 163 in the Calendar of State Papers for April 1667 is 'Advertisement of a reward for a white spaniel belonging to the King, stolen out of the Earl of Suffolk's stables in the Blue Mews, on April 20'

CHILDREN AND DOGS FIRST

When a family from Torquay in Devon set off for a short outing in their newly acquired speedboat, they weren't expecting problems – but when the engine cut out and the boat unexpectedly sprang a leak, they quickly realised they were in trouble. A quick search revealed there were only two lifejackets; as his wife made a frantic emergency call on her mobile phone, the father quickly assessed the priorities and strapped the jackets onto his twelve-year-old daughter – and their pet dog. They all jumped in the water as the boat sank, and luckily were picked up by a lifeboat thirty minutes later, suffering only from mild hypothermia from the cold water.

WHAT TO DO IF ATTACKED BY CATTLE

Take care when crossing fields with cattle whilst out walking your dog. They can sometimes be unpredictable in their actions; young cattle may be inquisitive and gallop up to investigate you, whilst cows with calves may become aggressive if they think you are a threat.

Never walk between a cow and her calf, and if you do feel threatened, don't shout, wave a stick or your arms, or try to protect your dog by placing yourself between him and any cattle: let him loose and head for the nearest exit.

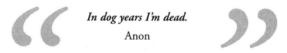

In dog years I'm dead.
Anon

⭐ HOW TO BREAK UP A DOG FIGHT ⭐

Always be careful when trying to separate fighting dogs, as aggression may be redirected towards you. The level of hostility may even increase if your dog feels he is fighting to protect you as well as defend himself.

- Try to stay calm. Do not scream or shout as this may make things worse. Avoid grabbing heads, shoulders or at collars as this is most likely to result in being bitten yourself.
- Surprise is usually the safest and most effective tactic. Use whatever tools you have available; throwing a blanket or jacket over the dog's heads may confuse or stop them long enough for you to separate them. Alternatively, if you're carrying a personal alarm, lock it on and throw it into the middle of the fight; blow a whistle; if water is available throw it over them.
- Once they break apart, co-ordinate your actions with those of the other owner, acting quickly to get them under control and out of range of each other.

⭐ ESCAPE FROM DEATH ROW ⭐

One of the saddest world records must be the one held by Word, a Lhasa Apso who spent a total of eight years and 190 days on 'Death Row'. After being accused of barking at and nipping two people, Word and his sister Parsheba were incarcerated at the Seattle Animal Control Centre in the USA whilst attorneys representing the owner argued their case all the way up to the State Supreme Court. In 2001 a decision was finally reached, and Word finally regained his freedom, on condition that he was kept in a secure environment and prevented from coming into contact with the general public. Although it was too late for Parsheba who had died in custody in 1999, Word went on to enjoy a happy and contented life at Pigs Peace Sanctuary, Washington USA until his death in Spring of 2004.

BLOWN AWAY

When Hurricane Katrina hit New Orleans in 2005, it was disastrous for humans and animals alike. After the storm hit, wreaking devastation and leaving the city submerged in 25ft of water, tens of thousands of pets had either been drowned or faced a desperate battle for survival, having been left without either food or water. The sound of howling from abandoned dogs was a haunting sound which rescuers say they'll never forget; although many owners wanted to keep their pets with them, rescue vessels refused to take animals on board – one man wishing to remain behind with his dog was forced at gunpoint to abandon it. When rescue workers headed for the worst of the flooded areas a week later, hunger and dehydration had taken their toll, leaving most of the dogs weak, and in some cases barely able to stand. Those that could be rescued were taken to safety at the Lamarr-Dixon Expo Centre, thirty five miles outside the city and more accustomed to housing horses – but the only immediately available shelter and holding centre able to cope with 5,000 dogs and cats, from which location they were then transported to other animal rescue facilities. Of all those rescued, only an estimated 20 per cent of dogs were ever reunited with their owners; and even after all this time there are still problems, with many of those animals which weren't rescued turning feral and eking out a precarious existence in the ruins of deserted streets.

 The more one comes to know men,
the more one comes to admire the dog.
Joussenel

WACKY DOGGY GADGETS 3

Invented in Japan, the 'Bow-lingual' is a translation device to let you know what your dog is trying to tell you. A special microphone is attached to the dog's collar and when it barks, the noise is transmitted to a hand held device which analyses and then categorizes it into one of six different emotional feelings: happy, sad, frustrated, on-guard, assertive or needy. The emotion is displayed and the most apt of one of 200 different phrases is selected, such as 'How boring' or 'I'm lonely'. The gadget claims to work on any breed of dog, but is intended more for entertainment purposes than to be used as a serious translation device.

❦ QUEEN'S CORGI ❦

As a child, the future Queen Elizabeth II fell in love with Dookie, the Corgi owned by her father in 1933, and which she and her sister Princess Margaret would feed by hand from a dish held by a footman. After being given a Corgi of her own, called Susan, as an 18th birthday present she has been associated with the breed ever since. She was accompanied by Susan on her honeymoon in 1947, and the royal pets still journey with her to each of her various residences, taking travel on planes, trains and cars all in their stride. Each sleeps in its own specially made wicker basket, and the Queen feeds them herself when her schedule allows; when she goes abroad, they stay at a special residence on the Windsor estates with a royal Corgi-sitter. Since Susan, the Queen has owned more than thirty Corgis, many of them descendants; she currently has five – Emma, Linnet, Monty, Willow and Holly. As well as Corgis she also has five Cocker Spaniels, Bisto, Oxo, Flash, Spick and Span, plus four 'dorgis'; a cross which first came about when Princess Margaret's dachshund Pipkin mated her sister's Corgi Tiny. The present dorgis are named Cider, Berry, Vulcan and Candy.

HOW TO GIFT WRAP WITH DOGS AROUND

- Gather presents, boxes, paper etc in middle of living room floor.
- Get tape back from puppy
- Remove scissors (plastic, paper-cutting variety) from older dog's mouth
- Open box
- Take puppy out of box
- Remove tape from older dog's mouth
- Take scissors away from puppy
- Put present in box
- Remove present from puppy's mouth
- Put back in box after removing puppy from box
- Take scissors from older dog and sit on them
- Remove puppy from box and put on lid
- Take tape away from older dog
- Go get roll of wrapping paper puppy ran off with
- Take scissors from older dog who took them when you got up
- Unroll paper
- Take puppy off box
- Cut paper, being careful not to cut puppy's foot or nose which keeps getting in the way
- Take puppy off box
- Wrap paper round box
- Remove puppy from box and take wrapping paper from his mouth
- Tell older dog to hold tape so he will stop stealing it
- Take scissors away from puppy
- Take tape older dog is holding
- Quickly tape one spot before taking scissors from older dog and sitting on them again
- Fend off puppy trying to steal tape, and stick down another spot
- Take bow from older dog
- Give pen to older dog to hold so he stops licking your face
- Take now soggy bow from puppy and tape it on
- Clean up mess puppy and older dog made playing tug-of-war with the roll of wrapping paper
- Realise puppy has chewed open box and taken gift out.
- Tell dogs what good helpers they are, put away rest of wrapping supplies and go out and buy gift vouchers instead.

WHY DO DOGS LOVE TO CHEW?

It's absolutely natural for puppies to chew, especially whilst teething when it can help relieve discomfort and aids in the process of shedding milk teeth and growing a permanent adult set. It's also one of the ways in which they learn more about their surroundings, and so you will often find that even after teething has ended, chewing continues on through into adolescence. Chewing in dogs of all ages can also be a coping mechanism when feeling bored, lonely, anxious or frustrated, as well as being an enjoyable activity – when gnawing at a bone for example – which can help keep teeth clean.

PRESIDENTIAL POOCHES 6

George Washington kept a pack of hounds with the names of Drunkard, Mopsy, Taster, Cloe, Tipsy, Tipler, Forester, Captain, Lady, Rover, Vulcan, Sweetlips and Searcher, plus five other French hounds. But of all the dog-loving US Presidents who took dogs with them to the White House, Calvin Coolidge had the most as pets including:

Peter Pan (terrier)

Paul Pry (Airedale, originally called Laddie Buck)

Rob Roy (white collie, name changed from Oshkosh)

Calamity Jane (Shetland Sheepdog)

Tiny Tim (Chow)

Blackberry (Chow)

Ruby Rough (brown collie)

Boston Beans (Boston Bulldog)

King Cole (Belgian Groenendael)

Prudence Prim (white collie)

Bessie (yellow collie)

Palo Alto (bird dog)

INSECT STINGS

Dogs will often snap at, or will try to investigate, buzzing insects more closely: but not all are harmless flies, and painful stings can result.

Wasp stings: apply vinegar to neutralize the chemicals and reduce pain and swelling.

Bee stings: remove the sting if still present, taking care not to squeeze the venom sac. Apply bicarbonate of soda, mixed to a paste with a little water.

Sometimes anaphylactic shock may occur; this is a life threatening allergic reaction, and you should get your dog to a vet as quickly as possible. Symptoms include agitation, scratching at the face, drooling, vomiting, diarrhoea, breathing difficulties, collapse, seizures and coma. You should also take your dog to the vet for emergency treatment if he is stung on the tongue, as swelling could block the airway.

A FINE THING

In Turin you can be fined if you don't walk your dog at least three times a day.

UNDER ARREST

In 1983 in Seville, Spain, a German Shepherd was arrested for snatching handbags from shoppers.

AGAINST ALL ODDS

If proof that miracles do happen were ever needed, the story of Dosha, a ten month old crossbreed puppy is a great example. After being hit by a car near her owner's home in California, a police officer shot her in the head to end her suffering. Her body was then put in a plastic canine 'body bag' and placed in a freezer at an animal control centre; when a vet opened the door two hours later, he was shocked to find Dosha standing upright. Incredibly, despite suffering from hypothermia, and the injuries she sustained, Dosha recovered.

QUESTION

What do you get if you take a really big dog out for a walk?

ANSWER

A Great Dane out!

❧ WHEN THE EYES GROW DIM ❧

As dogs grow older, very often their eyesight begins to fail; signs that there may be vision problems include:

- uncharacteristic clumsiness
- bumping into things
- becoming disoriented out on walks
- preferring to stay close to you, rather than investigating things further away
- hesitation and uncertainty when going up or down steps.

If a problem is suspected, consult the vet, but if nothing can be done, most dogs adapt fairly well to their new circumstances, especially since they rely as much on their hearing and sense of smell as their sight. An owner can help make things easier by:

- avoiding moving furniture around – dogs have a good memory for floor plans
- being tidy – don't leave things lying around where he might walk into, or trip over them
- padding the corners of coffee tables and other projecting edges of furniture
- allowing him plenty of room when passing through doorways and narrow openings when he's on the leash
- fencing off ponds and other garden hazards – he may know he's near but not necessarily how close until he falls in
- talking to him as you move around the house so he knows where you are – alternatively, tie a jingly bell to your leg with a bootlace
- being alert to dangers when out on walks, including other dogs running loose – keep him on a leash if necessary
- speaking to your dog before you touch him so he knows where and how close you are and isn't taken by surprise, which could provoke a defensive reaction
- placing different scent markers around the house to help him identify more precisely important areas in the house, such as a dab of vanilla essence by his water bowl, and a small shake of talcum powder in his bed. Avoid using strong smelling essential oils though, and having decided on a scent 'code', continue to use it consistently in the same places.

THE POWER OF LOVE

Love can make seemingly impossible feats and actions possible ... when a crocodile grabbed his dog, the owner stabbed it with a penknife until it let go and swam off. In another incident, when a black bear seized a dog, the owner refused to leave his pet to its fate, but leapt on the bear's back and – once again equipped only with a pocket-knife - stabbed the bear to death.

A good dog deserves a good bone.
Ben Jonson

TASTY SMELLS

In the roof the mouth is the vomeronasal organ, or Jacobsen's organ which allows dogs to 'taste' smells and enables them to respond in particular to pheromones, providing important sexual information about other dogs. The information is transmitted directly into the limbic system, which is the part of the brain that is involved with the emotions.

MISSING, PRESUMED EATEN

Villagers in Malaysia who had left their orchard being guarded by eleven dogs were dismayed when they returned to find that they had all completely vanished. The cause of their disappearance was soon discovered – they had been swallowed by a 22 ft python; said to be as big in diameter as a tree trunk, it was tethered to a tree before being handed over to wildlife experts.

URBAN MYTH 4 – NEUTERING AND SPAYING

Neutering or spaying will affect your dog's personality. No it won't – and not only will your dog still be the same lovable character, but it can actually have some positive effects. As well as the obvious – preventing unwanted pregnancies in females, and males being less likely to roam or be aggressive – there are some health benefits too. In males, castration eliminates the chances of testicular cancer developing, and can reduce the possibility of prostate problems; in females the risk of mammary tumours are lessened and eliminates the chance of life-threatening pyometra.

☙ ON THE TRAIL 2 ❧

In 1925 a Doberman Pinscher named Sauer tracked a stock thief 100 miles across the Great Karroo, South Africa, by scent alone.

☙ NOT LOST, JUST MISLAID ❧

Socialite Paris Hilton hit the headlines when she posted handmade signs advertising the theft of her pet Chihuahua Tinkerbell and offering a $5,000 reward. The dog was found shortly afterwards, safe at home.

☙ SENIOR CITIZENS ❧

Most dogs are classed as 'veterans' by insurance companies once they reach the age of 7 or 8 (human) years – or 6 years in the case of giant breeds.

DOGGY PLACE NAMES

Hound, Hants.	Houndsmoor, Somerset	Dog Village, Devon
Hound Green, Hants	Houndstone Camp,	Dogdyke, Lincs
Hound Hill, Dorset	Somerset	Dognersfield, Hants
Houndmills, Hants	Dog and Gun, Mersey	Dogridge, Wilts
Houndscroft, Glos	Dog Hill, Greater	Dogsthorpe, Peterborough
Houndslow, Scottish Borders	Manchester	

❀✿ HANGING ON ✿❀

A dog managed to cling to the grille on the front of a car after being hit by it: the driver heard a thump, but seeing nothing amiss, carried on. Only when he arrived in Belfast 60 miles later and heard the sound of barking coming from the bonnet did he discover the dog, who amazingly enough, suffered only minor injuries and hypothermia after his narrow escape.

Of all the dogs arrayed in fur,
Hereunder lies the truest cur
He knew no tricks, he never flattered:
Nor those he fawned upon bespattered.
Jonathan Swift

AMBI-PAWED

Like humans, dogs are either left or right pawed

QUESTION
Where does a Rottweiler sit in the cinema?
ANSWER
Anywhere it wants to!

SEE HOW THEY GROW

Compared to people, dogs pack a lot into a short space of time; born helpless, a puppy's senses develop rapidly until by the age of a year it's development is comparable to that of a 15-year-old human.

3 hours old: the puppy is able to turn himself the right way up again if he rolls over, and can raise his head. He is blind, deaf and toothless, although taste is present from birth, but his most efficient senses are those of touch, which together with scent and heat sensors in and on his nose help him to work out where his mother is and to crawl over to her. Close contact with her calms and relaxes both, and creates feelings of safety for the youngster.

1 week old: the puppy is still helpless and completely dependent on its mother. It spends around 90 per cent of its time sleeping and the rest eating. The mother stimulates her pups to urinate and defecate by licking, until they are around three or four weeks old, consuming their wastes in order to conceal their presence from possible predators

2 weeks old: the puppy is now able to stand up unaided on all four legs and to take his first steps, although he is rather wobbly and uncoordinated. At 8 – 10 days old, the eyes open, and at around 12 – 13 days the ear canals open and he hears sounds for the first time.

3 weeks old: steadier on his feet now, the puppy is able to move in the direction of his choice. At between 3 and 5 weeks, the milk teeth start to come through. He begins to interact with his littermates and to be taught basic behaviour disciplines from his mother, learning bite inhibition and how to play and be sociable with his own kind.

4 weeks old: the mother begins to spend more time away from the pups.

6 weeks old: better developed reflexes and increased balance, co-ordination and confidence, together with mature senses enable the puppy to investigate his environment. He can now be weaned.

7 – 8 weeks: the nervous system has reached maturity, and the puppy is ready to go to his new home; at this age he will easily be able to adapt to change. At 8 weeks he will be ready for his first vaccinations.

8 – 18 weeks: this is a period of rapid learning during which socializing the puppy is essential if he is to grow up to be a happy, well-adjusted and confident adult; a brief 'fearful' phase when he is easily scared often occurs at around 10 weeks old. Socialization is the process of introducing the puppy to a wide range of sights, sounds, noises, smells, places, people and situations, and teaching him to be comfortable with them. After this age, socialization should continue but the more which can be done before 18 weeks the better, as after this period it becomes harder for him to deal with new experiences. The better he is socialized as a puppy, the fewer fears he will have as an adult, and the more able he will be to cope with unusual things and take them in his stride.

4 – 6 months: adult teeth begin to come through. At around 4 months old, the puppy may go through a second 'fearful' phase when around new people or situations. The puppy may begin to show increased independence and to 'test the limits' of permitted behaviour.

6 – 9 months: adolescence. Puberty starts – females may have their first season, whilst males begin showing 'masculine' behaviour. Activity level peaks at around 8 months.

1-year-old: rapid growth phase ends and the puppy is now technically an adult – but a young one, and still not fully mature either physically or emotionally.

> *I've seen a look in dog's eyes,*
> *a quickly vanishing look of amazed contempt and am*
> *convinced that basically dogs think humans are nuts.*
> John Steinbeck

FRIEND TO THE END 5

Flying ace and fighter pilot Baron von Richthofen – known popularly as the 'Red Baron' due to his habit of painting his airplanes red – was a hero to millions of Germans, and achieved the admiration even of his enemies. Highly introverted, his best friend soon became a familiar sight by his side; they spent most of their free time together, shared a bed at night and even flew together on several routine patrol flights. The friend? A Great Dane named Moritz.

If your dog is fat, you aren't getting enough exercise.
Anon

FAMOUS OWNERS OF RESCUE DOGS 3

Drew Barrymore – Labrador cross Flossie repaid her rescue from a Pasadena flea market as a 6 week old pup by saving her owner's life when a fire broke out at her home during the small hours of the morning. Barking loudly and frantically clawing at Drew's bedroom door she succeeded in rousing her and her then husband Tom Green; as a reward, once the $3 million house was rebuilt, Drew left it to her in trust.

BONELESS

Dogs have no collar bone – this allows a greater stride length for running and jumping.

SPOT THE DIFFERENCE

As puppies grow older, not only do their eyes change from blue to a different adult colour, but their coats may also change in some cases. Kerry Blue Terrier puppies have black coats when they are born, which develop into the distinctive and attractive blue colouring with maturity, whilst Dalmatians are white at birth, with their spots appearing at two to three weeks old and continuing to develop usually up until two or three months old. Another characteristic which can change is ear shape – the German Shepherd for example, has floppy ears whilst very young, but which become erect as the ear cartilage strengthens with age.

TYPES OF TEETH

Most adult dogs have 42 teeth: 20 in the upper jaw and 22 in the lower jaw. These are made up of

12 incisors – used for nibbling
4 canines – used for grabbing and puncturing
16 premolars – used for tearing
10 molars – used for crushing

DOGGY EVACUEES

During World War II, playing on the anxieties many city-dwelling owners had for the safety of their pets in the event of an air raid, some farms advertised accommodation for animal evacuees.

*The dogs eat of the crumbs
which fall from their master's tables.*
New Testament

SUBLIMINAL ADVERTISING

Most pet advertising is aimed to appeal to owners, but one enterprising company dreamt up the idea of appealing directly to the dogs themselves – or at least of appearing to do so. A billboard in Holland was set up to emit an ultra-sonic sound that people couldn't hear, but which their pets could and responded to by barking. With a headline reading 'Bark if you love Bonzo!' it assumed that owners would think their dog was endorsing the product and would rush to buy it on his behalf.

WHY DO DOGS WAG THEIR TAILS? 2

After a busy day, sporting dogs with actively signalling tails can sometimes suffer from a condition known variously as 'cold water tail', 'limber tail', 'broken tail', 'dead tail', 'frozen tail' and 'broken wag'. The tail is held out horizontally from the body for a few inches, and then hangs limply. There is sometimes discomfort for a few days, after which it generally returns to normal.

ON TRACK

The long ears of scent hounds, such as those of the Bloodhound and Basset are supposed to help collect and channel scents towards the nose, aiding them in tracking.

EAR SHAPES AND DESCRIPTIONS

BAT EAR:
erect, broadest near to the head with a rounded tip and opening directly to the front eg French Bulldog

BUTTON EAR:
small ear where the tip folds forward, nearly to the skull eg Jack Russell

CANDLE FLAME EARS:
large, wide, erect and pointed ears which are specific to the English Toy terrier

DROP/PENDANT/PENDULOUS EARS:
ears dropping close to the head eg Labradors, Spaniels, Bassets

FILBERT EAR:
rounded off, triangular shape like a filbert nut eg Bedlington

FLYING EARS:
any characteristically drop or semi-prick ears that stand or 'fly'

NATURAL:
like a wolf's

PRICK EAR:
erect and pointed eg German Shepherd

ROSE EAR:
very small drop ear that folds back eg Whippets and English Bulldogs

SEMIPRICK EAR:
a prick ear but with the tip just beginning to fold forwards as in the Rough Collie
tulip ears: rose ears which are erect

RABIES

The first known written account of a canine ailment comes from Mesopotamia in 2,300 BC, and describes the risk of rabies to humans. Rather later on, around 350 BC, Aristotle also wrote at length about rabies in dogs, as well as other serious doggy diseases such as podagra and quinsy.

❧ BLUSHING ❧

When excited, a Pharaoh hound will 'blush', with the ears and nose turning a rosy pink colour.

❧ IDENTITY PARADE ❧

Dogs can distinguish by scent between different people at similar distances to ones we can accurately identify by sight.

❧ ON THE NOSE ❧

- The average dog has around 200 million scent detecting receptors in his nose, as compared to around 5 million in humans. One third of a dog's brain is set aside for scent detection alone.

- A damp nose makes it easier for a dog to smell; the moisture dissolves odours and pheromones, making them more easily recognizable.
- Using their scenting abilities, dogs can tell within five footsteps, in which direction someone is headed.

LIFE SAVER

Enjoying an outing in the countryside, university student Cheryl Smith was completely unprepared for what happened next. As her Assistance dog, a Golden Retriever called Orcajogged happily alongside, Cheryl's powered wheelchair suddenly hit a rock and catapulted her into a water filled ditch, before toppling fifteen feet after and effectively pinning her, face down, in the water and unable to move. It wasn't the sort of contingency that Orca, who had been taught to remain by Cheryl's side had been trained for, but obeying Cheryl's desperate command to go and fetch help, he deserted his post and set off. The first person Orca approached mistakenly thought he must be a lost dog, and attempted to walk him back home, but Orca managed to break free and ran back to check on his owner. Cheryl's heart sank when she saw him, thinking that he had been off chasing rabbits all the time; but Orca wasn't finished yet. Having made sure that Cheryl was still alright, he went off again into the rain, which was now pouring down, and by great good luck, the next person he met was Cheryl's neighbour Peter Harrison who was out jogging. Immediately recognising him and realising that something was wrong, Peter followed him along the path to where Cheryl lay, and was able to alert the emergency services and end her terrifying two hour ordeal. Orca, who was only 18 months old at the time and had only been partnered with Cheryl for 8 weeks, was deservedly awarded the PDSA Gold Medal for his life-saving actions.

THE SLOBBERIEST

Brandy the Boxer probably had the longest tongue in the world; measuring 17in, her owners commented that it had been fairly large when she was a puppy, and just seemed to keep on growing after the rest of her stopped.

❧ THE FASTEST 1 ❧

The fastest dog is the greyhound, which can reach top speeds of up to 40 mph; the fastest one ever timed was at 41.83 mph in Australia in 1994.

❧ COLLARS TO AVOID ❧

CHOKE CHAINS:

can damage the neck and throat;
even when fitted correctly they don't always release quickly.

ELECTRIC SHOCK COLLARS:

these deliver an electric shock when activated by a remote control or built in sensor,
and can be highly traumatising for the dog.

PRONG COLLARS:

made of interlocking steel links, each with blunt prongs that pinch
the neck when the collar is tightened

 You enter into a certain amount of madness when you marry a person with pets.
Norah Ephron

❧ THE STRONGEST TEAM ❧

The world record for the heaviest load ever pulled by a dog team was set in October 2000 during the 'Yukon Quest' sled dog race. Hooked up in tandem hitch to an 800 foot long steel cable, 210 huskies owned by local mushers successfully pulled a total weight of 145,002 lbs two thirds of a mile along Front Street in Whitehorse. It wasn't the largest dog team to pull a load however – that record was set in 1999 with 230 dogs.

❧ DOCTOR KING ❧

When Frederick the Great's dog Biche became ill in 1752, ten doctors were summoned to take care of her, but they were unable to save her life. After that, if any of his dogs became sick, Frederick nursed them himself.

HAIR TYPES

The skin is the largest organ of the body, and hair helps protect it from injury and UV radiation in sunlight, as well as providing insulation and warmth – although some coat types manage this more efficiently than others.

Dogs have three different types of hair

TACTILE HAIRS:

also called vibrissae, these are 'feelers', stiff sensory hairs found on the head as whiskers, eyebrows and on the chin and sides of the face. They are embedded three times deeper, and are twice as thick, as other hairs.

GUARD HAIRS:

these make up the top or outer coat covering the dog, and are the hairs found on single coated dogs. They form the outer, top coat of double coated dogs.

SECONDARY COAT HAIR:

these are soft, woolly hairs that make up the dense undercoat of double coated breeds.

Different hair textures also contribute to the appearance of some dogs, including

CORDED:

these are long, even strands of varying lengths which resemble dreadlocks and are a characteristic of the Komondor and Puli

WIRE HAIR:

coarse top coat hairs produce the distinctive appearance of the
Wire Haired Fox Terrier and Border Terrier

CURLY HAIR:

as well as the hair itself being curly, the follicle from which it grows is also curly, as seen in the Poodle.

DOG STAR

In Greek mythology, the huntsman Orion's dog became Sirius, where it is the brightest star both in the constellation of Canis major and in the night sky, and is often referred to as the 'Dog Star'. Popular superstition associated the appearance of Sirius with the 'Dog Days' of relentless summer heat thought to drive dogs mad – one of the meanings of the name Sirius is in fact 'scorching'. In 1844 it was discovered and in 1862 confirmed, that Sirius had a hidden companion, which was duly named Sirius B, but has more affectionately become known as 'the Pup'

❧ FOUR LEGS GOOD …
TWO LEGS JUST AS GOOD ❧

Dogs are often far better than we are at adapting to physical problems such as loss of eyesight or hearing; even those born without such senses learn to cope admirably well with specialised training and patience from their owners. Loss of a limb doesn't seem to bother them unduly either; 2006 for example, saw a team of three legged agility dogs demonstrating their skills before crowds of impressed spectators. Faith the bipedal dog is another example of how well dogs can overcome what appear at first sight to be overwhelming handicaps; born just before Christmas 2002 she was rescued as a three week old puppy. At the time she had three legs, but the front left one was so badly deformed that when it began to atrophy it was amputated at the age of seven months. Left with only her two back legs, Faith learned how to stand, hop and eventually walk on them, and has since made numerous appearances in public and on TV. Although two legged dogs aren't common, Faith is by no means the only one, although perhaps one of the best known.

✳✳ AMPUTEE DOGS ✳✳

When Dominic the Italian Greyhound was accidentally run over by a truck, he had to have two legs amputated, both on the same side, yet still leads an active and happy life. Similarly, Roadie – short for 'Railroad' - touched the hearts of those who heard of his plight. The son of a $10,000 champion hound, in 1992 at just nine months old he spent three nights lying between the rails of a railway track after a freight train mangled his rear right leg and front left leg. When a railway employee finally spotted him and stopped to put him out of his misery, the gun jammed; local vet Mike Griffit was called and the owner located, but noticing how he managed a grateful tail wag, rather than euthanize the pup, the vet asked if he might keep him. The two injured legs were amputated and before long he took his first steps, and far from feeling sorry for himself he never looked back and soon became a familiar sight lying on his bed behind the counter at the veterinary surgery.

After a news story about him was broadcast, donations flooded in from well-wishers, which were put into a Roadie fund and used to pay for treatment for pets whose owners couldn't afford a surgery or other expensive procedures. In his youth, his owner reckoned that even with only two legs, he could still run as fast as any four legged dog; he eventually lived to the ripe old age of 16, when old age finally caught up with him.

*The world was conquered through
the understanding of dogs;
the world exists through
the understanding of dog.*
Friedrich Wilhelm Nietzsche

✳✳ THE TINIEST ✳✳

The record for the smallest living dog in the world is shared between two Chihuahuas, Brandy from Florida, USA and Danka Kordak who lives in Slovakia. Danka Kordak is the smallest in terms of height, measuring just 13.8 cm at the withers. When Brandy's owner asked the breeder for 'a small one' she really did get what she asked for, with the diminutive dog weighing in at 1lb 13 oz and measuring 15.2 cm from nose to toe as compared to Danka Kordak's 18.8 cm.

DOG PLANT NAMES

Dog bane (Plectranthus ornatus)	Dog's mercury (Mercurialis perennis)
Dog berry (Ribes cynosbati)	Dog's tail (Cynosurus cristatus)
Dog chamomile (Chamaemelum nobile)	Dog's toes (Antenna plantaginifolia)
Dog daisy (Leucanthemum vulgare)	Dog's tooth violet (Erythronium denscanis)
Dog fennel (Helenium autumnale)	Dog wood (Cornus florida)
Dog rose (Rosa canina)	Hound's tongue (Cynoglossum officinale)
Dog's grass (Triticum repens)	Wolf's bane (Aconitum coctonum)

✳ WAG IF HE'S ALIVE ✳

Doctors in ancient Greece often used dogs to determine if a human patient was dead or deeply comatose. If the dog wagged its tail the person was alive.

QUESTION
What kind of dog does Dracula have?
ANSWER
A bloodhound!

✳ FOOD DETECTORS ✳

One of the tasks which sniffer dogs are perhaps less well known for, is that of finding food – and with their terrific sense of smell and voracious appetites, it's not surprising that despite an inclination to be stubborn, wilful and not always easy to train, Beagles are the breed of choice when it comes to detecting illegal edibles in luggage. As they are also small, easy to care for, and unlikely to intimidate people, it also makes them ideal for working in public situations where not everyone feels comfortable around dogs. Nicknamed the 'Beagle Brigade' in the US where they wear green jackets while on duty, they were first introduced in 1984 at Los Angeles International Airport, and over 20 years on, teams are now working at 21 international airports. On scenting the presence of a foodstuff, a Beagle will alert its handler by sitting next to the luggage; an experienced dog will have a 90 per cent success rate and can identify over 50 distinct smells. Their careers usually last 6 – 10 years, and on retiring they either go to live with their handlers, or are found an adoptive home.

❦ FIRST AID KIT ❦

You can either buy a ready-assembled first aid kit,
or put one together yourself; it's also a good idea to carry a basic kit containing a few
essentials with you when out on walks.

This should include:

STERILE SALINE

- for cleaning wounds.

COTTON WOOL

– soaked in water, sterile saline or diluted antiseptic to clean wounds.
Never use cotton wool dry.

STERILE DRESSINGS OF ASSORTED SIZES

BANDAGES

– to help hold dressings in place.

TAPE

– to keep bandages firmly in place.

TWEEZERS

– to remove foreign bodies such as splinters or insect stings.

SCISSORS

– for trimming hair away and cutting bandages and tape.

SPARE FABRIC TYPE LEAD

– can be used to control your dog, a stray dog,
used in an emergency as a tourniquet or emergency muzzle.

WATER

–for cooling down a hot dog, washing off hazardous substances, or offering a drink.

SMALL PEN TORCH

– even in daylight you may need an extra source of light; can also be used to check the
eyes of an unconscious dog for a reaction.

WHISTLE

– can be used to raise the alarm in remote areas; the noise carries better and is less tiring
than your voice.

KIT BAG

– something which is easy and hands-free to carry, such as a bum bag.

SIGNS OF DEHYDRATION

If a dog isn't getting enough water to replace that which is lost from his body – which may occur from overheating in hot weather, fever, excessive urination, bouts of severe vomiting or diarrhoea - he may become dehydrated. Signs include

- sunken eyes
- loss of appetite
- exhaustion
- depression
- dry mouth and nose
- reduced skin elasticity – check by picking up a fold of skin at the top of the base of the neck between a finger and thumb. It should flatten again the moment you release it; if it takes more than three seconds to flatten out, dehydration is present and you should consult your vet.

His name is not wild dog any more,
but the first friend, because he will be our friend for
always and always and always.
Rudyard Kipling

✺ PETS AS THERAPY ✺

Possibly the first example of a PAT (Pets as Therapy) dog was during the reign of Henry VIII when it was recommended that dogs be used to ease the suffering of patients by bringing them close to the sick person's chest or stomach – although the theory behind doing so was vastly different.

> *Alcibiades had a very handsome dog,*
> *that cost him seven thousand drachmas;*
> *and he cut off his tail, that, said he,*
> *the Athenians may have this story to tell of me,*
> *and may concern themselves no further with me.*
>
> Plutarch

✺ DOG DAYS OFF ✺

It's estimated that around 2.7 million working days are lost each year due to owners taking time off to look after poorly pets. Around 50 per cent of dog owners admit to paying more attention to an ill pooch than an ill partner, as well as to worrying more about their pet. And one in ten owners buy a gift for their dog when it's feeling under the weather to help cheer it up.

✺ EMERGENCY MUZZLE ✺

Even the best behaved of dogs may snap if they are in pain. If you need to examine an injury to your dog and he is likely to bite or snap, but you don't have a muzzle, you can improvise one using a bandage, scarf, or the leg from a par of tights. Make a large noose in the centre of the fabric, and slip it over the nose, tightening it sufficiently firmly to close the jaws, but not so much that the breathing is impaired. Bring the two ends down on either side of the muzzle, cross them under the jaw and then bring them up round the back of the head behind the ears, and tie in a bow.

Never muzzle a dog which has chest or jaw injuries or respiratory problems, if it is panting heavily or is convulsing, has vomited, or swallowed poison, or if it is a short nosed breed when it might impair breathing.

WHY DO DOGS CIRCLE BEFORE LYING DOWN?

Many dogs will also sniff at the area they are about to settle down on, and dig a little with the front paws before circling and eventually lying down – it's all part of the nesting instinct inherited from his wolf ancestors, even though he has no need to do it.

It is asserted that the dogs
keep running when drinking at the Nile,
for fear of becoming a prey to the
voracity of the crocodiles.
Pliny the Elder

FOOTNOTES

How often nails need clipping varies from one individual to the next – size, weight, diet and the amount of exercise taken on hard surfaces all play a part. The tips of the nails should just touch the ground when the dog is standing; if allowed to grow overlong, they can cause discomfort or could even lead to injury when moving.

Using guillotine type clippers, each nail should be clipped at a forty-five degree angle away from the dog, so that the tip lies flush to the floor. Clip just in front of the quick – cutting into it will hurt the dog, and bleed. The quick is easy to see as a line of pink tissue in white nails, but with black nails you will need to guess; if you cut level with the bottom of the pad, it should be fine. If the nails have been neglected, the quick will extend further down the nail however; if in doubt just nip off the curved hooks at the ends, but clip on a regular basis so that the quicks start to recede until eventually you can trim them safely to a more correct length. Finishing off any ragged edges with an emery board will help smooth them so they don't snag on carpets or fabrics.

If you find it too nerve-wracking a job to do yourself, either make an appointment for it to be done at a grooming parlour, or with one of the nurses at your vets.

TRUST YOUR VET

Pet owners tend to trust the advice, knowledge and skills of their vet over that of other healthcare providers, including doctors, dentists and opticians.

❖ PRESIDENTIAL POOCHES 7 ❖

When he became President Abraham Lincoln wanted to take the family pet, Fido, with him to the White House, but it was felt that the dog would be upset by all the noise and bustle. A brownish-yellow dog of mixed breed he was given into the care of neighbours in Springfield, whose boys had already become fond of him. Before they were able to leave him, the Lincolns asked that he not be scolded for having muddy paws, or left tied up in the back yard, and also gave Fido's new family a horsehair sofa he particularly liked to lie on. Fido settled in happily enough, but a year after his former master was assassinated he met his end, stabbed by a drunk when the dog playfully put his paws on the man's shoulders as he was sitting on a roadside kerb.

To mark a friend's remains these stones arise;
I never knew but one – and here he lies.
Lord Byron,
inscription on the Monument of a Newfoundland,

PARA PUPS

British 'para pups' were trained in World War II to parachute out of planes so they could accompany airborne and SAS units – but they weren't the first to do so. In 1785, a French balloonist used his dog to test out his idea for a parachute, dropping him several hundred feet. The parachute worked – but on reaching the ground the dog, probably sensibly enough in the circumstances, decided not to hang round to find out what would happen next, and ran off never to be seen again.

The dogs are useful but their expertise has been exaggerated. We feel that London is no place for police dogs.
1906 Metropolitan Police report on the use of dogs

HOLISTIC DOG CARE

Just as dogs have benefited from the availability of many of the latest treatments for humans, an increasing interest in holistic care has led to a number of these therapies also being employed or adapted from human usage especially for animals. Little is known about how some of these therapies work, although many owners nevertheless report positive experiences – but as not all animals respond in the same way to all treatments, different options may need to be explored. Some treatments are also more suitable for certain ailments, or their use may be contra-indicated by particular health problems. Because of this, as well as for legal reasons and to ensure that unnecessary suffering is not caused through misdiagnosis or inappropriate or incorrectly administered treatment, owners should either consult a vet who specialises in holistic medicine, or ask for referral to a qualified practitioner. Some treatments can legally only be carried out by a veterinary surgeon; and all reputable practitioners should in any case refuse to treat your pet unless it has first been seen by a vet and you have obtained a referral.

QUESTION
Why did the dog wear white sneakers?
ANSWER
Because his boots were at the menders!

❊❊ CONFIRMATION TERMS ❊❊

APPLE HEAD:

very domed, rounded skull

BITCHY:

feminine looking

BLOWN:

coat moulting or casting

BOSSY SHOULDER:

overdeveloped shoulder muscles

CHIPPENDALE FRONT:

elbows turned out, pasterns close and feet turned outwards

COW HOCKED:

hock joints turning in towards each other, causing the feet to turn outwards

CRANK TAIL:

sharply bent or angled tail

DEAD GRASS:

straw to bracken colour

DOGGY:

masculine looking

FLEWS:

pendulous upper lips

FOREIGN EXPRESSION:

an expression not typical of the breed

HALOES:

dark pigmentation round or over the eyes

HARE FOOT:

elongated foot, with the two middle toes noticeably longer than the outer ones

HERRING GUTTED:

flat ribs, without sufficient curvature

PLAITING:

crossing the front legs when walking or trotting

QUEEN ANNE FRONT:

the same as a Chippendale front

SNIPY MUZZLE:

pointed, weak muzzle

❀❀ URBAN MYTH 5 –
OLD DOGS AND NEW TRICKS ❀❀

'You can't teach an old dog new tricks' is a common enough expression, but one which doesn't hold any truth. Encouraging older dogs to use their brains is actually beneficial, as it helps rebuild connections between brain cells, keeping them mentally alert and helping to slow the onset of senility. Teaching new tricks, reviewing those already learnt and his obedience training, providing fun challenges and stimulating toys are all ways in which you can keep him from ageing faster than he should.

Although older dogs can happily learn new things, if you are trying to deal with a problem it may take longer to sort out than with a younger dog, but this is simply because existing behaviour patterns tend to be more deeply ingrained. With patience, perseverance and by providing the right motivation, it is still however, perfectly possible to overcome problems.

*A guide dog is almost equal in many ways
to giving a blind man sight itself.*
Musgrave Frankland

FRIEND TO THE END 6

Mary Queen of Scots (1542-1567) was a great lover of dogs, both hounds and the small lap dogs which kept her company during the long years she spent in prison. One little terrier – possibly a Cairn or a Skye – accompanied her to her execution, concealed under her skirts, and curling itself around her feet while she knelt at the block. Eyewitness Robert Wynkfield recounted how the dog was spotted when one of the executioners was pulling off Mary's garters: it "would not depart from the dead corpse, but came and lay between her head and body". Terrified and covered in blood, the terrier was quickly whisked away by Mary's ladies in waiting and bathed, but died just a few days later.

DEATH BY CHOCOLATE

For chocoholic humans the phrase may be a bit of a joke, but where dogs are concerned, it's no laughing matter; unless it is a product manufactured especially for pets, chocolate can be fatal. The cause of the problem is a substance called theobromine, found in the cocoa solids from which chocolate is made; it is also present in products such as cocoa powder and cocoa shell garden mulches. As little as 100mg per kilo of body weight can be fatal; that's approximately 32g of plain chocolate, 19g of cocoa powder and 17g of cocoa mulch for a Jack Russell Terrier.

Symptoms occur anywhere between 4 and 24 hours after eating and include vomiting, excessive drinking, hyperactivity, inco-ordination, and a racing heart. In severe cases these may be accompanied by muscle rigidity, panting, fever, convulsions, heart arrhythmias and ultimately kidney and heart failure.

There is no antidote for chocolate poisoning, but it may be possible to avert disaster if early veterinary treatment is obtained; if less than 2 hours have passed since it was eaten, inducing vomiting will help get rid of some of it. Thereafter, treatment is aimed at supporting life functions, preventing further absorption of the chocolate, hastening elimination and treating the symptoms.

Always contact your vet as a matter of urgency if you suspect your dog has managed to steal some chocolate, and never offer it to him as a treat.

Other foods which can be fatal for your pet include onions, avocado, grapes, raisins, macadamia nuts, cooked bones, walnuts, alcohol and raw potatoes.

PUG TO THE RESCUE

When William III and Queen Mary began their reign, it was with pugs by their sides rather than spaniels. Pugs were especially favoured by the House of Orange because of the role played by one called Pompey in saving the life of William's grandfather, when he awoke him from a deep sleep, averting an assassination attempt.

Other royal pug owners include Queen Victoria, who was particularly fond of a fawn pug called 'Bully', a gift from her adored husband Prince Albert. Edward VIII and Wallis Simpson were also notable pug fanciers, owning around 11 over the years, taking them along to almost all their social activities.

BLUE PETER 5

Bonnie, following the lead of Goldie also went on to have a litter of puppies that became successful guide dogs, and on her retirement after 1500 programmes and co-starring with 16 presenters she was given a special collar with an inlaid gold Blue Peter badge; she died in 2000 at the age of fifteen.

The greatness of a nation and its moral progress can be judged by the way its animals are treated.
Mahatma Gandhi

HAIR STYLES

Densely furred breeds such as the Spitz types can have as many as 600 hairs per square centimetre of skin, whilst fine haired breeds such as the Yorkie may have as few as 100.

Most breeds shed twice a year, in Spring and Autumn, with length of daylight hours generally being one of the most important factors in triggering the coat change.

Many owners opt for a plain 'lamb' clip (the same length all over) for their Poodles, but others favour the more sculptured look associated with the breed. The Poodle gained its name from the German word 'pudel' meaning to splash in water, referring to its original occupation as a water retrieving dog. Whilst the method of trimming may look fancy, it was intended to be practical, removing extra coat but still leaving vital organs and joints covered to help protect them against the cold.

HIGH STAKES

C M Coolidge is best known for the series of nine paintings he made in 1903 of anthropomorphized dogs playing cards; when two were sold at auction in 2005 they made over $500,000, far in excess of what had been expected. Coolidge's paintings went on to inspire many other imitators, the best of which are probably those produced by Arthur Sarnoff depicting dogs playing pool.

WACKY DOGGY GADGETS 4

An Australian invention called the Pet Loo sets it's sights a little closer to the ground and is aimed at owners who don't have access to a garden for their dogs to toilet in. An area of porous synthetic grass is provided, with a drainage tray placed beneath to catch urine.

VITAL SIGNS

Knowing how to take your dog's temperature, pulse and respiration can be useful in emergency situations and in monitoring health problems. Being able to provide this information when making a veterinary appointment can also help him in deciding how urgently your pet needs attention.

Always take readings when your dog is relaxed and at rest; stress, exercise and excitement will all increase rates and will lead to you getting an incorrect result. When taking respiratory or heart rate readings, it is easiest to use either a watch with a second hand, or a digital one which has a stopwatch function. You do not need to wait a full minute to get a reading – simply time the heart or respiratory rate for twenty seconds and then multiply by three in order to calculate the rate per minute.

Heart: To check a large dog's heart rate, press the fingers of one hand against the left side of the chest, just behind the elbow; you may need to press fairly firmly if he is a little overweight. With small dogs, place a hand on either side of the chest just behind the elbows and squeeze gently until you can feel the heartbeat. With overweight dogs it may be hard to feel the heartbeat, and easier to take a pulse reading instead. The best place to do this is by placing a couple of fingers over the femoral artery on the inside of the thigh, close to the groin. Don't press too hard, otherwise you will stop the flow of blood and won't be able to feel the pulse.

Temperature: Ask someone to hold your dog securely in a standing position; if he is likely to become fractious or to snap, don't be insistent about it – leave it to your vet. A digital thermometer is easier and safer to use than an old-fashioned glass one and is also easier to read. Before using it, read any accompanying instructions and check that it is registering zero. Lubricate the end with a little petroleum jelly or K-Y Jelly, then hold the tail near it's base with one hand and gently insert the thermometer about 1" (2.5cm) into the rectum, using a slight twisting action. Hold it in position for 90 seconds, or until it beeps if it is one which alerts you when a reading is ready to be taken. Remove it, not the readout and then wipe clean using a mild antiseptic.

Breathing: You can calculate the respiratory rate by watching and counting the chest movements – either count the movements in, or the movements out, but not both. Also look and listen for any abnormalities in the breathing, such as if it's shallow, irregular, laboured, gurgling or wheezy.

If the breathing is very shallow, or the chest movements are hard to see because of a shaggy coat, rest a hand lightly on the chest so you can feel the movement instead.

QUESTION

What is a dog's favourite food?

ANSWER

Anything that is on your plate!

SPACE AGE DOGS

Throughout the 1950s and '60s the USSR used a number of dogs in their space programme in order to determine whether spaceflight would be safe – or indeed possible – for humans. Many missions were flown by the dogs, some of them travelling on several occasions; strays were chosen as it was thought they would be better able to deal with the stresses and rigours involved, and females were also preferred as they didn't need to cock a leg to urinate. During their training they had to endure such privations as being placed in small boxes for up to 20 days at a time, chained so as to be able to sit, stand or lie down but otherwise unable to move or turn round. The first flights were sub-orbital, and there were several runaways; when Smelaya escaped the day before a launch was due, it was at first feared that she had been eaten by wolves, but she was found later and subsequently made a successful flight with a fellow canine companion Malyshka. Bolik also ran away days before her flight, and an untrained stray dog took her place which had been found running around the barracks.

REASONS TO HAVE A DOG 1

Because they're better than women

Dogs don't shop

Dogs never expect gifts

Dogs think you have a great singing voice

Dogs love it when your friends come round

Dogs don't spend hours in the bathroom

Dogs never criticize

Dogs never invite their mothers round

Dogs don't expect you to call when you're running late. And the later you are, the more excited they are to see you.

Dogs can keep a secret

And in that town a dog was found,
As many dogs there be,
Both mongrel, puppy, whelp and hound,
And curs of low degree.
Oliver Goldsmith

❧❧ DONOR DOGS ❧❧

Blood transfusions for dogs haven't always been easy to accomplish in the past, with vets having to rely in emergencies on local owners with donor dogs, prepared to make themselves available often at short notice. A register set up on the Internet made the search for potential donors easier, but the obvious answer – a canine blood bank - was out of the question until legislation changed in 2005. This legislation had stated that vets were only allowed to take blood for use in a specific dog; they were only allowed to store it if there was some left over, or if the originally intended recipient no longer needed it.

With a change in law, a national blood bank for dogs has now been set up; as with human donations, it relies on a system of voluntary donors.

Donating blood is not painful or detrimental to the donor dogs' wellbeing, the actual process taking around 5 – 10 minutes, although a visit will last slightly longer to allow for health checks to be given and a rest period afterwards. Donors should have a god temperament, be aged between 1 – 8 years old and weigh a minimum of 25 kgs; they shouldn't have travelled abroad and should be up to date with all their vaccinations. Blood is usually taken from the neck, which sounds unpleasant, but doesn't seem to bother the donors; once finished they are given a goody bag, a drink and a biscuit.

The blood collected is then processed and stored ready for distribution to wherever it is needed.

They dogs never talk about themselves
but listen to you while you talk
about yourself and keep up an appearance of
being interested in the conversation.
Jerome K Jerome

❧❧ FIRST TRANSFUSION ❧❧

The first record of blood transfusions involved dogs, when physician Richard Lower drained a medium sized dog of a substantial amount of its blood, replacing it with that from a large mastiff. Both dogs apparently survived.

Just like humans, dogs have a number of different blood groups. A first transfusion can be of any type, rarely causing a reaction - but it's essential that any further blood that is needed is typed and cross-matched to the recipient otherwise it could kill.

Greyhounds can make good blood donors, not just because of their large size and generally amiable personalities, but because they have higher levels of red cells and lower levels of white cells and platelets than other breeds.

Dogs weighing over 25 kg can donate up to 450 mls of blood. A single donation has the potential to be able to help up to four dogs in need.

Show a dog a finger,
and he wants the whole hand
Yiddish proverb

DOGS AND THE LAW

There are many laws concerning dogs, which cover your responsibilities as an owner both to your pet and to the community. By law, you must care properly for your dog, must not allow him to roam on his own, or allow him to bite or frighten anyone. In addition, you should also be aware that Under the Control of Dogs Order 1992, all dogs in the UK must wear a collar and ID disc at all times (even if micro chipped or tattooed) when in a public place; that includes times when your dog is sitting inside your car, if the car is in a public place. If a collar is not worn, the dog can be seized and treated as a stray. The only exceptions to the collar and tag law is for dogs which are engaged in work when wearing a collar could be dangerous.

FOOD FACTS 2

- 9 per cent of owners feed commercially prepared pet food at least once a week.
- Dogs eat around 785,000 tonnes of commercial pet food in the UK each year.

EYE SPY

- Flatter lenses plus weaker muscles to change their shape mean that dogs don't see in such sharp detail as we do – which possibly explains why they often don't see a toy which is lying right in front of them.
- Eyelashes grow only on the upper lids
- Dogs can see colour, but it's thought to be much more muted than our own

perception. They cannot tell the difference between green, yellow-green, orange or red colours in a similar way to people who are red/green colour blind. Neither can they differentiate between greenish blue and grey, but are much better than us at distinguishing between subtle shades of grey.

- Dogs don't cry, but do produce a continual film of tears to keep the eye from drying out, fight infection and ensure clear vision; any excess tears collect in the corner of each eye closest to the nose and drain through a channel called the nasolacrimal duct into the nasal cavity.
- A third eyelid, also called the nictitating membrane or haw, acts as a kind of windscreen wiper, brushing any foreign bodies away from the surface of the eye. Normally you can't see it, although you may be able to spot it moving across the eye as your dog falls asleep and shuts his eyes.
- Dogs are much better at detecting movement than us.
- They also have better vision in conditions of low light; this is due to the tapetum lucidum, a reflective layer of cells behind the retina, which acts like a mirror to increase what light there is. You can see this if you shine a torch at your dog at night, when you will see an eerie green glow as heir eyes reflect back at you.

✦ BRAIN POWER ✦

It's not enough to exercise your dog's body – giving his brain a workout is important too. Especially if he's bright, failure to provide sufficient mental stimulation could lead to him becoming bored and possibly developing a problem behaviour. Good ways to engage his mind as well as his body include

- Introducing an activity such as agility, heelwork to music or tracking.
- Teaching a few tricks such as giving you a high five or rolling over on command.
- Taking basic obedience training up a level and trying more advanced work.
- Increasing his vocabulary – teach him the names of different toys and objects and ask him to find them and bring them to you.
- Trying clicker training, which will really encourage him to use his brain to work out what you want him to do.
- Giving him some fun and rewarding problem solving tasks, such as popping a tasty treat or favourite toy under a towel, or in the bottom of a large cardboard box filled with crumpled balls of newspaper, and encouraging him to retrieve it.
- Providing interactive toys – these generally require him to work out how to extricate food from their interiors.

 To err is human, to forgive is canine.
Anonymous

✦ PET CALL ✦

An American Animal Hospital Association survey showed that 37 per cent of pet owners left messages for their pets on answering machines while they were out.

✦ GOOD TO THE LAST DROP ✦

Tap water isn't enough for some pampered pooches to drink; nothing will do but that they have water especially produced and bottled for them. One company produces flavoured and vitamin-enhanced water with jokey names such as 'Puddle water', 'Hose water', 'Gutter water' and 'Toilet water'. And if your dog feels left out when you settle down with a well-earned drink, it's even possible to buy non-alcoholic, non-carbonated 'beer' for him – 'Happy Tail Ale' in the US, and 'Kwispelbier' in Europe.

☙ THE NAME GAME ❧

It's vital to choose the right name for your dog – once he's learnt to respond to it, you're stuck with it. Apart from suiting him, a good name should be easy for you to call and easy for him to recognize, so one or two syllables is best. It is also a good idea to avoid names that might be embarrassing to use in public, or which sound like, and might get confused with, commands such as Joe/No, or Kit/Sit.

☙ EYE SHAPES ❧

Although eyeballs are round, the eye rims can give different breeds distinctive eye shapes

ALMOND EYES:

oval shape, bluntly pointed at both ends eg Akita

GLOBULAR:

round, prominent but not bulging eg Pug

GOGGLE:

protruding eye – considered a fault

OVAL:

the most common shape; egg shaped eg Schnauzer

ROUND:

circular eg Weimaraner

TRIANGULAR:

more angular in contour than oval eyes eg Afghan

☙ ON THE ROAD ❧

Under the Road Traffic Act 1988 it is an offence to have a dog on a designated road without it being held on a lead. Also under this Act, if a dog is injured in a car accident, the driver must stop and give his or her details to the person in charge of the dog. If no-one is around, the incident must be reported to the police within 24 hours.

☙ FRIEND TO THE END 7 ❧

King Charles and his wife Henrietta Maria loved their little spaniels; when the queen returned from Holland in 1643 where she had been selling her jewellery to help finance the war at home, Parliamentary ships opened fire as her luggage was being unloaded. She took refuge in a field ditch before realising she had left her dog behind; ignoring all advice and warnings, she went back and rescued her pet before fleeing to safety.

Charles's pet spaniel Rogue kept him company during his imprisonment at Carisbroke Castle, and later on, as the king walked to his execution the dog managed to escape and raced after him. He was persuaded to go back, but it's said that after his master was dead, he was taken by a Roundhead soldier and paraded around the city.

Dogs who are loved soon acquire nicknames Jilly Cooper
His name is Rufus II – the II is silent Winston Churchill
Dogs feel very strongly that they should always go with
you in the car, in case the need should arise for them to
bark violently at nothing right in your ear.
Dave Barry

THE HIGHEST

When greyhound Cinderella May a Holly Grey – Cindy to her friends – was born, no-one could have guessed that she would become a double record breaker. She was born in 2000 in Florida at one of the sixteen dog tracks in the US where racing is legal, the result of an illicit liaison between two racing dogs and as a result the track had no use for her. Luckily, along with the other pups in the litter, Cindy was rescued by Hollydogs Greyhound Adoption and eventually adopted out. After three months she was back again, as the family she had been rehomed with simply found her too energetic to cope with. At 6 months old she was adopted once again, this time by Kathy Conroy and Kate Long – aided in their choice, naturally enough, by their pet collie Colleen. In 2003 she claimed the World Record for the dog high jump, clearing 5ft 6 in, and then went on again to break her own record by two inches, clearing a height of 5ft 8 in on her first attempt.

QUESTION
What is the only kind of dog you can eat?
ANSWER
A hot dog!

❋❋ HOT STUFF ❋❋

San Franciscans already recycle more than 60% of their rubbish, but moves are currently afoot to try and increase this still further, with the introduction of a plan to re-use dog waste produced by the city's pets. With dogs producing 6,500 tonnes of faeces each year, animal waste accounts for almost 4% of residential waste, and the plan is to use it to help keep the city running. The waste will be placed in a methane digester, and the methane produced will be used for appliances powered by natural gas such as cookers and heaters, and can also be used to generate electricity.

When a dog runs at you, whistle for him.
Henry David Thoreau

❋❋ EXPENSIVE GIFTS ❋❋

Owners spend around £294 million each year on gifts for their dogs. Men tend to spend more than women, but tend to select practical items such as collars and leads, whilst women pick luxury presents such as gourmet treats, or cosy beds.

❋❋ HOW TO ORGANIZE A DOGGY BIRTHDAY PARTY ❋❋

- Find a suitable venue – outdoors in a park, large garden, at a beach, or even a hydrotherapy pool if the weather is nice, or undercover if it's likely to be cold or wet: village halls and covered riding schools can be good choices if your house isn't big enough. Arrange hire and sort out any permission needed in plenty of time to avoid disappointing the guests.
- Make out a guest list; invite those people and dogs most likely to be compatible, as you don't want any fights to break out at what should be a happy event for all concerned.
- Invite the guests; buy cards or print out your own bone shaped invitations. Include time, date, venue and directions if needed and ask for confirmation of attendance so you know how many to cater for.
- Ensure that those areas which can be used for dogs to relieve themselves are clearly signed, and provide a bin and some bags for scooping any poop.

- Provide some party food; sandwiches, quiche, sausages, crisps and other nibbles for the humans and separate (labelled) bowls with canine treats and snacks. Make sure plenty of water bowls are also available.
- Plan some party games which both two and four legged guests can take part in, such as a Bonio and Spoon race, Musical Sits, Frankfurter Bobbing, Obstacle and Dressing-up race.
- At some point during a lull in proceedings, bring on a cake for the special birthday dog; either buy one from a canine supplier or make your own.
- Make up some 'doggie bags' of goodies for each guest to take home at the end, containing a few treats and maybe a toy.

❄ ☃ ONE OF EACH ☃ ❄

As well as one child, families in Beijing, China are only allowed to have one dog each. Large and dangerous dogs are also banned, and anyone caught breaking the regulations faces a fine of up to 5,000 yuan (around £400) plus having the pet taken into custody.

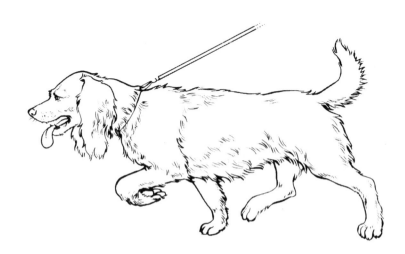

✦ ONE OF THE FAMILY ✦

A Spaniard was given visiting rights to see his dog Yako, a Golden Retriever, when he separated from his wife and she prevented him from seeing him. The decision was later overturned by a higher court which ruled that dogs should not be treated like children in divorce cases.

Yet most owners – 9 out of ten according to one survey – do consider their dogs to be as important a part of the family as human members. In December 2006 a New Zealander did in fact claim that his Border Collie Sally should not have to be registered because she was not a dog, but a 'living being who is loved and cared for as part of the family, and should not as such be subject to regulation'.

✦ CELEBRITY CANINE CUSTODY CASES ✦

Jessica Simpson and Nick Lachey: Jessica got custody of *Daisy* the Maltipoo.

Jennifer Aniston and Brad Pitt: Jennifer gained custody of *Norman*, a Corgi cross dog.

Will and Julia Carling: Julia kept Labrador *Biff.*

Les Dennis and Amanda Holden: both wanted Westies *Nobby* and *Fudge,* allegedly they eventually agreed to keep one each.

Kirsten Dunst and Jake Gyllenhaal: Gyllenhaal kept German Shepherd *Atticus,* but Kirsten was given partial custody.

George and Alex Best: Alex was given custody of Irish Red Setters *Red* and *Rua.*

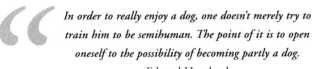
> *In order to really enjoy a dog, one doesn't merely try to train him to be semihuman. The point of it is to open oneself to the possibility of becoming partly a dog.*
> Edward Hoagland

✦ SPELLING IT OUT ✦

In 1975 Scottish comedian Billy Connolly recorded a parody of Tammy Wynette's hit single 'D.I.V.O.R.C.E' which became a popular hit in its own right. In it the husband spells out the word so that their dog, rather than child, can't understand what he's saying about an impending marital split, following a visit to the vet which goes wrong and ends up with both wife and dog biting him.

CANNY CUSTOMER

When Lele the dog is hungry, he barks to let his owner know; but instead of giving him some food, Wu Qianhe from Chengdu city in China gives him a one yuan note and sends him off to the shops to buy a sausage. Lele isn't a customer who can be conned – he won't surrender the note until he's been given the sausage, and can even tell the difference between money and a piece of plain paper.

ONE FOR THE KIDS

In keeping with the times, Mattel's doll 'Barbie' proudly introduced her latest acquisition to the world in 2006 – Tanner, her pet Labrador. Along with accessories such as a leash, dog toys, feeding bowl, a bone and biscuit treats, Tanner also has that other essential piece of kit – a pooper scooper. When 'fed' he produces poop from the other end, which Barbie can then clean up and place in the bin.

WHY DO DOGS SMELL DOGGY?

- Older dogs and uncastrated males often smell more than younger, neutered ones; generally though, they shouldn't have a strong or unpleasant smell – if they do, it could be a sign of ill health. Help keep your mutt smelling sweet by
- Grooming regularly.
- Checking round the bottom of hairy dogs as faeces can sometimes become trapped in the fur there.
- Bathing every 2 – 3 months, or treat him to a session at a grooming parlour.
- Giving breath freshening treats and chews; although if halitosis is a constant problem it could be a sign of dental or other health problems which need investigating by a vet.
- Drying off your dog as thoroughly as possible if he's been swimming or out in the rain – wet dogs always smell more than dry ones.
- Laundering pet bedding regularly.

PRESIDENTIAL POOCHES 8

If a dog saved the career of Nixon, it very nearly ended that of Lyndon B Johnson when he picked up one of his Beagles, Edgar, by the ears to pose for a picture. It sparked off horrified protests and accusations of cruelty, and following the incident his popularity plummeted.

Dogs don't feel threatened by your intelligence

Dogs never laugh at you

Dogs love all your cooking – even the mistakes

Dogs are never late for dinner

Dogs miss you when you're out

Dogs think that snuggling up on the sofa with a DVD is a great way to spend the evening

You can train a dog

Dogs don't hog the TV remote control

Dogs don't have problems expressing affection in public

❋ URBAN MYTH 6 ❋

St Bernards never carried small brandy casks around their necks.

❋ CHARLIZE'S COCKER ❋

Charlize Theron's Cocker Spaniel Denver landed a part in the film 'The Legend of Bagger Vance'; in his big scene he had to react to the sound of a gunshot by getting up and standing behind his mistress' legs – and managing it perfectly first time. Charlize got Denver as a three month old puppy, after responding to an advert for unwanted puppies just after she had moved to Los Angeles.

Bark bark bark bark bark bark BARK BARK
until you hear them all over the park.
T S Eliot

❋ POOP SCOOPING ❋

With UK dogs producing an estimated 1000 tonnes of poo every day, and leaving a considerable proportion of it behind in parks, on pavements and other public places, the Dogs (Fouling of Land) Act 1996 Act was introduced to try and clean things up. This act has since been superseded by the Clean Neighbourhoods and Environment Act 2005, but the intent is the same: it makes it an offence not to clear up after your dog in public places – and this requirement can also apply to certain areas of private land as well.

Failure to comply can result in a fine of up to £1000; the only time when no offence is committed is either if the owner of the land has given permission for the dog waste to be left or if the person in charge of the dog is a registered blind person.

MOLLY

As LS Lowry is renowned for his pictures of 'matchstalk' dogs (as well as men and cats), it seemed appropriate for the Lowry Arts Centre to celebrate it's 4th birthday in 2004 by adopting a suitable mascot. A nationwide search was duly launched, discovering Molly, a five-year-old ex-rescue dog, who fitted the bill perfectly.

QUESTION
What kind of dog sounds like you can eat it?
ANSWER
A sausage dog!

ARTIST'S MUSE

Other famous artists who have portrayed their pets include Hogarth, who included his Pug, Trump in a self-portrait, and Lucian Freud whose images of his own whippet Pluto, and of Eli, belonging to his studio assistant David Dawson are extraordinarily tender and affectionate.

MAKING A SPLASH

Big dogs, little dogs, hairy dogs and even bald ones ... all got a thorough soaking in 2003, when twelve veterinary students from the University of Sydney set a record for bathing dogs when they scrubbed 848 dogs in eight hours.

ON A ROLL

Elvis Presley's first public performance in front of an audience, aged ten years, was singing 'Old Shep' in a talent contest. He won $5. Later on in his career, 'Hound Dog' became a huge hit for him, selling over 4 million singles on its first release.

❖❖ A MATTER OF TASTE ❖❖

Just like humans, Dogs are sensitive to different tastes – sweet, sour, bitter and salty – using taste buds to help in detecting them. The taste buds are located mainly on the tongue, but although dogs have more than cats, there are far fewer than in humans, with around 1,706 as compared to about 9,000. As a result, they rely more on smell to provide information about food than taste. Warming food will make it smell better and therefore be more tempting to a dog with a poor appetite.

❖❖ LICENSING ❖❖

The only part of the UK where dog licences are required by law is in Northern Ireland; introduced in 1983 it costs £5, and a tag is issued with an ID number.

In Great Britain, dog licences were abolished in 1987; only around half of all owners bothered to purchase one and the annual fee of 37p became less than the administrative costs.

In Germany, dog ownership is regulated by a dog tax rather than licence, with the amount depending on the breed of dog. Those considered to be dangerous are taxed at a higher rate.

In the US, the cost of dog licences can vary not just between different states, but also according to which sex the animal is and whether it is neutered or not. Licensing is not just about complying with the law, but also offering a degree of protection for the dog;

those with licence tags are not only more likely to be reunited with their owners, but will be held for a longer period whilst waiting to be claimed than those without. If not wearing a tag, some states will euthanize the dog within just a few days, and in those states that allow it, unlicensed dogs may be used for vivisection.

PM'S CHOICE

The first British female to have a No.1 hit was Lita Rosa in 1953 with 'How Much is that Doggie in the Window?' In 1990, British Ex-Prime Minister Margaret Thatcher declared that it was her favourite pop song of all time, and Irish Prime Minister Bertie Ahern has also admitted that it is a favourite of his.

> *Newfoundland dogs are good*
> *to save children from drowning, but you must have a*
> *pond of water handy and a child, or else there will be no*
> *profit in boarding a Newfoundland.*
> Josh Billings

WAYS TO BE YOUR DOG'S BEST FRIEND

- Be a leader your dog can look up to, trust and respect.
- Always be consistent in your actions and behaviour.
- Set aside a period of time each day for spending quality time with your dog, playing and interacting with him.
- Don't leave him on his own for long periods: If you're going to be out for more than 4 hours arrange for a friend, relative or pet walker to visit and let him out in the garden or take him or a walk.
- Provide opportunities for him to socialise and play with other dogs.
- Make sure he gets sufficient mental stimulation as well as physical exercise.
- Praise your dog every time he does something right – not just when he's learning something new, but for behaviours which are already established too.
- As he grows older, be sensitive to changes in his needs and ready to adapt to them.
- Learn to do Tellington-Touch, Shiatsu or massage to help make him feel good and which will also deepen the bond between you.

FAT CAN BE FATAL

Being overweight could have been the fatal for Oscar the St Bernard when he fell into a canal, because at 15 stone, he was too heavy to swim, and nearly drowned; luckily he was rescued in time by a team of firemen equipped with ropes and pulleys – but even then, two of them had to don wetsuits and help push from behind.

No stone stands over where he lies.
It is on our hearts that his life is engraved.
John Galsworthy

DOGS ARE GOOD FOR YOU

According to research published in the British Journal of Health Psychology, although pet owners generally tend to be healthier than non-owners, those who have a canine companion in particular are likely to have lower blood pressure and cholesterol levels, fewer minor ailments, and are less likely to suffer serious medical problems. There even seems to be evidence to indicate that dogs can play a part in helping owners recover from illness if it does strike – even from serious physical ailments such as heart attacks.

LAB OR WALRUS?

In January 2007, two brothers were successfully prosecuted by the RSPCA for allowing their 11-year-old Labrador Rusty to get too fat. His weight had ballooned to a massive 11 1/2 stones (69.8 Kg) causing RSPCA officials to describe him as being 'hugely and grossly overweight' and a vet to comment that he looked like a walrus. The normal weight for an average Labrador is 25-36 Kg (55-80 lb)

WAR VETERAN

In spite of the lack of any official US war dog programme during World War I, American dogs nevertheless played crucial roles in the conflict – although those that were present were invariably dogs which had either been smuggled over with their owners, or found as strays in France and adopted by soldiers. One of these was Stubby, an American Pit Bull Terrier cross found by John Robert Conroy towards the end of his training. When his division was shipped out to France, Conroy smuggled him aboard and over the next year and a half Stubby took part in four offensives and seventeen battles. He learnt how to warn his unit of incoming gas and shell attacks, located wounded soldiers and even apparently captured a German spy, as well as saving a young girl from being run over while on leave. At the end of the war he was smuggled home again, having become the most decorated dog of the war; he was introduced to three US Presidents – Calvin Coolidge, Warren Harding and Woodrow Wilson, who solemnly shook his paw.

RESPONSIBLE OWNERSHIP

Owning a dog involves effort and commitment for many years. Your obligations aren't just to your pet, but also to the community in which you live, so being a responsible owner means you should be prepared to

- Devote time as well as money to his daily care
- Make sure he has some form of ID
- Never allow him to roam on his own
- Know about the law as it affects you both
- Ensure adequate exercise and play
- Clean up after him on walks
- Teach him basic obedience
- Control him properly when out in the countryside
- Register him with a veterinary surgeon
- Provide a balanced, nutritious diet and access to fresh clean water at all times
- Worm regularly
- Groom regularly
- Ensure he is protected against major canine diseases
- Discourage him from making a nuisance of himself with strangers or other dogs
- Take out an adequate insurance policy

QUESTION
What do you do if your dog eats your pen?
ANSWER
Use a pencil instead!

❄ ❄ DANCING WITH DOGS ❄ ❄

'Doggie dancing' as it's sometimes called, is a fairly new sport, but one which is catching on fast all over the world – as with agility and flyball, it's something which appeals to pet owners as a fun competition, and in which dogs of all sizes, types and breeds can compete.

The idea of working to music had already been in use for several years by training clubs to enhance rhythm and balance, but following a couple of public performances by training virtuoso Mary Ray, and especially after one display was televised nationwide at Crufts in 1992 it caught the imagination of owners everywhere.

Officially recognized as a sport by the Kennel Club in 2002, it has since evolved to include different divisions such as Musical Dressage, Heelwork to Music and probably everyone's favourite, Freestyle. Freestyle routines – where the dog isn't constantly maintaining a heelwork position - are particularly popular as they allow everyone to compete on a more equal footing, as well as allowing greater scope for creative expression.

Any dog, pedigree or crossbreed, large or small can participate; each individual has their own natural pace and behaviour, and a part of the skill and enjoyment comes from creating a routine and selecting a piece of music which suits these characteristics and succeeds in bringing the performance to life. It is also a sport which is suitable for handlers of any age.

Each of the moves used are taught step-by-step, and once each has been mastered are then put together to form a routine; some of the moves include twists, standing up,

REASONS TO HAVE A DOG 3

Because they're better than kids

Dogs don't want to spend all their free time in front a computer screen

Dogs get up before midday

Dogs eat everything you put in front of them, and what's more, enjoy it

Dogs don't want all the latest and most expensive toys and clothes

Dogs don't play loud music while you're trying to relax

Dogs aren't embarrassed to be seen out with you by their friends

Dogs never say 'I hate you' or slam doors

Dogs like to go out and get some fresh air

crawling, rolling over, bowing, reversing, circling, weaving through the handlers legs and jumping through his/her arms, and are cued through subtle use of verbal and body signals, or use of a 'prop' such as a walking stick.

Even if you don't want to actually compete, joining a class purely for pleasure can be just as satisfying as well as having many benefits: the variety involved, including changes of direction and pace and moves you'd never normally see in an obedience class can all add a bit of excitement, mental stimulation and pose a few new challenges to training sessions. Many dogs and owners find it more appealing than traditional obedience work, and it can help hone communication skills and to maintain motivation to continue beyond the basics with training, as well as simply being a fun way of spending time interacting with your dog.

To compete in competitions organised under Kennel Club rules, dogs need to be registered on the Activity Register. Independent competitions are also held nationwide.

Classes cater for all levels of experience, beginning with 'Starters' and routines of up to two and a half minutes in length and going on through to 'Advanced' level where routines may be up to four minutes in length.

Marks are awarded for programme content, accuracy and musical interpretation.

In Heelwork to Music classes, at least two thirds of the routine must be heelwork and only one third freestyle movements. In Freestyle classes, the reverse applies – two thirds freestyle movements, and one third heelwork. Both are calculated on the length of time spent doing them, rather than on the number of moves performed.

The main difference between heelwork in Heelwork to Music classes and obedience classes is that there are no compulsory movements - the content is chosen by the handler; and there can be backing and sidestepping as well as going forward.

✺✸ FAMOUS OWNERS OF RESCUE DOGS 4 ✸✺

Michael Schumacher - adopted 'Floh' a stray dog he found wandering around in the paddock at the Brazilian grand prix in 2004. He also owns 4 other dogs: a Westie, a crossbreed and two Belgian Shepherds.

✺✸ TIPS FOR SAFE CAR TRAVEL FOR DOGS AND DRIVERS ✸✺

- Travel your dog in a crate, with a seatbelt, or at least behind a dog guard for his own safety as well as to prevent him from distracting the driver and possibly being responsible for causing an accident.
- If using a crate, secure it firmly so it can't shift around.
- Teach your dog to sit and wait while you clip a lead on before getting out of the car.
- Always invite your dog to get into or out of the car from the kerb side, not the road side, so he is not endangered by passing traffic.
- Never leave a dog in a car; in hot weather interior temperatures rise rapidly even with windows left open and can kill a pet left inside within minutes. In cold weather interior temperatures drop equally fast, turning cars into fridges and dogs may become hypothermic.
- Don't feed your dog immediately before a car trip.
- Remember that your dog can't anticipate what's going to happen, so try and make his journey more pleasant by driving considerately
- Allow more time to accelerate and decelerate
- Don't take turns too tightly as this also makes it hard for your dog to balance
- Try to make smooth gear changes
- On long journeys stop every two hours to allow him to stretch his legs, spend a penny and have a drink.

✺✸ HITLER'S FIRST DOG ✸✺

Blondi wasn't Hitler's first dog; during the First World War, he had been besotted by his dog Fuchsl (little fox). The small white terrier was probably a mascot belonging to the British soldiers, and while busy chasing a rat in No Man's Land jumped into a German trench and was promptly caught by Hitler. Although he tried to return at first, Fuchsl soon became accustomed to his new master, sleeping beside him in the trenches and sharing his rations. 'When I ate he used to sit beside me and follow my gestures with his gaze' Hitler wrote later, 'If by the fifth or sixth mouthful I still hadn't given him anything he used to sit up on his rump and look at me with an air of saying 'And what about me, am I nothing at all?'" He adored the dog, writing 'I can look at him like I look at a human being. It's crazy how fond I am of the little beast'; it appears that the feeling was mutual, since when Hitler returned after two months away receiving treatment for a shrapnel injury, Fuchsl was delighted to be reunited with him.

In 1917 whilst waiting on a train station, Hitler was approached by a railway employee who offered him 200 marks for the dog, to which he replied that he wouldn't sell Fuchsl, 'not even for 200,000 marks'. When the troops arrived at their destination and left the train Fuchsl was nowhere to be found and Hitler was distraught at his loss; despite doing his best to find the dog, he never saw him again. Hitler was convinced that the 'slacker' who had tried to buy Fuchsl earlier had stolen him and wrote bitterly 'The swine who stole my dog doesn't realise what he did to me'.

 A dog is the only thing on earth that loves you more than he loves himself.
Josh Billings

PRESIDENTIAL POOCHES 9

President Thomas Jefferson was responsible for introducing dog licences in the US.

DEWCLAWS

Although most dogs have fully formed, or rudimentary dewclaws on the forelegs, they are also present on the back legs of some breeds – and others, such as the Pyrenean Mountain Dog, Lundehound and Beauceron even have double dewclaws. Dewclaws are said to brush the dew off the grass, which is where they get their name from, although in Europe they're often referred to as 'wolf claws' instead. As they often don't come into contact with the ground as the other nails do, they may need to be clipped more often; sometimes they are removed, especially if loose and floppy, to reduce the risk of injury should they become caught on something. A superstition about dewclaws is that a dog which still has them it will be immune to snake bites.

❧❧ SWEPT AWAY ❧❧

Zoe the Pyrenean Mountain Dog had a close brush with death when she was literally swept off her feet after running straight at a huge street sweeping machine in Missouri, USA. Her owner, 70-year-old Gene Fee feared the worst, and went home thinking that he'd never see his pet again; luckily for Zoe, truck driver John Reutter who'd been behind the sweeper saw what happened, and called for help. He climbed up on the sweeper and looked inside between the conveyor and the bloom, and spotted her, stuck in a small space, but still very much alive and looking up at him.

Six city workers, three maintenance vehicles and twenty minutes later Zoe was freed, unhurt but covered from top to toe in dirt and grease and asking to be petted and reassured. A vet said that all she needed following her ordeal was some painkillers and a good shampoo to restore her to her usual white colour; Gene was contacted, and the two were reunited.

QUESTION
What do you get if you cross a cocker spaniel, a poodle
and a rooster?
ANSWER
Cockerpoodledoo!

❧❧ FRIEND TO THE END 8 ❧❧

James I had a 'most special and favourite' hound called Jewel, which was accidentally shot by the queen whilst aiming at a deer, causing him to rage and swear at her; although later he repented of his loss of temper and gave her a £2000 diamond by way of apology.

❧❧ THE GRAVE OF GELERT ❧❧

Given as a gift by King John to Prince Llewelyn, Gelert was an Irish Wolfhound of huge strength and great intelligence. Although Llewelyn had plenty of other hounds, Gelert soon became his favourite, and in return, Gelert was devoted to his master. By day he would accompany him out hunting, and at night would sleep at the foot of his bed; but one morning Gelert refused to join Llewelyn when he was ready to set out. When Llewelyn returned that evening after a less successful hunt than usual, he was cross with the dog for having deserted him. Calling his name, his anger turned instantly to fear as

Gelert came to greet him, appearing from the door of the chamber where the prince's young son slept, with his muzzle covered in blood. In horror, Llewelyn rushed into the room to discover the cradle overturned, bedding strewn across the floor and covered in blood, and the child missing. Believing there could be only one explanation he drew his sword and plunged it into the dog's body. Gelert gave a great shriek of anguish and then, eyes fixed reproachfully upon his master's face, sank to the floor and died. Suddenly, another cry was heard – the child had crawled into a closet and fallen asleep there, only waking when he heard Gelert's dying scream. Hugging the child to him in relief, Llewelyn righted the overturned bed, and found the dead body of a grey wolf hidden beneath. In remorse he erected a tomb and chapel to the memory of the faithful hound and the place is called Bedd-Gelert to this day.

He never judges me, never looks away
because of my condition ...... I can put my hand out
to my side day or night and he is always there.
He has taught me to love, laugh and live again.
Allen Parton, talking of his assistance dog, Endal

❋❋ AWFUL TRUTH ❋❋

In 1937 film 'The Awful Truth', Wire Haired Terrier Asta plays the part of 'Mr. Smith' who becomes the subject of a custody battle when his owners decide to divorce.

THE FASTEST 2

In a bid to discover the fastest animal in the racing world, eight-year-old greyhound Simply Fabulous took on six-year-old racehorse Tiny Tim over a 2 furlong (400 m) course at Kempton Park, Middlesex. Tiny Tim was the 8-11 favourite with the bookies, and a split second race was predicted. In the event, Simply Splendid crossed the line in a time of 23.29 seconds, with Tiny Tim trailing in 15 dog lengths (or 7 horse lengths) behind, in a time of 24.63 seconds.

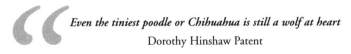

Even the tiniest poodle or Chihuahua is still a wolf at heart
Dorothy Hinshaw Patent

RIGHT TO ROAM

Charles II and James II both inherited their father's love for spaniels, and it is after Charles that both the Cavalier King Charles and King Charles Spaniels take their name. Samuel Pepys recorded that Charles paid more attention to his dogs than to the business of a Privy Council meeting; he also wrote that they were allowed the run of the court - although not, as popularly believed, granting them the right to go into any public place and into the House of Commons. The bitches were allowed to give birth and then bring up their puppies in the royal bedchamber, 'and indeed made the whole court nasty and stinking'.

When James was caught in a terrible storm at sea, it was said that as the orders were given to abandon ship he shouted "Save the dogs!" followed, almost as an afterthought, by the command "... and Colonel Churchill"

CLEAR IT UP

Dog fouling laws apply to the person in charge of the dog at the time, even if they aren't the owner.

Ignorance of the law is no excuse; not being aware that your dog has relieved himself, or not having anything with which to clear it up is not considered to be a reasonable excuse for failure to 'bag it and bin it'.

Poop scoops and refill bags can be bought from pet shops, or you could use nappy sacks or recycle old plastic carrier bags to pick up and dispose of the mess in a dog waste bin. Each special bin costs around £200, and about £3 to empty.

❧ TEN FAT FACTS ❧

- Obesity is the most common form of malnutrition in dogs.
- Fat dogs aren't happy dogs, but likely to have health problems and a shorter lifespan – and it's reckoned that around 50 per cent of all pet dogs are overweight. Health problems are a virtual certainty in dogs 30 per cent or more over their ideal weight; they are more at risk in the operating theatre, more prone to injury, have more stress on their organs and joints and are more susceptible to diabetes.
- Overweight dogs should always be taken to the vets for a health check and advice taken before putting them on a diet, as obesity can sometimes be due to disease. Eight out of ten vets now operate clinics for chubby pets.
- As little as a 1 per cent calorie excess on a daily basis can cause obesity by middle age.
- 15 per cent over the ideal bodyweight is clinically defined as the beginning of obesity.
- The risk of becoming overweight increases throughout life.
- Neutering is not directly a cause of weight gain, but can in some cases cause a reduced metabolic rate and thus a decreased food requirement.
- Nearly a third of dogs put on weight over Christmas. Almost two thirds of owners admit to preparing a special Christmas dinner for their pet in addition to giving treats as gifts.
- Fat puppies become fat adults – overfeeding a youngster is likely to predispose him to being overweight when he reaches maturity and it will be harder for him to shed the pounds.
- Breeds most at risk of developing weight problems include: Labrador Retriever, Cairn Terrier, Long Haired Dachshund, Basset Hound, Cavalier King Charles Spaniel, Beagle, and Shetland Sheepdog.

❧ NOSE COLOURS ❧

Self coloured nose: same colour nose as coat
Winter or Snow nose: dark coloured nose
that fades to brown during the winter due to lack
of sunlight
Liver nose: brown pigmented
Flesh coloured nose: an even, but light colour
Butterfly nose: parti-coloured nose; dark and
light speckles or patches
Dudley nose: entirely pink

❋ VITAL SIGNS ❋

Normal heart/pulse rates can vary – it may be as slow as 50 beats per minute in a large dog or as fast as 90 – 120 per minute in small ones, while a puppy's heartbeat may be as rapid as 200 per minute. It's helpful to know what is normal for your individual pet.

A high heart rate can be a sign of heart problems, pain, fever, and will increase during the early stages of shock. A rapid but weak pulse may indicate blood loss following an accident, or anaemia.

Large dogs usually have a respiratory rate of around 10 breaths/minute while very small dogs may have a rate of 30 breaths/minute. Respiration will increase with shock, pain, lung and heart problems. After exercise, the breathing of a healthy dog should return to normal within minutes.

A dog's temperature is higher than ours and is usually in the region of 100.5 F (38.1 C) and 102.5 F (39.2 C). Puppies have slightly higher temperatures than adult dogs. A high temperature may indicate problems such as infection, fever or heatstroke; if below normal it may be due to problems such as hypothermia or shock. If the temperature is

- 105 F or higher: take action to cool dog immediately and seek emergency veterinary attention as soon as possible.
- 103 – 104 F: get veterinary attention the same day
- 99 F: get veterinary attention the same day
- 98 F or lower: keep warm and seek emergency veterinary attention

QUESTION
What do you call a sheepdog's tail that can tell tall stories?
ANSWER
A shaggy dogs tale!

❋ UNDER CONTROL ❋

You must by law control your dog so that it doesn't scare, worry or disturb wildlife or farm animals; on most areas of open country and common land, you must keep your dog on a fixed lead of no more than 6ft in length between March 1st and July 31st, and at all times when near livestock. The Animals Act 1971 makes it legal for a dog to be shot, without warning, by a farmer for worrying livestock. The owner can also face criminal prosecution under the Dogs (Protection of Livestock) Act 1953.

WHY DO DOGS NEED TO HAVE THEIR TEETH BRUSHED?

Looking after your dog's teeth is an important but often neglected part of caring for a dog; by the age of three years, around 70% of dogs in the UK are in need of dental attention. Preventive care doesn't take long, and can lead to fewer traumatic trips to the vet. Regular toothbrushing is one of the most effective ways of removing plaque and delaying the formation of tartar, which can lead to gum infections and dental disease, which can in turn lead to other serious problems such as heart, liver and kidney disease. Plaque is a combination of food debris, oral bacteria and salivary secretions deposited as a film on tooth enamel; if not removed, it becomes mineralised and eventually forms hard yellowish brown coloured deposits of tartar. Once this has occurred, no amount of brushing will remove it, and descaling and polishing under anaesthesia by your vet will be required.

Brush the teeth on a daily basis, using a pet toothbrush with soft bristles; you can either use clean water or buy special doggy toothpaste which is made in tasty flavours such as vanilla, malt, beef or chicken to help make the process more pleasant for your pet. Human toothpaste should never be used as it can cause gastric irritation and vomiting.

Providing chewy items can also help – there are a whole range which aim to provide a flossing action to help clean the teeth, exercise the gums and offer a safe outlet for natural chewing instincts.

ON THE TRAIL 3

The first recorded arrest of a criminal tracked down by a Bloodhound was in 1810, and took place in the New Forest, Hampshire. The culprit was convicted of sheep stealing and condemned to death.

HOW TO WEIGH A DOG

- Pick up the dog and stand on your bathroom scales. Read off your combined weights.
- Weigh yourself again, this time without the dog, and subtract this reading from the other one.
- If the dog is too big or heavy, or dislikes being picked up, ask if you can use the walk-on scales at your local veterinary practice.
- Monitor weight on a monthly basis.

FIRST VET SCHOOL

The first veterinary school was established in 1764 in Lyons, and others soon followed across Europe – in Britain the Royal Veterinary College was established in 1791 and another opened shortly after in Edinburgh. In what was perceived as a male profession, it wasn't until 1889 that the first woman graduated from a British veterinary school.

THE DOG SAINT

In a similar legend to that of Gelert, a thirteenth century greyhound in France called Guinefort saved an infant from a large serpent, but was killed by his owner who failing to spot the snake, but seeing blood on the dog's muzzle initially thought that he had eaten the baby. Realising his terrible mistake, the owner placed the unfortunate Guinefort's body in a well and planted a grove of trees around it. Peasants soon began to visit and to pray to the canine martyr, referring to him as 'Saint Guinefort'. Not even the Inquisition were able to put an end to what they considered a heretical practice; even though they disinterred Guinefort's remains and cut down the trees, people continued to visit the site of the shrine until as recently as 1940, praying for protection for their children.

HIP DYSPLASIA

The discovery of hip dysplasia – a problem affecting several breeds, and which is nowadays screened for in those known to be affected by it – was first made during the Second World War, when it was noticed that some large breed dogs which 'broke down' during training had abnormal hip joints.

POSERS

Andy Warhol had been a renowned cat lover, but in the 1970s discovered the joy of dogs after buying a dachshund puppy called Archie. He took him everywhere – to the studio, openings, dinners and photo shoots – and found him indispensable during interviews: if asked a question he didn't want to answer, he simply passed it over to Archie. When Archie was three years old, he was joined by another dachshund, Amos. Warhol produced a series of dog paintings as did David Hockney, another dachshund fan, although he found that they didn't always make easy subjects, with Stanley and Boodgie being all too inclined to leap up at the slightest distraction.

✦ DOGS ON FILM ✦

Recognition for canine film stars and their on-screen talents finally happened in 2001 with the inception of the 'Palm Dog' Trophy – the canine equivalent of the Oscars. Fox Terrier Mutley presides over the jury each year at the event which is held alongside the Cannes Film Festival with it's own Palme d'Or awards for two legged stars. The inaugural winner was Otis, who received the Palm Dog Trophy collar for his performance in the film 'The Anniversary Party'.

Winners in subsequent years have been

2002: Tahti as 'Hannibal' in 'The Man without a Past'

2003: Moses in 'Dogville'

2004: All the dogs in 'Mondovino'

2005: Bruno in 'The Cave of the Yellow Dog'

2006: Mops in 'Marie Antoinette'

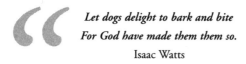

Let dogs delight to bark and bite
For God have made them them so.
Isaac Watts

✦ LET SLEEPING DOGS LIE ✦

According to most trainers and canine behaviourists, allowing your dog to share your bed is highly likely to lead to problems of some kind at some point in your relationship with each other; yet around half of all owners admit to actively encouraging their pet to snuggle up at night.

✦ LUCKY JASPER ✦

When Jasper, a down-and-out Labrador/Dobermann cross from Battersea Dogs and Cats Home was adopted by Diana Myburgh, he had hardly had time to find his paws in his new surroundings when his benefactor died. But instead of being back on the street again, Jasper's future had been secured by a £25,000 legacy, which doubled to £50,000 when his fellow beneficiary, Jason the whippet, died not long after. His guardian, Diana's son-in-law, has taken good care of his investments, with the result that he is now worth an estimated £130,000.

✵✵ DOG SUPERSTITIONS ✵✵

- Three white dogs together is a good omen.
- If a dog is seen eating grass, it means rain is on the way.
- A dog howling when a baby is born indicates that the child will have an unhappy life.
- If a dog runs under a table, a thunderstorm is on the way.
- Being followed by a strange dog will bring good luck.
- Should a black and white dog cross your path, then whatever business you are engaged upon at the time will have a favourable outcome.

✵✵ NEWTON'S LOSS ✵✵

"Oh Diamond! Diamond! Thou little knowest what mischief thou hast done!" was the exclamation supposedly uttered by the famous physicist and mathematician Sir Isaac Newton(1642 – 1727). It seems remarkably restrained considering the circumstances which caused it; perhaps foolishly as it turned out, he kept a pile of papers on his table upon which were written calculations which had taken him twenty years of work to make. One evening he left the room for a few minutes, only to discover on his return that his little dog Diamond had knocked over a candle, setting fire to the precious paperwork of which nothing was left but a heap of ashes.

The little dogs and all,
Tray, Blanch, and Sweetheart, see, they bark at me.
William Shakespeare

✦ LUCKY DOGS ✦

Two thousand years ago, Tibetan Terriers were being raised in monasteries, where the monks often called them 'Little people' although they were also popularly known as 'Good Luck Dogs' or 'Luck Bringers'. They were never sold, but were sometimes given as gifts, or to travellers undertaking perilous journeys as no-one would harm a person fortunate enough to have been given one.

✦ BREAKING UP IS HARD TO DO ✦

When partners separate and the time comes to agree over division of possessions, the whole matter can rapidly develop into an acrimonious dispute if there's a shared dog involved. A survey conducted on behalf of Direct Line Pet Insurance revealed that 39% of owners would be prepared to fight a custody battle over ownership, with a similar number being prepared to pay off their partner in order to secure guardianship of the pet; nearly a third were prepared to offer £1000, and just over a sixth as much as £10,000 to guarantee custody. One in ten were willing to resort to blackmail tactics if necessary, whilst one in six owners admitted to already having had the 'custody conversation' about what would happen to the dog should they separate from their partners. In addition, further research on the subject by Sainsbury's Bank found that one in five owners believe that couples should be bound by law to provide maintenance for pets in the event of a divorce.

✦ BORN AGAIN ✦

Practicing Tibetan Buddhists believe that the soul is frequently reborn in a dog as the last stage before becoming human.

✦ TITANIC MYTH ✦

Of all the myths which have sprung up around the sinking of the Titanic, one of the most enduring and a favourite amongst dog-lovers is that of Rigel, a large Newfoundland dog allegedly owned by the First Master, William Murdoch. He was said to have barked to warn the crew of Carpathia of the presence of the lifeboats when the survivors were too weak to call out a warning, and to have then guided them through the dark to safety. After spending three hours in the icy water he was brought on board the Carpathia apparently none the worse for wear, and he continued to stand vigil on the deck, looking through the rails for a sign of his missing master until removed to a cabin to be checked over. Sadly, although heart-warming, this account is actually the fictitious invention of a certain seaman called Jonas Briggs who apparently furnished several tall tales for the press.

> *I wish I were doing what my dog is doing at this moment, rolling in something ripe he has found on the beach in order to take on its smell. His is such an easy, simple way to increase one's stature and enlarge one's personality.*
> EB White

BASIC GROOMING EQUIPMENT

SLICKER BRUSH:
used to remove dead hair from curly, double and long coats.

RUBBER SLICKER:
suitable for wiry and fine, smooth haired coats.

METAL TOOTH COMB:
wide toothed for curly, double and long coats, narrower for smooth and wire haired coats.

SHEDDER:
a tool with serrated edges which remove loose hair.

GROOMING MITT:
rubber pimple covered glove to remove hair and mud from short, smooth coats.

CHAMOIS LEATHER:
to add a final polish to fine, smooth coats.

NAIL CLIPPERS:
for keeping nails trimmed to a suitable length.

CANINE TOOTHBRUSH AND PASTE

COTTON WOOL:
to clean ears, eyes and bottoms.

SCISSORS:
for any trimming necessary.

ANTI-STATIC SPRAY:
to help keep long haired coats from becoming too fly-away whilst working on them.

◦✿ FIREWORK FRIGHT ✿◦

Many dogs are frightened by fireworks or loud thunderstorms. Sometimes their fear can be traced back to a previous scary experience, but sometimes they can become frightened for no apparent reason. Things you can do to help include

- Don't cuddle and reassure as this will reinforce the dog's belief that something awful is happening. Ignore all fearful behaviour, but praise calmness. Try to pretend nothing is wrong, and behave normally.

- Offer long lasting chewy treats or a favourite toy to distract him. Chewing is also a 'stress busting' activity.

- Draw the curtains to block out any flashes of light and muffle the noise as much as possible.

- Provide your dog with a den – use a crate covered with a blanket or improvise with a table or couple of chairs – which he can use as a refuge. Some dogs feel safer if they have such a retreat available, but never shut him in.

- Feed a stodgy meal earlier in the day if fireworks or a storm are anticipated. Including pasta or rice so he has plenty of carbohydrates will help him to relax and sleep.

- Invite over a canine friend who isn't bothered by noises to set a good example.

- Give plenty of exercise early on in the day so he is physically and mentally tired and more likely to sleep.

- Using a close fitting T shirt, or a 'bodywrap' as used by Tellington-Touch practitioners can sometimes help to calm an anxious dog; preferably put it on before any noise is expected.

- Consult your vet about the use of short term medications or alternative remedies which may help.

- Find out about desensitisation and conditioning programmes using realistic sound effect CD recordings.

❧ BERTIE'S FAVOURITE ❧

Edward VII was devoted to his wire haired Fox Terrier Caesar, a gift from the Duchess of Newcastle in 1902; Edward's mistress, Violet Keppel, was not at all amused to find that the little dog was allowed to sleep in a chair by the side of the bed. At his master's funeral in 1910, led by a royal ghillie, Caesar accompanied the royal family, nine kings and numerous princes and nobles from all over the world.

QUESTION
Why do dogs run in circles?
ANSWER
Because its hard to run in squares!

❧ COLD COMFORT ❧

A 'Three Dog Night' is a phrase attributed to the Australian Aborigines, referring to sleeping outdoors with their dogs. The colder it is, the more dogs you need to stay warm.

❧ HOW TO STORE DOG FOOD ❧

- Check 'Use by' dates and use within the period stated – foods using natural preservatives may have a shorter shelf life than you anticipate.
- Buying in bulk can be cheaper – but buy only as much as you can use up within the use by dates. Foods used after this period may deteriorate in palatability and nutritional quality, and could upset your dog's stomach.

- Cover half full cans and place them in the fridge to keep them fresh – but allow to stand until they have reached room temperature before feeding.
- Use opened cans of food within 24 hours
- Store dry foods in a cool, dry place, out of contact with the floor and away from strong smelling things.
- Once opened, ideally keep dry foods in a container with an airtight seal. If this isn't possible, fold the top of the bag over and use bulldog clips or clothes pegs to keep it closed.
- A clean dustbin or large plastic toy box with a snap-on lid can make an ideal container for storing big bags of dry food, helping to minimise the danger of tears in the packaging or dropped morsels which can attract vermin and insects.
- Don't mix old and new batches of food. Topping up an older supply with fresh can lead to premature staleness, decay and the build up of bacteria.
- Regularly clean out storage containers and allow to dry completely before refilling.
- Keep crunchy biscuit type treats separate from semi-moist ones.
- Ensure all foodstuffs are kept where your dog can't access them and help himself.

 A dog can express more with his tail in a minute than a human can express with his tongue in an hour.
Anonymous

❧ FLYBALL ❧

Like Frisbee, another doggy sport which started out as a demonstration, flyball is hugely popular all round the world, with tournaments run throughout the round. First seen in California in the early 1970s, when Herbert Wagner first invented a ball launcher for displays, the dogs loved it, the owners loved it, and so did the onlookers. After appearing on TV, this fast and furious sport grew from there, really taking off in Canada and North America in the 1980s and in the UK in the early 1990s.

A team sport, each squad consists of up to six dogs, four of which run in a relay against another team; each dog races up a straight lane, jumping four hurdles on the way and then using it's paws to hit a pad on a spring loaded box which releases a tennis ball into the air. The dog catches the ball, and then runs back down the lane of hurdles, and the next dog in the team sets off. The winning team is the one with the fastest time with no penalties incurred. Tournaments are usually organised on a 'best of three' or 'best of five' knockout system of heats. Dogs must be 12 months old to begin competing in Starter classes, and 18 months old to compete in sanctioned classes, and hurdle height is determined by the size of the smallest dog in the team - so smaller members aren't discriminated against and can in fact be an asset since the others benefit from the lower height too.

 The most affectionate creature in the world is a wet dog.
Ambrose Bierce

MAYHEW ANIMAL HOME

Originally starting out as a stray cats home, this charity soon developed into a refuge for 'the lost and starving dogs of London' too; founded by the West London Society for the Prevention of Cruelty to Animals it's first permanent home came three years later in 1889 when a local clergyman generously donated a plot of land. Like most of the early charities, fundraising was a struggle but despite the odds against, by 1894 it was flourishing and had gained a reputation for excellence under the management of Superintendent Annie Mayhew, who the home was later renamed after. As with many other animal rescue organisations, the Home is actively involved in education and animal welfare, in addition to rescuing and rehoming stray and unwanted pets and offering low cost vaccination, neutering and micro chipping services; all of which results in daily running costs of £3000.

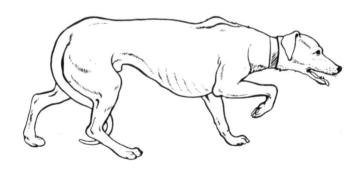

❄❄ SAFE SWIMMING ❄❄

Many dogs love to paddle or swim, and in the summer it can be a fun activity for owners to share – but it's also important to be aware of some of the hazards

- It's not a good idea to encourage dogs to take a dip in human swimming pools as the chemicals used in them can cause gastric, eye and skin irritation. If you do own a swimming pool, fence it off securely so your dog cannot jump into it – steep or slippery sides may make it impossible for him to get out. Garden ponds are also best fenced off.
- Always supervise swimming activities – never leave your dog to his own devices.
- Swimming can have wonderful therapeutic benefits, but if taking your dog swimming for health or fitness reasons or following injury, it's best to take him to a proper hydrotherapy centre where the water will be warm and he will be properly monitored by experienced staff.
- When swimming outdoors, be aware of dangers posed by boats and other vessels, fishing activities, tides, weeds and other vegetation, pollution, algae poisoning and unseen underwater hazards. Observe and obey all warning signs, and assure yourself that the area is safe before allowing your dog in the water. If visiting a beach, bear in mind that not all are dog-friendly, so check before you set out.
- Unlike people, dogs can't tread water – if they stop swimming, they sink. Swimming can be a very tiring activity, but some dogs love it so much they keep going even when fatigued and may then get into difficulties; keep a careful eye on him and stop before this happens.
- If your dog is not a very proficient swimmer, is old or weak, or if at the seaside, it's a sensible precaution to put a flotation jacket on him. These can be bought in a range of sizes to fit all sorts of dogs.
- Discourage your dog from drinking the water; take along your own supply for him.
- Even in warm weather, the slightest breeze can rapidly chill, so take along plenty of towels to dry your dog off with. If he's been swimming in the sea, rinse the salt out of his coat as soon as you are able.

❄❄ FRIEND TO THE END 9 ❄❄

Frederick the Great adored his dogs, and wishing to be buried near them, had a special mausoleum built on the palace lawn where it would overlook the graves of eleven of his pets. He now rests inside, next to the body of his last dog.

✴✺ URBAN MYTH 7 – TOP DOG VERSUS THE UNDER DOG ✺✴

The descriptive terms 'top dog' and 'underdog' are popularly believed to refer to the practice of two men using a two handed saw in the days when wooden planks were sawn by hand. One man stood on top, and the other underneath in a pit – a much more uncomfortable position, with the added bonus of sawdust falling onto him as well. The irons used to secure the wood were called 'dogs' and the word 'dog' was also sometimes used to refer to menial workers. However, although it's a nice explanation, all the printed references of the time when such pits were in use are all in the context of dog fights.

QUESTION
How did the little Scottish dog feel when he saw a monster?
ANSWER
Terrier-fied!

✴✺ HOLIDAY CHECKLIST ✺✴

Taking your pet with you on holiday means you can spend quality time together, and you will be able to enjoy your break without being troubled by a guilty conscience at having left him in kennels. As well as throwing a few things in a bag for yourself, you'll need to take some essentials for your pet; it's a good idea to make out a list beforehand, and you can tick off each item as you pack it. Basic things to include are

- Bedding – the familiarity of his own bed will help your dog settle in a strange new place.
- Towels to dry wet or muddy feet and coats.
- Dog food plus can opener if needed, fork and measure.
- Food and water bowls.
- Water container - for the journey and any long outings you go on.
- Poo bags.
- First aid kit.
- Grooming kit.
- Treats.
- Toys.
- Stain remover – just in case of any accidents.

- An old sheet to spread over your bed if your dog is likely to join you on it.
- Documentation – very important if travelling abroad, so best kept together in a special wallet where it's easy to find.
- Bumbag or rucksack – for carrying all the doggy things you'll need whilst out and about each day.
- Collar with ID and leash – not items which need to be packed, but which you do need to remember to take with you.

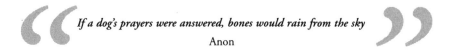

If a dog's prayers were answered, bones would rain from the sky
Anon

LIGHT AT THE END OF THE TUNNEL

The Bendigo Branch of the German Shepherd Dog Club of Victoria, Australia thought they'd celebrate their 10th Anniversary in style and make it a particularly memorable event by setting a world record. They decided to take a crack at the longest human dog tunnel, a record first set in the UK in 2004, with 222 pairs of straddled human legs, through which 4 dogs ran. All the preparations were going well, and plenty of volunteers had been recruited, with the aim of beating the record using 230 pairs of legs and five dogs – and then the bad news arrived. With little time left before the event, the club learned that the record had already been broken, just two months previously, in the USA when a dog called 'Nightie' ran through a tunnel formed by 382 pairs of legs. With the clock ticking away, a frantic search for more volunteers followed, and finally they were able to collect together 387 pairs of legs, together with 7 dogs who were to make the attempt. As the first dog started his run, to emerge victorious at the end of the tunnel, followed in succession by the other six, a cheer went up and another record – albeit a strange one – was toppled.

FOOD FACT

The first commercial pet food was manufactured by lightning rod salesman James Spratt in the 1860's after he noticed stray dogs eating discarded ship's biscuits. He decided he could come up with something better for pet owners, and went on to produce 'Patent Meat Fibrine' cakes.

BLUE PETER 6

Compared to previous canines, pedigree Golden Retriever 'Lucy' was a late starter, recruited to the show at the age of 5 months old in 1999 when Bonnie retired; a well trained and amenable character, she has achieved her Kennel Club Good Citizen Gold Award. Sharing the dressing room with her is 'Mabel', a Border Collie cross who was rescued after she had been abandoned, locked in a bare basement flat with no food or water.

The best thing about a man is his dog.
French proverb

A CHANCE TO SHINE

Recognising that rescue dogs so often have so much to give, but all too often never get the chance to do so, The Sam Simon Foundation in the US aims to give them a chance to shine. Selecting them from shelters where many would otherwise be put to sleep, they are trained to be Hearing Dogs, with those that don't quite make the grade being adopted out as 'career change dogs' to families who want a canine friend. The foundation also runs a programme which rescues elderly dogs which are hard to adopt, plus a mobile clinic which offers spay and neuter surgery free of charge to pets of low income families, plus free vaccinations, flea control, worming treatment and nail trims. The foundation costs millions to run, but is entirely privately funded by self-styled 'dog nut' Sam Simon, TV writer and producer of shows such as 'Taxi', 'Cheers', and 'The Tracey Ullman Show'. Simon was also the co-creator of 'The Simpsons', which of course, is famous for the family dog, Santa's Little Helper, adopted (naturally) from Springfield Downs dog race track.

ON HOLIDAY

According to a Travelodge survey, 2 million UK owners take their dogs away on holiday with them each year. Another survey, by a pet insurance company, revealed that whilst their owners are on holiday:

2.2 per cent of pets fell pregnant

18.2 per cent put on weight

12.2 per cent lost a significant amount of weight

❄❄ THE ORIGIN OF MODERN DOG TRAINING ❄❄

Modern training methods all started with dribbling dogs – strange but true. Russian scientist Ivan Pavlov was studying the digestive system in mammals when he noticed that the dogs he was using in his experiments investigating saliva started to drool even when food wasn't present. Curious, he looked into the cause of this mysterious phenomenon and discovered that it was the sight of the lab coats that his assistants wore which was triggering the response. This was because everyone time the dogs were given food, the person serving it up was wearing a lab coat, and they associated the two. Intrigued by this, Pavlov experimented further, ringing a bell at the same time as the food was given, and after a while every time the dogs heard the sound they would begin to salivate, whether food was present or not. As well as bells, Pavlov also used other types of stimulus, such as whistles, tuning forks, metronomes and various visual stimuli.

This kind of learned response is called a conditioned reflex, and the process whereby the association is made between the stimulus (in this case the bell) and the reflex (the salivation in anticipation of food) is called conditioning.

Another scientist, BF Skinner, became interested in Pavlov's work and further developed it by looking at ways in which specific behavioural actions in response to a stimulus could be created by adding a 'reinforcer'. A reinforcer is either a reward or a punisher; a reward will increase the desire to repeat the action which achieved it, whilst a punisher will decrease the desire to repeat the action.

HOLIDAY ETIQUETTE

It's fun going on holiday with your pet, and hotels and Bed & Breakfast accommodation are increasingly catering for four as well as two legged guests. Make sure your dog is a welcome visitor by:

- making sure his training is up to scratch and that you can control him easily. If he isn't housetrained, don't even consider going to a hotel or B&B.
- giving him a good groom to remove loose hairs, or possibly a bath before you go if he's a bit smelly.
- finding out what areas your dog is allowed in, and keeping him on the lead unless the proprietor invites you to let him loose.
- scooping your dog's poop outside and asking about where you should dispose of it.
- not allowing your pet to annoy other people; not all the guests may be dog-lovers.
- Exercising caution around other guests' dogs who may not be as friendly and sociable as your own.
- Ensuring you have adequate insurance which will cover you just in case he does damage something.

COOL TREAT

A cool treat on a warm day is an ice cream you can share with your dog – and it's very easy to make. In a food processor blend together one large banana, one tablespoonful of peanut butter, and one tablespoonful of honey until smooth. Add one large tub of natural yoghurt, and blend again until smooth. Pour the mixture into a container and freeze. Allow to stand for ten minutes or until beginning to soften slightly before serving so it isn't too cold for your dog.

DANGEROUS DOGS

Be prepared when walking your pet in areas where other dogs are off-leash, as not all are well behaved. If a dog which appears threatening runs towards you, place your dogs in a sit-stay and step forward toward the aggressor. Startle him and discourage him from coming any closer by using a quick jet from a canister of compressed air when he's within around 20 feet of you; alternatively, toss a plastic bottle or tin with pebbles in it towards him, or an activated personal alarm. Pointing and opening an umbrella can also be effective in persuading an onwards bound dog to back off.

❊ DOG HOUSE RULES ❊

The dog is never permitted in the house. The dog stays outside in a specially built kennel.

… Okay, the dog can enter the house, but only for short visits, or if his kennel is under renovation.

… Okay, the dog can stay in the house on a permanent basis, provided his kennel can be sold on to a rookie dog owner.

… Inside the house, the dog is not allowed on the furniture.

… Okay, the dog can get on the old furniture, but not the new furniture.

… Okay, the dog can get up on the new furniture until it looks like the old furniture and then we'll sell the whole works and buy new furniture … upon which the dog will most definitely not be allowed.

… The dog never sleeps on the bed.

… Okay, the dog can sleep at the foot of the bed.

… Okay, the dog can sleep alongside you, but he's not allowed under the covers.

… Okay, the dog can sleep under the covers, but not with his head on the pillow.

… Okay, the dog can sleep alongside you under the covers with his head on the pillow, but if he snores he's got to leave the room.

… Okay, the dog can sleep and snore and have nightmares in the bed, but he's not to come in and sleep on the couch in the living room where I'm now sleeping …

(Author unknown)

❊ THE LONGEST ❊

The longest jump ever was allegedly by a greyhound named Bang who cleared a 4 ft 6 in gate and covered a distance of 30 ft whilst chasing a hare at Brecon Lodge in Gloucestershire, England. Unfortunately whilst managing this feat he landed on a hard road and damaged his pastern bone.

THINGS TO LOOK FOR IN A TRAINING CLASS

Happy, relaxed looking owners and dogs

No shouting or lots of noise

Interested and approachable trainers

Firm but fair and humane training methods

Safe, well organised classes

Classes small enough to ensure adequate attention for everyone

TOY STORY

Buying toys for your pet isn't just about showing him how much you care. He probably just thinks they're fun, but they're actually a vital necessity for his mental and physical health; as well as helping prevent boredom, they can be used as training aids, to raise the level of exercise he gets, may be able to discourage some problem behaviours, and can help establish your own status and increase the interaction between you and your pet.

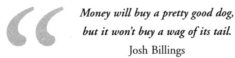

Money will buy a pretty good dog, but it won't buy a wag of its tail.
Josh Billings

THE PRICE OF A WOMAN

On 7 April 1832, a certain Cumberland farmer called Joseph Thomson took his wife to Carlisle where he sold her by auction for the sum of twenty shillings and a Newfoundland dog.

WACKY DOGGY GADGETS 6

'Neuticles' - prosthetic implants for dogs - came into existence when Greg Miller's Bloodhound 'Buck' disappeared on the scent of a female dog in season. After he was finally located, twenty miles and several days later, Miller had Buck neutered to prevent such an event from happening again. Horrified to discover that prosthetic testicles didn't exist for dogs, Miller promptly decided that he'd better invent them himself so that dogs could continue to look the same after the snip – or even be slightly 'enhanced' if wished.

ALL WASHED UP

Some time around the 15th century, or so the legend goes, some little white dogs - thought to be related to the ancestors of the modern day Bichon Frise - were accompanying some ladies on board a ship sailing between France and the West Indies. During the voyage there was a violent storm and the ship sank, with all on board perishing, save for the little white dogs who swam for their lives, coming to shore at the Port of Tulear on the southwest coast of Madagascar. There they went native, using their wits to survive such problems as how to cross crocodile infested rivers (their solution was to create a diversion) until they eventually became popular as pets, acquiring the name of the Coton de Tulear in acknowledgement of their origins on the island.

SEAMAN

Bought for $20 by Captain Meriwether Lewis, Seaman the Newfoundland accompanied his owner on the Lewis and Clark expedition to the Pacific coast from 1804 -1806, to become one of the furthest travelled dogs of his time. During the expedition, Seaman had to deal with all manner of discomforts – being tormented by mosquitoes, scared by buffalo, overheating in his thick coat and being bitten on a back leg by a beaver, resulting in a severed artery. Having survived that, he was then kidnapped by Indians, only being returned when Lewis threatened to burn the village down.

No-one knows for certain what happened to Seaman once the party reached their destination as the references to him in Lewis' journals taper off, but there does seem to be some evidence to suggest that he continued to accompany his owner on further journeys until Lewis' death in 1809. A mere five years later, Timothy Alden, a scholar with a reputation for meticulousness noted an inscription on a dog collar in a museum in Virginia which read: 'The greatest traveller of my species. My name is SEAMAN, the dog of Captain Meriwether Lewis, whom I accompanied to the Pacifick ocean through the continent of North America'. Alden added the following note regarding the collar and the dog who had once worn it: "The foregoing was copied from the collar, in the Alexandrian Museum, which the late gov. Lewis's dog wore after his return from the western coast of America. The fidelity and attachment of this animal were remarkable. After the melancholy exit of gov. Lewis, his dog would not depart for a moment from his lifeless remains; and when they were deposited in the earth no gentle means could draw him from the spot of interment. He refused to take every kind of food, which was offered him, and actually pined away and died with grief upon his master's grave'.

✹ HOLIDAY HOUND ✹

Prime Minister Harold Wilson was incensed when he heard that his yellow Labrador Paddy might not be allowed to accompany him to his holiday home on the Isles of Scilly due to the Island's Councils plans to ban visitors pets in order to keep rabies at bay. His private secretary leapt into action, firing off a memo to the Department of Environment giving them a 48 hour ultimatum to respond, but the premier couldn't wait that long. He phoned his own contacts on the Scillies, who told him that as a resident, Paddy would naturally always be welcome. Paddy was, incidentally, at one time accused of trying to drown his master by tipping him out of a rubber dinghy, but this was simply a scurrilous piece of hearsay aimed at concealing the fact that his master was too portly to climb back in when he had lost his balance and fallen out. At the time of the alleged incident, Paddy was in fact tied up elsewhere.

✹ HAPPY HUNTING ✹

In the 19th century, a Mr Thomas Nevill from Hampshire kept a tame stag and a pet hyena, both of which lived in the house with him. They were regularly hunted by his pack of Bloodhounds, travelling to the meet along with the hounds and setting off from there with the pack following in full cry. When they felt the hunt had gone on for long enough, they would either head for home, or stand at bay, after which they would trot docilely back home alongside the hounds.

❖ PRESIDENTIAL POOCHES 10 ❖

James Garfield named his dog Veto to warn Congress not to send any more bills to the White House that he didn't want to sign.

> *He is very important, a dog is; he never makes it his business*
> *to inquire whether you are in the right or wrong, never asks*
> *whether you are rich or poor, silly or wise, sinner or saint.*
> *You are his pal. That is enough for him.*
> Jerome K Jerome

❖ SORTER ... SORTED ❖

One night in 5 BC, when the garrison of Corinth had all fallen asleep after an evening's carousing, a flotilla of enemy Athenian ships landed on the shore and began to stealthily make their way towards the city, thinking to catch them unawares and unprepared. Luckily the Corinthians had left 50 dogs in kennels along the shoreline, and as the soldiers began to creep forward the canine sentries attacked ferociously. All but one were killed in the melee, but the sole survivor, a dog called Sorter, fled back to the city and roused the drunken soldiers to battle. Victorious over the Athenians, the grateful populace gave the dog a collar inscribed *'Sorter, Defender and Saviour of Corinth',* and erected a monument to him and his fallen fellows.

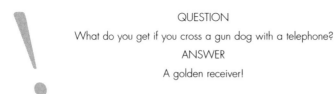

QUESTION
What do you get if you cross a gun dog with a telephone?
ANSWER
A golden receiver!

❖ FIRST CASUALTY ❖

The first British dog to be killed in action during World War II was Bobbie, a white German Shepherd who carried messages between military units whilst in France. As soon as darkness fell a sergeant major and three other men recovered the body of their fallen four legged comrade and buried it with full military honours.

HOME SWEET HOME

Whilst accompanying his owner who was visiting relatives in Wolcott, USA in 1923, Bobby the collie was set upon and chased away by a pack of local dogs. Despite searching, his owner was unable to find him, and sadly set off on the journey home again. Six months later, Bobby arrived back home under his own steam; on arrival he headed for the farm where he had lived as a puppy, and it was there, just a few miles from his home, that he was discovered, sleeping on the grave of a fox terrier who had been his youthful playmate.

 If I had a dog I would not feel so lonely, but I suppose that is asking too much.
Eva Braun

SOUNDS LIKE

One of the most famous brand names to feature a dog is the HMV label – but it very nearly didn't happen. The dog in the picture is 'Nipper' a stray dog found and adopted by scenic artist Mark Barraud in 1884. When Mark died in 1887, Nipper went to live in Liverpool with his younger brother Francis, also an artist. Along with Nipper, Francis also inherited a cylinder phonograph and recordings of Mark's voice, and he noticed how when he played them, Nipper would cock his head to one side and look puzzled as to where the voice was coming from. It wasn't until three years after Nipper's death in 1895 that Francis committed the scene he remembered so well to canvas, calling the finished painting 'Dog Looking at, and Listening to a Phonograph'. He submitted a picture for copyright, and showed it to several publishers who showed little interest in it, commenting that 'dogs don't do that'. When a friend suggested that repainting the black horn as a shiny brass one might make it more attractive, Francis called at the offices of The Gramophone Co, hoping to borrow one to use as a model. He showed a photograph of the picture to the Manager, William Barry Owen, who immediately offered to buy it provided he replaced the phonograph with a gramophone. The changes were made, and Nipper's image made it's first appearance in advertising literature in 1900. The US rights to the picture were obtained by the Victor Talking Machine Company which used a simplified drawing of the dog and gramophone on their records from 1902 and urged buyers to 'look for the dog'. In 1909 the picture was also used on record labels in the UK, and Francis went on to paint 24 more copies of what became his best known work for branch offices around the world.

HOMELESS HOUNDS

Of all the breeds, greyhounds are probably the most numerous of all those in search of new homes. Over 10,000 greyhounds retire each year due to injury, old age, or simply not being fast enough, many of them still very young. Not all trainers or owners keep them, and consequently a large number are either abandoned or destroyed; the Retired Greyhound Trust rehomes around 2,000 every year, and numerous other charities do what they can to help, but inevitably there are always more dogs than places available for them in shelters.

RIN TIN TIN

Found as a shell-shocked pup during the last days of World War II, Rin Tin Tin and his sister were rescued by serviceman Lee Duncan who took them back to the US with him at the end of the war. Sadly, the sister died of distemper, but Rin Tin Tin (named after the tiny puppets given to US soldiers for luck by French children) thrived and learned a number of tricks. After being spotted by a film producer, Rinty as he became nicknamed, went on to make 26 films for Warner Brothers before he died in 1932, when his body was returned to the country of his birth for burial. At the height of his fame he received 10,000 fan letters a week, and was considered to be just as much a top Hollywood star as any two-legged actors; he is even credited with having helped save the film studio from financial ruin. Rinty's bloodline has continued, with the current Rin Tin Tin being the tenth to carry the name.

SPOT'S DAY OUT

No-one quite knows what the motive for Spot's journey was, only that he seemed to have a sense of purpose and was quite determined about it. The 8 month old collie cross jumped onto a coach at Cardiff, bound for London, and no amount of coaxing and cajoling would persuade him to disembark. Firmer measures didn't work either, but produced a sufficiently threatening growl that no-one was prepared to push matters further. Eventually, fifteen minutes late, the coach set off with its extra passenger; on arriving at Victoria, Spot jumped off and disappeared but half an hour later, he was back again, just in time for the return journey. Settling back down again on the same seat he enjoyed the fuss and attention lavished on him by the other passengers until reaching Cardiff, when he was taken to an animal shelter.

❧❧ MATCHMAKER ❧❧

When Luath, the favourite dog of poet Robert Burns tripped up Jean Armour at a wedding, it gave him the chance to speak to the woman who was to become his wife and the other love of his life. He was heartbroken when the little collie was killed by the 'wanton cruelty' of someone the night before his father's death, and went on to immortalise him in the poem 'The Twa Dogs'. A statue of Burns in Dumfries shows a dog sitting at the poets feet which is reputed to be Luath.

Whosoever loveth me, loveth my hound.
Sir Thomas More

❧❧ THIS IS HEAVEN ❧❧

A man and his dog were walking along a road. The man was enjoying the scenery, when it suddenly occurred to him that he was dead. He remembered dying, and that the dog walking beside him had been dead for some time also.

After a while, they came to a high, white stone wall along one side of the road. It looked like fine marble. At the top of a long hill, it was broken by a tall arch that glowed in the sunlight.

When he was standing before it he saw a magnificent gate in the arch that looked like mother-of-pearl, and the street that led to the gate looked as though it were paved with pure gold. He and the dog walked toward the gate, and as he got closer, he saw a man at a desk to one side.

When he was close enough, he called out, 'Excuse me, where are we?'

'This is Heaven, sir' the man replied.

'Would you happen to have some water?' the traveller asked.

'Of course, sir. Come right in, and I'll have some iced water brought right up.' The man gestured, and the gate began to open.

'Can my friend come in too?' asked the traveller, gesturing toward his dog.

'I'm sorry, sir, but we don't accept pets.'

The traveller thought a moment, and then turned back toward the road and continued the way he had been going with his dog. After another long walk, and at the top of another long hill, he came to a dirt road leading through a farm gate that looked as though it had never been closed. There was no fence.

As the traveller approached the gate, he saw a man inside, leaning against a tree and reading a book.

'Excuse me!' the traveller called to the man. 'Do you have any water?'

'Yeah, sure, there's a pump over there, come on in.'

'How about my friend here?' The traveller gestured to the dog.

'There should be a bowl by the pump'

They went through the gate, and sure enough, there was an old-fashioned hand pump with a bowl beside it. The traveller filled the water bowl and took a long drink himself, then offered some to the dog. When they had satisfied their thirst, he and the dog walked back toward the man who was standing by the tree.

'What do you call this place?' asked the traveller.

'This is Heaven' the man answered.

'Well, that's confusing' said the traveller. 'The man down the road said that was Heaven, too.'

'Oh, you mean the place with the gold street and pearly gates? No, that's Hell disguised as Heaven.'

'Doesn't it make you angry that they're using your name like that?' asked the traveller.

'No, we're just happy that they screen out the folks who would leave their friends behind.'

(Author unknown)

✻ SMART DOGS ✻

Some of the smartest dogs can understand up to 200 verbal commands.

DOGS AND THE UNDERWORLD

In Greek mythology, Cerberus is the three headed dog with a snake for a tail, who guarded the gateway to Hades, allowing all to enter but none to return. He wasn't always altogether successful at his job, being foiled on several occasions by the resourcefulness or cunning of various heroes: as the last of his twelve labours, Heracles captured him by wrestling him into submission, and Orpheus lulled him to sleep using his musical skills. Hermes also sent him to sleep, this time with water from the river Lethe, as did Psyche with drugged honeycakes.

Garm was another sentinel of the underworld, this time in Norse mythology, standing guard at the gates of Helheim. With four eyes and a chest drenched in blood, the end of the world will be heralded by the sound of his howling.

The Egyptian god Anubis was variously depicted as having the head of either a jackal or a dog, and as guardian of the boundary between the realms of the living and dead was able to move freely between the two. Revered by high and low alike, he presided over funerary ceremonies, greeted new souls arriving in the underworld, ensured the accuracy of the scales on which they were weighed and protected them on their journey.

MOUSTACHE

Moustache, a black Barbet Spaniel had a distinguished military career with the French Army. Born in 1799 he became the pet of a regiment of French grenadiers and took an active part in the Napoleonic wars; he is supposed to have discovered a spy and saved a detachment of his company from a surprise attack. His greatest triumph happened at Austerlitz, when a young ensign bearing the regimental colours was mortally wounded and surrounded by the enemy. Under fire, Moustache raced to the rescue and retrieved the flag from the boy's dead body and triumphantly carried it back to his own lines. In recognition of this act he was awarded a medal for gallantry and his name laced on the regimental books as a full-fledged soldier and entitling him to draw rations and pay. On being presented to Napoleon he performed tricks such as saluting with a paw, after which he continued to accompany his battalion; but at the siege of Badajoz in 1811 he was hit by a cannon ball. He was buried where he fell and a stone to his memory raised over it bearing the simple words 'Ci git le brave Moustache'. His grave was destroyed by the Spaniards after the war, but in 2006 his memory was honoured and a plaque erected on the wall of the pet cemetery at Asnieres-en-Seine in Paris, also the last resting place of fellow canines Barry the heroic St. Bernard and film star Rin Tin Tin.

❖❖ FRIEND TO THE END 10 ❖❖

The Duchess of Bedford built a temple as a memorial to her Peke 'Che Foo' at Woburn Abbey, Bedfordshire. Corinthian pillars surround a bronze effigy of the little dog, of whom the duchess wrote disconsolately in her diary, "My little Che Foo died. He has been my constant companion for over eleven years – a more faithful and devoted one I shall never have."

❖❖ MISGUIDED ❖❖

A blind person walking along the street commanded his dog to turn right into what he thought was the subway entrance. He had miscalculated however, and found himself completely disoriented in a dead end alley. A passer-by saw his dilemma and asked if he could be of help.

"Yes, thank you" the blind man replied. "I was trying to get to the subway."

The man leaned over to the dog and said slowly and distinctly into the dog's ear, "Take … him … to … the … subway."

(Unknown guide dog trainer, reporting a story told to him)

QUESTION
What do you get if you cross a Beatle and an Australian dog?
ANSWER
Dingo Starr!

❖❖ THE BIG SIT ❖❖

The 'Big Sit' was an attempt on the Guinness World Record for the greatest number of dogs to do a sit/stay exercise for two minutes and which took place at the Wag and Bone Show in August 2003. When planning for the record attempt started, the figure stood at 76 dogs, but as the day drew closer a new record claim was made for 337 dogs. Requests for participants were made, and dogs and owners responded in their hundreds; after the final count the record had been smashed, with 514 dogs performing the world's largest simultaneous canine sit-in. This success was repeated at the same show two years later in 2005, when the record was once again resoundingly cracked, this time with a count of 627 dogs.

HOW TO GIVE VERBAL COMMANDS:

- Choose command words which are short and easy to understand. Single words are best.
- Be consistent – always use the same words for each action.
- Speak clearly.
- Prefix commands with your dog's name so you get his attention first.
- Don't keep repeating the same command; saying 'down down down' is likely to confuse him.
- Use the appropriate command for the action you want your dog to take. For example, if you'd like him to remove himself from the sofa, using the word 'Down' might just encourage him to get more comfortable!
- Be authoritative or enthusiastic according to the situation, but try never to sound cross or angry.
- Don't forget to use your voice to give praise as well as commands!

MOTHER LOVE

Molly the Rottweiler decided to lend a helping paw when farmer Maria Foster brought two newly born lambs into the house to try and warm them up. Molly took over without any urging, sleeping with them at night and protecting them from the family cat. The sheepdog was allowed to take a peek – but only for a short while; when Molly decided it was time for some peace and quiet for her woolly charges, she firmly pushed him away.

WELL-COLLARED

Leather collars began to appear in Victorian times, but from the 17th to 19th centuries, adjustable brass collars were popular, fastened with a brass padlock and often bearing inscriptions. According to Jonathan Swift, Mrs Dingley's lap dog Tiger wore a collar with the words 'Pray steal me not: I'm Mrs. Dingley's, whose heart in this four footed thing lies'. Probably the most famous inscription is that on a collar presented to the Prince of Wales by Alexander Pope and bearing the legend: "I am his Highness' dog at Kew; Pray tell me, sir, whose dog are you?"

My name is Oprah Winfrey. I have a talk show. I'm single.
I have eight dogs – five Golden Retrievers, two black Labradors,
and a mongrel. I have four years of college.
Oprah Winfrey,
when asked to describe herself during jury selection

TRAINING TREATS

Around 90 per cent of dogs are motivated by food, which makes it a very effective reward to offer when training. Training treats should be divided into tiny pieces so the dog doesn't become full too rapidly (when he may then lose interest in earning any more), and preferably quick and easy to eat rather than needing a lot of chewing. Grade treats according to how much your dog likes them, keeping those which are tastiest for when he's done something really well, or those occasions when he needs a little extra motivation.

BABY LOVE

When a two week old baby girl was abandoned in woodland outside Nairobi in Kenya, no one noticed … except a stray mixed breed dog. She carefully picked up the baby, wrapped in a dirty cloth, and carried her across a busy road and through a barbed wire fence back to where her litter lay. Two days later, a group of children playing nearby heard a baby crying, and on investigating, found the baby nestled in amongst the puppies. Whilst the baby recovered in hospital, the dog was given the name Mkombozi (Saviour) and taken into the care of the Kenyan Society for the Protection of Animals.

Shania Twain: Tim, a German Shepherd; a special doggie door was fitted to the tour bus for him.

Sheryl Crow: Scout, a crossbreed

Billy Joel: Fionula the Boston Terrier and Sabrina, a Pug

Elton John: Arthur the Cocker Spaniel, who was best man at the civil partnership ceremony of Elton and David Furnish

Geri Haliwell: Harry the Shih Tzu, and Daddy the Pomeranian

Samantha Mumba: Foxy, a Pomeranian

Elvis Presley: Sweet Pea, a Pomeranian he acquired when his mother died was the first of many dogs he would own.

Mariah Carey: Jack the Jack Russell

Joss Stone: Dusty Springfield the Poodle

Barry Manilow: Bagel and Biscuit, both Beagles. Bagel appeared on the back cover of three albums, and one of Manilow's most loyal followings is the self-styled 'Beagle Bagels' fan club.

A JOY FOREVER

A well trained dog can be a joy to live with; but no matter how responsive or smart he is, he can't train himself – it requires effort, time and patience from you on a daily basis.

WHY DO DOGS EAT THEIR OWN POO?

Dogs are by nature scavengers, and eating their own faeces, or those of other animals may be a way of topping up on nutrients, particularly when they are from herbivores such as horses. It can also be due to health problems, boredom or hunger, and isn't generally a habit to be encouraged as it increases the risk of parasite infection. Another habit some dogs develop is called 'pica' which is the ingestion of unnatural, inedible objects such as stones, paper and soil, and can be potentially health threatening. Boredom, or an attempt to gain attention can be causes, but as with poo-eating it can also be due to a medical problem or related to diet, so it's a good idea to seek veterinary advice.

DOUBLE DUTCH

When three new, fully trained police dogs joined the Avon and Somerset police, the handlers found themselves with a little communication problem: the dogs came from Holland and didn't understand English. The difficulty was solved by giving the handlers a crash course in Dutch commands.

PRESIDENTIAL POOCHES 11

Lucky the Bouvier was exiled to the Reagan's California ranch after becoming too large for the White House. He departed amidst rumours that his boisterousness (he was once photographed towing the President across the lawn in front of a bemused Margaret Thatcher), combined with lack of housetraining contributed to his departure.

McCARTNEY'S MUSE

Paul McCartney of Beatles fame was inspired to pen the 1968 song 'Martha My Dear' by his Old English Sheepdog Martha. She is also said to have been the inspiration behind 'Fool on the Hill' following an early morning walk, and McCartney is also popularly supposed to have included a high pitched sound at the end of 'A Day in the Life' audible only to dogs. Martha died in 1981 at the age of 15 years, but one of her offspring is featured on the cover of McCartney's 1993 album 'Paul is Live'.

To the memory of my dear Emma – faithful and sole companion of my otherwise rootless and desolate life.
From a dog's gravestone

LUSCIOUS LIVER BREAD

Ingredients:

8oz liver

4 oz Self Raising flour

2 eggs

2 cloves of garlic

Method

Place the liver in a food processor or liquidizer and puree.

Add the remaining ingredients to the liver puree, mix well until smooth.

Pour into a greased Swiss roll tin.

Bake at 180 C, Gas Mark 4 for 30-40 minutes.

Allow to cool, then cut into tiny pieces for use as an irresistible training treat.

Store in the fridge and use within 3 days. The remainder can be kept in the freezer until required.

✧✦ DACHSHUND TRAINING? FORGET IT ✦✧

E B White, author of the classic children's stories *Charlotte's Web* and *Stuart Little,* once wrote that he'd rather train zebras to balance clubs on their noses than attempt to teach a dachshund anything.

✧✦ WACKY DOGGY GADGETS 7 ✦✧

Invented by Eduardo Segura and Andres Diaz, the 'Lavakan' is the world's first side-loading washing machine for dogs (and cats). A programme is selected, and the pet is then soaped, rinsed and dried in under thirty minutes. Both the 'Lavakan' and 'Neuticles' were recipients of 'Ig Nobel' prizes – a parody of the Nobel prizes and awarded for achievements that 'first make people laugh, and then think'.

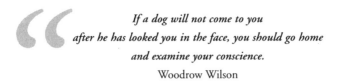

*If a dog will not come to you
after he has looked you in the face, you should go home
and examine your conscience.*
Woodrow Wilson

✧✦ HOW TO GET THE MOST OUT OF TRAINING CLUBS AND CLASSES ✦✧

- Turn up regularly for classes.
- Arrive in plenty of time before your class starts.
- Work on training exercises at home between classes.
- Write a diary so you can keep track of how you are doing.
- Pay attention to what's going on rather than gossiping with others.
- Choose a club which caters for different levels and encourages you to progress further.
- Watch other classes if you have time before or after your own.
- Find a club which offers classes in other activities if you're interested in trying something new such as agility, heelwork to music, or tracking.
- Ask if any certification schemes are run, such as the Good Citizen Dog Award, so you have goals to work towards.
- Enquire about, and join in other activities which may be on offer, such as club outings, barbeques and fundraising events – socialising isn't just something for your dog!

LAZIEST DOG?

Yorkshire Terrier Spike earned himself the title of world's laziest dog when his owner, comedienne Joan Rivers hired a man to carry him around in a Louis Vuitton carrying case.

WHY DO DOGS WAG THEIR TAILS? 3

After studying tail wags from a variety of dogs, Italian researchers found that in situations where dogs were confronted by something which made them feel anxious, the wag was to the left. When shown something familiar the trend was for the tail to wag to the right instead; when shown humans the wagging to the right increased still more if it was the owner instead of a stranger. In humans, strong activity in the left side of the brain (which controls the right side of the body) is usually linked to a happy, amiable disposition, and is also associated with approach behaviour, and right-brain activity is associated with retreat; and it would appear that dogs are no different.

AUSSIE SNIFFERS

Quarantine Beagles are a familiar sight at airports in Australia, where in any one month a team will intercept around 33 kg of fresh fruit and 9 kg of meat, as well as plant material, eggs, live plants and plant cuttings - even though items may have been packaged in sealed containers or concealed under several layers of clothing. During each 4 – 6 hour shift, each team seizes between five and ten items – around seven seizures per thousand passengers, with four out of every five items seized being undeclared.

EVERYTHING I REALLY NEED TO KNOW I LEARNED FROM MY DOG

- Never pass up the opportunity to go on an outing
- When loved ones come home, always run to greet them
- Take naps and stretch before rising
- Run, romp, and play daily
- Be loyal
- Never pretend to be something you're not
- Eat with gusto and enthusiasm
- Avoid biting when a simple growl will do
- Thrive on affection and let people touch you – enjoy back rubs and pats
- No matter how often you're scolded, don't pout but run right back and make friends
- When someone is having a bad day, be silent, sit close by and nuzzle them gently
- On cold nights, curl up in front of a crackling fire
- When you're excited, speak up
- When you're happy, dance around and wag your entire body
- Delight in the simple joy of a long walk

ASSISTANCE DOGS

Guide dogs may have been the first, but since then, their role as canine helpers has expanded to include Hearing Dogs who are able to alert deaf owners to noises they would otherwise be unaware of, seizure alert dogs for sufferers from epilepsy, and assistance dogs who possess a wide and remarkable range of skills. Each of them are canine heroes in their own rights, devoted to their duties and enabling their owners to achieve a greater degree of independence and quality of life than would otherwise be possible.

❖❖ CAREER CHANGES ❖❖

- Former Olympic diver Greg Longanis now trains dogs and works with the AKC to promote responsible dog ownership. He owns four dogs, including a Bouvier called Speedo.
- After leaving the Irish band Boomtown Rats, which he had been a driving force in forming, bassist Gerry Cott also became a successful dog trainer; his own pet Westie 'Bobby' is one of the four dogs to play the role of Greyfriars Bobby in the 2005 film of the same name.

Calling a tail a leg doesn't make it a le.
Abraham Lincoln – supposedly inspired by his dog Fido

❖❖ CHIPS WITH EVERYTHING ❖❖

The first US war dog to be sent overseas during World War II was a German Shepherd cross called Chips, who also went on to become the most decorated. After landing in Sicily in 1943, he found himself and his handler pinned down on one occasion by enemy gunfire. Pulling himself free, he jumped into the pillbox where the machine gun was situated and attacked the four hapless Italians he found there, who were forced to abandon their position and surrender. Later on that day he helped to take ten more Italians prisoner. For his actions during the war, he was awarded the Silver Star and Purple Heart, but these were later revoked as being inappropriate and 'contrary to Army policy'; for some reason the powers that be felt that awarding them to a dog devalued them in some way. His unit didn't care, and unofficially awarded him with a Theater Ribbon with an Arrowhead, plus a Battle Star for each of his eight campaigns. He was discharged in 1945 and returned to the family who had originally donated him, but died 6 months later, due to his war injuries. He was only 6 years old.

❖❖ YUM YUM ❖❖

Dogs tend to use their lips, tongues and teeth in much the same way that we use our hands, to investigate and learn more about objects they encounter; it's therefore very important to be careful not to leave things lying around which could be dangerous to them if chewed or accidentally swallowed.

✿ HONEY TO THE RESCUE 1 ✿

When an 11-year-old Abraham Lincoln discovered an injured brown and white dog, he named her Honey and nursed her back to health, and they soon developed a close bond. Some time later, the future president fell into a deep underground hole whilst exploring a cave system, from which he was unable to climb out; a passing farmer was alerted to his plight by the dog's frantic barking and able to effect a rescue.

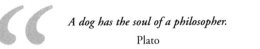

A dog has the soul of a philosopher.
Plato

✿ CANINE HONOURS ✿

The highest award for canine bravery in military conflicts is the Dickin Medal, instituted in 1943 by Maria Dickin, founder of the PDSA. It acknowledges outstanding acts of heroism and courage displayed by animals serving with the Armed forces or Civil Defence units worldwide, and is recognised as the Animals' Victoria Cross.

The medal has been awarded 62 times, the first 54 occasions being between 1943 and 1949, with 14 of the recipients being dogs. In October 2000, a Canadian dog named Gander was posthumously added to the roll of honour, following which five other dogs also received the award; three for life saving action and devotion to duty after the terrorist attacks in New York and Washington, and two related to military conflicts in Kosovo and Iraq. The two most recent awards were to Sadie, an arms and explosives dog for her gallantry in Afghanistan, and posthumously to Lucky, a RAF police tracker dog on behalf of himself and three other dogs, Bobbie, Jasper and Lassie, who worked in Malaysia between 1949 and 1952.

The first Dickin medal was awarded to Rob, a black and white collie, War Dog No. 471/322, for making over 20 parachute jumps into North Africa and Italy during World War II – although there is some doubt as to whether his celebrated exploits ever really happened. It's suspected that they may have been fabricated by a quartermaster who had become fond of the dog, as a way of keeping him by his side after he had received a letter from the family who had donated him when they wrote enquiring if they might have him back if he was of no further use. Whether it was a hoax or not, no-one will probably ever know for sure; but what is true is that Rob was trained as a parachute dog, and that many other dogs whose names are long forgotten, did make numerous jumps.

HONEY TO THE RESCUE 2

When Michael Bosch set out for a drive with Honey the Cocker Spaniel one sunny morning, he could hardly have imagined that the next few hours would be so dramatic, or that he would owe his life to his passenger. A stray beam of sunlight momentarily blinded him, he misjudged his steering and ended up crashing down into a ravine, rolling the car five times before it dropped fifty feet to land upside down. Still recovering from a heart attack he'd had two months previously, Bosch dangled upside down for the next eight hours, trapped by a tree that had penetrated through the car roof and crushing his legs.

In such an isolated area, there was little chance of rescue unless the alarm could somehow be raised – Honey was his only chance of surviving. Realising he had no other choice, he managed to clear a hole in the smashed windscreen through which she squeezed, and then urged her to go and get some help. Honey made her way through dense thickets of brambles and forest for over half a mile, finally ending up at the door of Robin Allen, where in true Lassie style she whimpered and pawed at him and managed to make it very clear that she was to be followed.

By the time they reached the car Bosch was in a serious state and had help not arrived when it did, would almost certainly have died. One of the most remarkable aspects of the story is that Honey was only five months old at the time, still very much a puppy – and had been rescued herself, from an animal shelter, just two weeks before the accident. Recognition of her deed came when she was awarded the USA's 2006 title of 'Rescue Dog of the Year'.

✿ SAVING THE DAY ✿

After a disabled woman's cat knocked over a candle, setting fire to the house, her specially trained assistance dog didn't panic, but calmly took charge. She fetched her owner's artificial limb, brought her a phone she used to ring emergency services, and then helped her outside. Once safe, the dog then returned to try and save the cat – sadly she didn't succeed and both perished.

✿ ALPINE HERO 1 ✿

The St Bernard has for a long time been associated with the hospice and way station at the isolated mountain pass of the same name in the Alps, founded and named after St Bernard of Menthon in 1049. The first reports of the dogs being used to help rescue stranded travellers or avalanche victims date back to 1750, since when they are estimated to have saved over 2000 lives. Of all these dogs, Barry is perhaps the best known, reckoned to have saved 40 lives; legend has it that the 41st person he tried to rescue was a soldier who mistakenly thought he was about to be attacked and killed him with his bayonet. Happily this is untrue – in 1812 Barry was taken to Berne by a monk, and died there at the age of 14 after a happy retirement.

> *All trees have bark*
> *All dogs bark*
> *Therefore, all dogs are trees.*
> *The fallacy of barking up the wrong tree.*
> Anon

✿ YOUR COUNTRY NEEDS YOUR DOG ✿

When the US Army War Dog Program was expanded in 1942, James Austin proposed setting up a War Dog Fund to help raise money for the Dogs for Defense organization which had been asked to assist in finding around 40,000 dogs. He initially sent letters to over a hundred dog fanciers asking if they would like to 'enlist' their dogs and offering a variety of ranks according to size of donation – one dollar for a private and one hundred dollars to be made up to an admiral or general. In this way, 112 dogs were signed up, 54 of them as generals, whilst Austin's own dog Saddler became a general and the chief canine recruiter. The War Dog Fund offered a certificate confirming rank, plus a window sticker and collar tag to all those who enlisted; President Franklin D. Roosevelt's dog Fala was one of the first to sign up as an honorary private, after which owners all over the country enthusiastically followed suit. Within 14 months another 25,000 dogs had been enlisted, raising $75,000.

❈❉ THE LONG AND THE SHORT OF IT ❈❉

Extending or retractable leads were invented by Manfred Bogdahn in Germany around 30 years ago. They have a spring action which controls the length of the lead; as your dog walks away from you it becomes longer, and as he returns it retracts back into the casing. A braking system allows you to prevent your dog from going further or to lock the lead at your preferred length. They can be useful when teaching recalls and retrieve exercises, or for permitting your dog more freedom of movement than is possible with a conventional fixed leash on those occasions when he cannot be allowed to roam loose.

RACE AGAINST TIME

In 1925 the serum run to Nome, or the 'Great Race of Mercy' as it is often called was an act of tremendous courage and bravery on the part of both the humans and dogs who took part. The services of 20 mushers and around 150 sled dogs were called upon when the isolated town of Nome in Alaska was under threat from a diphtheria outbreak. Icebound, with no planes able to fly in the severe cold, and with the nearest railway station over 650 miles away, things looked grim unless the relay of dogs could succeed in collecting the serum from Nenana. Without it, the mortality rate in Nome and the surrounding population was expected to be 100 per cent.

The first musher, 'Wild Bill' Shannon left Nenana in temperatures of –45C, developing hypothermia along the way, and on arrival at Tolovana 52 miles later, parts of his face were black with frostbite, and three or possibly four of his dogs died from the effects of frostbite. By the time the second musher in the relay, Edgar Kallands took over, things hadn't improved greatly and when he reached Hot Springs, hot water had to be poured over his hands to free them from the sleds handle bars. And so the desperate race continued, a battle against the elements as well as time: when Charlie Evans' two lead dogs collapsed with frostbite he harnessed himself up in their place: Gonangen travelled through a whiteout: Ivanoffs team had barely even started when it collided with a reindeer: Olsen was blown off the trail by the wind and suffered severe frostbite to his hands while putting blankets on his dogs.

Seppala and his lead dog Togo had the longest and most treacherous stretch of the journey – 91 miles, nearly double that of all the other teams – yet succeeded despite travelling directly into storm conditions with a wind chill factor of –65C caused by gale force winds. Last in the relay, Kaasen also had his problems; visibility was so poor that at times he couldn't see the dogs harnessed closest to the sled, but his lead dog Balto kept them safely on course. One heart stopping moment occurred when strong winds flipped the sled over and the cylinder containing the precious serum fell off; Kaasen acquired frostbite digging in the snow with bare hands to feel for it.

The serum finally reached Front Street in Nome at 5.30 am, with not a single ampoule broken after covering a total of 674 miles, travelling day and night in extreme subzero temperatures and near blizzard conditions. It took an incredible one hundred and twenty seven and a half hours, considered a record at the time, and when a re-enactment of the run was held in 1975, it took six days longer.

Following the mercy dash, Kaasen and Balto became celebrities and spent a year touring, and even starring in a film. Subsequently however, Kaasen sold the team to a travelling sideshow where they lived in appalling conditions for the next two years until spotted by George Kimble, who organised a fundraising campaign to free them. Having raised the $2000 necessary to buy the team, they received a heroes welcome when they arrived at their new home at Cleveland Zoo. Balto died in 1933, when he was put to sleep due to old age. Seppala took his own dogs on tour, and Togo received a gold medal from Roald Amundsen; his owner often maintained that many of his exploits were frequently incorrectly attributed to Balto, and was heartbroken that Togo never received the amount of credit that he felt he deserved.

Winston's feelings for animals was passionate. I have watched him mobilize tired notables at a house party to seek a lost poodle in twilight, and he once held up a meeting of urgency to wait for a vet's visit.

Lady Diana Cooper, speaking about Winston Churchill

ALPINE HERO 2

In 2004 the future of the St. Bernards looked to be uncertain when the monks announced that they could no longer cope with the drain on resources, but 33 local villages rallied round and contributed towards the cost of setting up a foundation. One of the kennel dogs is always called Barry in honour of his heroic ancestor, and as well as continuing this tradition, the foundation bears his name too.

DOG PROPERTY LAWS

- If I like it, it's mine.
- If it's in my mouth, it's mine.
- If I can take it from you, it's mine.
- If I had it a little while ago, it's mine.
- If I'm chewing something up, the pieces are all mine.
- If I saw it first, it's mine.
- If you are playing with something and put it down, it automatically becomes mine.
- If it's broken, it's yours.

(Author unknown)

❧ HOW TO GREET A STRANGE DOG ☙

- Ask the owner or handler before you touch.
- Approach from the side; this is less threatening than moving towards him head-on.
- Turn your head slightly and avoid making direct eye contact, which may make him feel intimidated or threatened. Use peripheral vision to watch him.
- Speak to the dog, using a normal, friendly, conversational tone, not a high-pitched, squeaky, excitable voice.
- Allow the dog to approach and check you out by having a sniff.
- Offer a hand for him to sniff at, with fingers curled in a loosely clenched fist.
- Making your movements slow and quiet, gently stroke under the throat and the front of the chest, using the back of your hand. Stroke, rather than pat.
- Don't force your attentions on a dog if the owner tells you it isn't friendly, if it appears to be ignoring you or if it tries to move away.

If you get to thinking that you are a person of some influence, try ordering someone else's dog around.
Will Rogers

❧ WOOF, WOOF ☙

Dogs can produce a variety of noises including whining, grunting, yipping, howling, yelping, growling and moaning. They have a fairly limited vocal 'vocabulary' compared to humans, able to communicate an estimated 39 different meanings by varying and modulating each sound.

Some breeds tend to be noisier than others; excessive barking is more likely to occur in smaller dogs such as Terriers and Toys, whilst beagles and some herding breeds also tend to bark more. One breed doesn't bark at all though – the Basenji makes a chortling or yodelling noise instead.

- When listening to recordings, even non-dog owners are able to fairly accurately match different types of bark to a list of various causes.
- Actively encouraging – or simply allowing – your puppy to bark increases the likelihood that he'll grow up to be a noisy adult too.
- Barking can sometimes be a sign of senility in older dogs.

10 WAYS TO PROTECT YOUR DOG FROM THEFT

- have him microchipped, and put up notices at your home to this effect to act as a deterrent.
- install security lighting and alarms around your property if you don't already have any.
- make sure all access gates and fencing is secure.
- never leave him unattended in the car, or tied up outside a shop.
- vary the times and routes when you take your dog out for exercise.
- teach him to respond really well to a recall signal so he'll come back to you promptly when out on a walk
- keep him within sight at all times when he's running loose outdoors
- treat with suspicion any strangers who approach you to chat about your dog.
- don't allow young children to walk the dog unaccompanied by an adult.
- keep your hand through the loop of your dog's lead so he can't be snatched from you.

ALPINE HERO 3

The last St. Bernard was used around 1975; they have largely been replaced since then by Golden Retrievers and German Shepherds to run over the avalanche debris and search for victims.

DOGS TRUST

In 1891, whilst visitors and exhibitors were enjoying the first ever Crufts Dog Show, a meeting chaired by Lady Gertrude Stock was being held in an adjoining room and which was to result in the National Canine Defence League being formed. Its first campaigns were against vivisection, unnecessary muzzling and chaining for excessive lengths of time, and cruel treatment of dogs by railway companies, as well as providing care for stray dogs. By 1902 membership totalled 1000, and today the charity – now known as Dogs Trust – has over 300,000 members and supporters and is the largest dog welfare charity in the UK. Claiming never to put a healthy dog down, Dogs Trust tries to rehome most of the dogs it cares for, with a sponsorship scheme to help support those who for some reason cannot be adopted.

One of the charity's primary aims is to solve the problem of why there are so many unwanted dogs in the UK, and seeks to address this through providing advice, raising awareness, promoting responsible ownership and implementing practical measures – for example, over £3million has been invested in a neutering and microchipping scheme.

✵✵ FAMOUS OWNERS OF RESCUE DOGS 5 ✵✵

Anthony Head: passionate about rescue dogs, Tony is an active supporter of Dogs Trust, the Blue Cross, Mayhew Animal Home and Battersea Dogs and Cats Home. He lives with Sarah Fisher, a TTouch instructor and three dogs, two of whom are from Battersea, London. When Archie, a lurcher, was found as a stray at 6 months old in a pitiful state, he was noise sensitive to the point of phobia and had a long list of behavioural problems; thanks to TTouch and the efforts of Tony and his partner, these issues are now a thing of the past and he has matured into a dog with a hugely entertaining character. Ginny is Tony's other rescue dog, an elderly mixed breed found as a stray, again in an appalling state. Tony reckons that "there is nothing better than coming home at the end of a long, tiring day and being greeted by happy dogs; watching them playing in the sun or sleeping by the Aga in the evening brings a sense of peace and fulfilment that can never be matched."

✵✵ DOGS TRUST FACTS ✵✵

- Over 187,500 dogs have been neutered and 206,814 microchipped through Dogs Trust.
- The charity has 17 rehoming centres all around the country.
- Over 13,500 dogs are cared for each year.

❧ PRESIDENTIAL POOCHES 12 ❧

Abraham Lincoln's pet, Fido was the first Presidential dog to be photographed.

❧ TAIL SHAPES AND DESCRIPTIONS ❧

Tails come in all sorts of shapes and lengths, and are carried in a variety of ways including

CORKSCREW TAIL:

short and twisted eg Pug

DOCKED TAIL:

shortened by surgery or other means, usually around 2-3 days after birth. The practice is banned in many countries including the UK.

GAY TAIL:

carried higher than the ideal carriage stated in the Breed Standard.

ODD TAIL:

uncommon - twisted, but not short eg Tibetan Terrier

OTTER TAIL:

very thick at the base, with a rounded appearance and gradually tapering towards a rounded tip eg Labrador Retriever

SABRE TAIL:

gently curving like a sabre eg Basset

SCIMITAR TAIL:

similar to a sabre tail, but more pronounced eg Gordon Setter

STERN:

the name given to the tail of a sporting dog or hound

WHIP TAIL:

a relatively long, thin, pointed tail carried stiffly out in line with the back eg Greyhound

❧ PAINT JOB ❧

The Old English Sheepdog has become so inextricably linked with the name of a brand of paint after being used in advertising campaigns, that it is often referred to as a 'Dulux dog'. The original Dulux dog was 'Shepton Dash' who held the post for eight years, followed by 'Fernville Lord Digby' who acquired fame for both himself and his owner. When filming, Digby was treated like a star, travelling in style in a chauffeur driven car; Barbara Woodhouse was employed as his trainer, and he had three stunt 'body doubles'.

> *To his dog, every man is Napoleon: hence the constant*
> *popularity of dogs.*
> Aldous Huxley

✧ IT'S IN HIS KISS ✧

When asked about the best kiss he'd ever had, singer Justin Timberlake replied that it had been from his Boxer dog Buckley, commenting that "When he kisses you it's like a shower over your face"

✧ A MAN'S BEST FRIEND 1 ✧

George Graham Vest served as a US Senator from 1879 to 1903, becoming a noted and eloquent orator of his time. Earlier in his career, while practicing as a lawyer he was asked to represent Charles Burden, whose favourite hunting dog 'Old Drum' had been killed by a neighbour. The dog had been accidentally shot by the neighbour, Leonidas Hornsby, while attempting to scare him off after he was discovered stealing milk and other dairy products. Rather than admitting what had happened, the Hornsby family hid the body; when it was later discovered by the Burdens the matter developed into a bitter feud, and legal action was taken, with both families determined to win the case. During the trial, Vest announced that he would 'win the case or apologize to every dog in Missouri'; in his closing speech he made no reference to any of the testimony which had been offered but instead offered a eulogy that apparently swung the matter in Burden's favour, and which has since become famous as a tribute to the dog as man's best friend. A statue of Old Drum now stands in front of the courthouse at Warrensburg, Missouri, and a TV movie ('The Trial of Old Drum') loosely based on the trial was made in 2002.

✧ CHAT SHOW GUEST ✧

A regular guest on Paul O'Grady's teatime chat show is his own dog, Buster, a nine-year-old grey Shih Tzu/Bichon Frise cross. Paul adopted him as a four week old puppy after he had been dumped on a motorway, nursing him constantly until he was fully recovered. Buster's full name is Buster Elvis Savage, and he has applied to register his name as a trademark; and when his owner was given an honorary fellowship to Liverpool University, Buster also received a matching gown.

THE PRICE OF FAME

After socialite Paris Hilton appeared on the front cover of the US edition of Seventeen magazine with her pet Chihuahua Tinkerbelle, demand for the breed suddenly increased. Dogs previously available for hundreds of dollars began fetching thousands instead, and for the first time ever the breed made it into the top ten list of registered dogs in America.

QUESTION
What do you get if you cross a dog with a frog?
ANSWER
A dog that can lick you from the other side of the road!

COMMON DOGGY SAYINGS

Give a dog a bad name
One barking dog sets the street barking
It's a dog eat dog world
Sly dog
Hang-dog
Top dog
Tail wagging the dog
Lucky dog
As happy as a dog with two tails
As sick as a dog
As crooked as a dog's hind leg
As fit as a butcher's dog
Not fit for a dog
Barking mad
One man and his dog

FEISTY

The word 'feisty' comes from the Middle English 'fist' or 'fisting dog', a derogatory term for a small lapdog.

STILL ROLLING ON

Another enduring advertising image is that of the Andrex puppies who for the last 35 years have been amusing and entertaining viewers of the TV adverts for toilet tissue. The yellow Labrador pups have appeared in over 120 commercials since their first appearance in 1972 where a mischievous pup leaves a trail of unravelled toilet roll all over a family house. As well as helping to sell the product, they have also sold themselves; it's estimated that one in ten homes now owns merchandising spin-off in the shape of an Andrex puppy soft toy. In 2004, a figure of an Andrex puppy was inducted into Madame Tussauds, the famous London waxwork display, joining a line-up including such celebrities as Kylie Minogue, Madonna, George Clooney and Brad Pitt.

 Beware of a silent dog and still water.
Latin proverb

MAN'S BEST FRIEND 2

"Gentleman of the Jury: The best friend a man has in the world may turn against him and become his enemy. His son or daughter that he has reared with loving care may prove ungrateful. Those who are nearest and dearest to us, those whom we trust with our happiness and our good name may become traitors to their faith. The money that a man has, he may lose. It flies away from him, perhaps when he needs it most. A man's reputation may be sacrificed in a moment of ill-considered action. The people who are prone to fall on their knees to do us honor when success is with us, may be the first to throw the stone of malice when failure settles its cloud upon our heads.

"The one absolutely unselfish friend that man can have in this selfish world, the one that never deserts him, the one that never proves ungrateful or treacherous is his dog. A man's dog stands by him in prosperity and in poverty, in health and in sickness. He will sleep on the cold ground, where the wintry winds blow and the snow drives fiercely, if only he may be near his master's side. He will kiss the hand that has no food to offer. He will lick the wounds and sores that come in encounters with the roughness of the world. He guards the sleep of his pauper master as if he were a prince. When all other friends desert, he remains. When riches take wings, and reputation falls to pieces, he is as constant in his love as the sun in its journey through the heavens.

"If fortune drives the master forth, an outcast in the world, friendless and homeless, the

faithful dog asks no higher privilege than that of accompanying him, to guard him against danger, to fight against his enemies. And when the last scene of all comes, and death takes his master in its embrace and his body is laid away in the cold ground, no matter if all other friends pursue their way, there by the graveside will the noble dog be found, his head between his paws, his eyes sad, but open in alert watchfulness, faithful and true even in death."

(George Graham Vest's summing up in the Trial of Old Drum)

ENGLAND'S FINEST HOUR

When the Jules Rimet World Cup trophy was stolen from under the noses of guards whilst on display prior to England hosting the tournament in 1966, there were red faces all round. More than that, panic began to set in as it began to look as though it had gone for good; but whilst the police were trying without success to recover it, a black and white canine sleuth was on the job. Out for a walk in the London suburb of Norwood, he spied a parcel under a bush in a front garden and dragged his owner over to it. Unwrapping it to see what was intriguing his dog so much, David Corbett removed a last layer of newspaper to reveal the missing trophy in all its glory.

Pickles instantly became a celebrity, making the front pages of newspapers, starring with June Whitfield and Eric Sykes in the film 'The Spy with the Cold Nose', appearing on TV programme Blue Peter, and sharing the same agent as Spike Milligan.

Bizarrely, when the gold medals belonging to Olympic rower James Cracknell were stolen in 2006, they were also discovered and returned courtesy of a dog which sniffed them out, lying under a bush in a garden.

OLD SHEP

When a shepherd fell ill during the summer of 1936, he was accompanied by his dog Shep when he went to Fort Benson for treatment. A few days later he died, and when arrangements were made for his body to be returned to his relatives, Shep anxiously followed the box containing his owner's body to the train depot. He watched as it was put on board a train, and then settled down to wait ...... and wait ...... and wait. The name of the shepherd is now long forgotten, but not that of the devoted Shep as he waited at the station for the next five and a half years, greeting each train as it arrived and looking hopefully for his returned master. By the time he had maintained his vigil for two years, Shep had not only become a familiar sight, but famous too; fan mail poured in, children sent gifts and travellers would even make detours from the main line in order to see for themselves this faithful dog.

Tragedy struck a few years later, in 1942; old and deaf now, Shep failed to see or hear the 10.17 train arriving, and he slipped on an icy rail trying, too late, to get out of the way. His obituary was published across America, and the funeral held for him a few days later was attended by hundreds; appropriately enough he was buried on a hill overlooking the train depot. An obelisk to his memory was built, which was refurbished in 1988, and in 1994 a bronze statue was erected in the town.

❀ "EXCUSE ME..." ❀

"I just need to go and see a man about a dog" is a frequently used excuse by men to absent themselves; the phrase was in vogue in the US in the mid- 1800's, although no-one is quite sure how it came into being. Its first appearance in print was in a play called 'The Flying Scud, or a Four Legged Fortune' by Dion Boucicault when a character exclaims 'Excuse me, Mr Quail, I can't stop; I've got to see a man about a dog'

❀ URBAN MYTH 8 – MILLIONAIRE DOG ❀

Gunther the multi-millionaire German Shepherd made newspaper headlines around the world when it was made known that with funds of around $150 million at his disposal he was the world's richest dog. After he was bequeathed the estate of German Countess Karlotta Liebenstein, five staff were especially employed to attend to his every whim and he allegedly dined in style on steak and caviar every night. Gunther's story came to the attention of the press in 1999 when his offshore holding company attempted to buy Sylvester Stallone's house; failing to do so he settled for Madonna's $7.5 million villa in Florida. After being taken seriously by the media around the world, the hoax was revealed when an attorney for the Gunther Corp admitted to the Italian press that Gunther wasn't rich, and that Countess Karlotta Liebenstein had never even existed.

❀ FOOD FACTS 3 ❀

The first canned dog food appeared in the 1920's, made by Chappel brothers and using horsemeat.

✺✺ DOG IN THE MANGER ✺✺

This phrase dates all the way back to around 600 BC, being derived from one of Aesop's fables. In the tale, a dog was taking a nap in a manger; when an ox came along and tried to eat some of the hay the dog was lying on, the dog barked and snapped furiously. Prevented from being able to eat any of his food – which was useless to the dog – the ox left, grumbling 'People often grudge others what they cannot enjoy themselves'

✺✺ SEA DOGS ✺✺

Dogsbody – meaning a lowly, menial person – originates from the British Royal Navy of Nelson's era. The sailors lived on a diet consisting of such culinary delights as boiled salt beef and weevil infested ships biscuit; another staple foodstuff was dried peas boiled in a bag. Officially called pease pudding, the sailors referred to it instead as 'dogs body'; eventually it became a phrase applied to lowly members of the crew and finally the term jumped ship in the 1930s to become a part of the civilian vocabulary.

> *Every dog is allowed one bite, but a different view is*
> *taken of a dog that goes on biting all the time. He may*
> *not get his licence returned when it falls due.*
> Harold Wilson

✺✺ IT GREW IN THE TELLING ✺✺

A 'shaggy dog story' is a long-winded tall story which generally has an absurd or anti-climactic ending that confounds the expectations of the listener. The original shaggy dog story was told sometime around the 1930's but varies according to different sources; in one version someone advertises a competition to find the shaggiest ever dog. After much searching, when the winner is finally presented to him, he comments 'I don't think he's so shaggy.' The alternative version tells of a London family who lose their shaggy dog, and place an advertisement in the paper. An American businessman spots the advert; feeling sorry for the family he hunts for another dog which matches the description given, and after a long search discovers one which he personally brings across the Atlantic. When he arrives at the house he is received by the butler who takes one look at the dog and shuts the door in his face saying 'But not that shaggy, sir!'

❧❧ HUSH PUPPIES ❧❧

Hush puppies are little balls of deep-fried seasoned dough, usually made with cornmeal and sometimes served as a side dish in Southern USA. Legend has it that during the American Civil War, Confederate soldiers kept their dogs quiet while they were cooking by feeding them these little snacks – and hence, "Hush, puppy". More likely, they came about during the day long fishing and hunting expeditions which were popular amongst Southern gentleman, and which generally ended with a barbeque; left-over cornmeal from dredging the fish before cooking were fried up and tossed to where the hungry hunting dogs had been tied up, instantly quieting their barking.

If your dog doesn't like someone,
you probably shouldn't either.
Anonymous

❧❧ QUIET PLEASE ❧❧

The proverb 'Let sleeping dogs lie' meaning that some things are best left alone, stems back to Geoffrey Chaucer's 'Troilus and Criseyde' in 1380 where it appears as 'It is nought good a slepyng hound to wake'.

'You don't keep a dog and bark yourself' is another proverb which has roots lying far in the past; in 1583, in Brian Melbancke's 'Philotemus: the warre betwixt nature and fortune' the original version read 'It is small reason you should kepe a dog, and barke your selfe'

❧❧ MORE HUSH PUPPIES ❧❧

'Hush Puppies' is also the name of the range of casual shoes created in 1958, and which has a Basset Hound as a mascot. After an employee was served the fried corn balls known as hush puppies by a friend, and remembering that the common idiom for sore feet was 'barking dogs' the canine connection was complete and a brand name was born.

❧❧ FRIEND TO THE END 11 ❧❧

When Gianfranco Brillantini developed a severe asthmatic condition, his 15 -year-old mixed breed dog Juna was also taken ill with the same problem; while the 67-year-old

owner was rushed to hospital by paramedics, his pet was taken off in the opposite direction, to the vets. She managed to escape and raced to Brillantini's side at the hospital, but staff dragged her away, and desolate, she remained outside his window howling. Her owner died three days later, and the lifeless body of the faithful Juna was found soon afterwards.

CANINE WISDOM FROM AROUND THE WORLD

A dog knows the places he is thrown food (Africa)

If a sane dog fights a mad dog, it is the sane dog's ear that is bitten off (Burma)

From the lowly perspective of a dog's eye, everyone looks short (China)

The barking of a dog does not disturb a man on a camel (Egypt)

It is home to a dog after he has been there for three nights (Finland)

A dog in the kitchen asks for no company (France)

The fatter the flea, the leaner the dog (Germany)

A dog with two homes is never any good (Ireland)

There is no dog so bad that he won't wag his tail (Italy)

If a man be great even his dog will wear a proud look (Japan)

A house without a dog is the house of a scoundrel (Portugal)

If you are a host to your guest, be a host to his dog also (Russia)

If skill could be gained by watching, every dog would be a butcher (Turkey)

10 WAYS TO KEEP YOUR DOG SLIM

- Don't feed left over scraps from meals.
- Manufacturers recommendations are only guidelines – adjust them as necessary to suit each individual dog. Neutering can cause a reduced metabolic rate and therefore a decreased food requirement
- Weigh out dry feeds or use a measure, as it's easy to overfeed them if judging by eye alone.
- Don't share your own snacks which are high in fats and sugars.
- Insist he stays out of the kitchen so you aren't tempted to toss him the odd morsel when preparing food.
- If using food treats during training sessions, reduce the food ration accordingly.
- Use low-calorie food treats such as carrot sticks and ice cubes on other occasions.
- Check he eats only his own food ration and doesn't help himself to that of other pets.
- Ensure he gets enough exercise.
- Switch to a life stage or diet food if age or ill health prevent your dog from taking much exercise.

NAME CHANGES

The National Canine Defence League (NCDL) changed its name to Dogs Trust in 2003, a name with a more modern and friendly feel.

Cruft's: Cruft's lost its apostrophe in 1974, to become Crufts.

German Shepherd: Worried about anti-German feeling following the First World War, the German Shepherd was renamed the Alsatian in 1919; the original name wasn't reverted to until 1977.

Dachshund: During both World wars, many Americans referred to their Dachshunds as 'liberty pups' for similar reasons as with the German Shepherd.

CAVE CANEM

On a fence: *Salesmen welcome. Dog food is expensive.*

In a vet's waiting room: *Back in five minutes. Sit! Stay!*

DOGGY INSULTS

DOG:

unattractive or dull girl or woman

DOG'S DINNER:

something messy or bungled

DOG'S LIFE:

a wretched, miserable existence

GOT UP LIKE A DOG'S DINNER:

dressed ostentatiously

GOT THE DOG ON:

behaving sulkily

DOG-EARED:

shabby or worn

DOGGEREL:

nonsense

DOGGONE:

exclamation of annoyance

IN THE DOGHOUSE:

out of favour

DOG LATIN:

incorrect Latin

GOING TO THE DOGS:

going to ruin

DOGSBODY:

a drudge

DOG TIRED:

exhausted

HOUND:

chase relentlessly

DOGGY BAG:

a bag into which the leftovers of a meal are put, ostensibly to be given to the diners' dog

UNDERDOG:

person in an inferior position

> *I know not why God gave the dog this spark of humanity*
> *that has made him kin to man. I only know this – that*
> *when we shall have learned from the dog the beauty of*
> *his virtues of honesty, fidelity and courage, the world will*
> *be a better place for it.*
> Walter A Dyer

❖ DOGGY PLACES 1 ❖

The Isle of Dogs is a peninsula located in the East End of London, and surrounded on three sides by the River Thames. The name is thought to either be a corruption of 'Isle of Ducks' as it used to be an area plentiful in wildfowl, or to have arisen because greyhounds belonging to Edward III were kept there; Henry VIII is also thought to have kept hunting dogs there.

❖ FIRST AMONG EQUALS ❖

The RSPCA Dog of the Year competition is the UK's largest national competition exclusively for rescue dogs – and one at which crossbreeds and pedigrees of all ages, shapes and sizes can compete together on equal terms.

✦ CANINE CRIME FIGHTERS ✦

Members of the London Watch sometimes took along a dog during the course of their duties, but more for company than any crime fighting skills. In the 1890's a Fox terrier called Topper was kept at Hyde Park Police station, but as far as the public were concerned, he was a favourite to be fondled rather than feared. Although the French and the Germans conducted a few experiments, it wasn't until 1899 that the idea of using dogs for police work was seriously pursued, with the establishment of a training school at Ghent in Belgium.

The programme attracted attention from other police forces, and by 1910 there were 600 towns in Germany using police dogs, with France, Hungary, Austria and Italy following suit soon after. The New York City programme was developed in 1907, and in 1908 the first British police force to employ dog and handler teams was the Hull and Barnsley Railway Police, using Airedale Terriers. From such small beginnings, the use of dogs in law enforcement became more widespread and commonplace and nowadays they are used for patrol work, in apprehension of criminals, tracking, and in the detection of drugs and arms.

QUESTION
When does a dog go "moo"?
ANSWER
When it is learning a new language!

✦ BLUE PETER 7 ✦

Other Blue Peter hounds include presenter Matt Baker's dog 'Meg', who first appeared in 2000, and left with him in 2006, and a series of guide dogs which have been puppy walked by various presenters on the programme since 1965. Honey was the first, followed by Cindy in 1968, Prince in 1981, Honey (so named in honour of the first one) in 1991 and Magic in 2006. When viewers were asked to save milk bottle tops and other pieces of aluminium foil which could be sold to sponsor a guide dog in 1964, they succeeded in collecting seven and a half tons – enough to pay for two dogs. This appeal was followed more recently with 'Bark in the Park' fundraising events during the Guide Dogs for the Blind Association's 75th anniversary year in 2006.

❁❁ BLACKBALLED ❁❁

When it comes to rehoming, black dogs are frequently passed over for adoption in favour of those with lighter coloured coats. No-one entirely knows why …… possibly because people are subconsciously superstitious, or maybe wary of them since black dogs are invariably portrayed as baddies in horror and ghost films. Many shelters go to great lengths to increase their desirability by dressing them in colourful bandannas to attract the attention of potential owners and encourage them to take a closer look.

❁❁ CANINE COMMUTER ❁❁

When Sixty, a four-year-old greyhound cross was left on her own for the night by her owner, she wasn't too thrilled about it. Using her initiative, she set out to rejoin him, showing up at 3am the following morning at the home of her master's sister-in-law, 20 Km away. As she didn't appear to be tired and wasn't dirty and travel stained after her journey, it was assumed that she took her usual route – by Barcelona commuter train.

❁❁ DOGGY PLACES 2 ❁❁

Dogger Bank is a large sandbank situated in a shallow area of the North Sea off the eastern coast of England; the name is derived from the old Dutch word 'dogge' meaning fishing boat. The largest earthquake ever recorded in the UK occurred under the bank in 1931, measuring 6.1 on the Richter scale.

 A dog is for life, not just for Christmas.
Dogs Trust slogan

❁❁ PDSA FACTS ❁❁

- The PDSA is the largest private employer of fully qualified vets and veterinary nurses in Europe.
- Each year 1.3 million treatments are provided.
- More than 4,650 animals are seen each working day.
- The charity employs 230 vets and 257 veterinary nurses.
- The average cost of treatment for each pet is £143.

GROMIT: SUPERSTAR

Gromit, the smart canine sidekick of inventor Wallace, was voted British Dog of the Century in 2000, seeing off fierce opposition from the likes of the Blue Peter dogs and Dougal from the Magic Roundabout. The Plasticene hound was also instrumental in helping creator Nick Park win 3 Oscars.

ON THE NOSE

Although rudimentary gas masks for dogs had been made by several companies during the First World War, they were only introduced for British dogs during World War II after the capture of certain documents revealed that German dogs were equipped with them. The Chemical Weapons Unit at Porton Down in Wiltshire were asked to devise something suitable, and having done so, the new gas masks were tested on 120 dogs. Most were easily coaxed into wearing them, but according to reports, one of the dogs initially became 'obstreperous and refused to wear any respirator' although eventually he was 'persuaded to wear one satisfactorily ie without wanting to bite the handler'.

PRESIDENTIAL POOCHES 13

Spot is the only dog to have lived at the White House under two different presidential administrations. One of the puppies of George Bush's Springer Spaniel Millie, he was born there in 1989 and given as a gift to son George W. Bush; he died, aged 14 at the White House.

CARROT OR NO CARROT

Modern, humane and effective dog training is based on 'positive reinforcement' – a pleasant reward for an action, such as the dog sitting on command and then receiving a treat, toy, praise or a pat. Every time the dog does something we find desirable it gets something it finds rewarding; if the action asked for doesn't happen, then no reward is given. In other words, rather than a 'carrot or stick' attitude, it is more a case of 'carrot or no carrot'. Obviously however, it is important to try and set up training in such a way as to enable the dog to succeed as often as possible; where a more complicated behaviour is required, this may involve breaking it down into smaller, easy steps, each of which leads in turn to the eventual finished behaviour.

✤✤ DOGGY PLACES 3 ✤✤

Hound Tor is a large and impressive tor on Dartmoor. Legend has it that it was created when a huntsman and his pack of hounds disrupted a coven of witches whilst chasing a hare. In revenge, one of the witches turned herself into a hare and first led both huntsman and hounds into a bog, and then transformed them into stone – the huntsman himself is located about a mile away, and known as 'Bowerman's Nose'

✤✤ ALL AT SEA ✤✤

When Todd, a two-year-old Labrador fell overboard from his owner's boat in 2002, he showed a remarkable sense of direction, if not a great deal of commonsense. When the accident happened, the boat was just one mile away from the Isle of Wight; but instead of swimming towards land, Todd set off in the opposite direction. What was more, he wasn't wearing his usual orange lifejacket, as due to the heat of the day, it had been taken off. Fearing the worst, his distraught owner sent out radio messages asking other boat crews to keep an eye out for the dog, and then spent four hours searching himself before stopping, convinced that he had drowned. Incredibly, after swimming against strong currents and managing to avoid ferries, tankers, ocean liners and yachts, Todd staggered ashore six hours later, having crossed ten miles of one of the busiest waterways. Still heading in the direction of home, he was discovered in a state of exhaustion soon after, and taken to a local vet who was able to identify him from his microchip and reunite him with his delighted owner.

WHO NEEDS PARTIES?

Actress Renee Zellweger was renowned for her devotion to her dog Dylan, a Golden Retriever/collie cross; after acquiring him as a puppy in 1988 he accompanied her everywhere, becoming quite at home on set wherever she was working. He gained his chance to appear in front of the cameras rather than behind them during the filming of 'Nurse Betty', playing the part of a 'seeing-eye' dog. Originally, Renee hadn't planned on getting a dog at all: when she visited Austin Animal Shelter, it was in search of a cat – but then Dylan emerged from a group of gambolling puppies and rested his muzzle on her foot. Renee felt a dog was too much responsibility and that she wouldn't have enough time, but Dylan had other ideas, and when she moved off, made his point by following and sitting firmly on her foot. When Renee was nominated for an Academy Award in 2003 Dylan was by this time becoming elderly and in ill health; after the ceremony the combination of a torn dress and concern about Dylan made her decide to return home to check on her pet before changing and going on to the attendant parties. Finding that he had been ill in several rooms, she changed her mind about going out again, staying in instead to clean up, bathe Dylan and spend the rest of the night comforting him. Sadly, Dylan passed on in November of the same year.

*The gift which I am sending you is called a dog,
and is in fact the most precious and
valuable possession of mankind.*
Theodorus Gaza

PDSA

While visiting the poor in London's East End, Maria Dickin was appalled by the dreadful poverty and living conditions she witnessed – and equally horrified by the sight of their animals suffering in silence when the owners couldn't afford veterinary care. Haunted by the problem she determined to do something about it and after a long and difficult struggle to acquire funding she was finally able to open her first 'People's Dispensary for Sick Animals of the Poor' on the 17th November, 1917. Encouraged by a sign outside which read 'Bring your sick animals. Do not let them suffer. All animals treated. All treatment free' owners overcame their initial suspicions and a trickle of clients rapidly became a flood and soon larger premises were required to accommodate treatment of over

100 animals a day. Dreaming of reaching out to animals all over the country, Maria converted a horse drawn caravan into a mobile dispensary and accompanied by a vet, travelled the length and breadth of Britain, treating animals and setting up clinics along the way. By 1923 there were 16 dispensaries, and the first overseas dispensary had been set up in Tangiers. Today there are 43 PDSA Pet Aid hospitals and 4 PDSA PetAid branches around the UK which provide a range of medical and surgical services for sick and injured pets; treatment is free for eligible clients, but all are encouraged to contribute whatever they can afford towards the cost, in order to help the charity to continue it's work.

He is gentle, he is kind –
I shall never, never find
A better friend than old dog Tray.
Stephen Collins Foster

HAIR OF THE DOG

It was once a popular belief that taking a few hairs from a dog which had bitten you and applying them to the injury would help to heal the wound. By mediaeval times taking a 'hair of the dog' was more likely to refer to a hangover; it was thought that the best cure was a drink of the same potion which had made you ill in the first place. The first mention of this phrase occurs in 1546 in John Heywood's Proverbs: "I pray thee, let me and my fellow have a haire of the dog that bit us last night, and bitten were we both to the braine aright."

BACK TO THE FRONT

When Private James Brown was posted to France in 1914 with his regiment, the 1st North Staffordshire, he had to leave behind his dog Prince, an Irish Terrier. Disconsolate at the absence of his master, Prince disappeared shortly after, and Brown's wife had the unenviable task of having to write and tell her husband the news that his beloved dog had gone missing. But by the time her letter arrived, Prince had already been reunited with his owner in the trenches; somehow he had managed to travel over 200 miles through the South of England, crossed the English Channel, and then walked across 60 miles of battlefield to reach his master's front line position at Armentieres.

CARTOON CAPERS

Pluto: Mickey Mouse's dog was named after the dwarf planet which had just been discovered.

Snoopy: the Beagle with the Walter Mitty complex in the Peanuts cartoon strip made his first appearance in 1950, first walked upright in 1956, and was first animated in the mid-1960's

Huckleberry Hound: the blue dog appeared in the first animated show to win an Emmy

Fred Basset: appearing in an animated TV series in 1970, Fred first appeared as a cartoon strip in The Daily Mail, modelled on cartoonist Alex Graham's own dog Freda. Freda was supposedly a gift following complaints that his early drawings didn't look much like a Basset.

Gnasher: pet dog of comic strip and animation character Dennis the Menace, he is supposedly an Abyssinian Wire-haired Tripehound.

Scooby Doo: originally called Too Much, and playing the bongos in a band called Mysteries Five, the ghost busting Great Dane was rewritten to become Scooby Doo after the executive in charge of developing the programme heard the 'doo-be-doo-be-doo' refrain in a Sinatra song.

Droopy: low key but persistent and shrewd Basset Hound with a surprising amount of strength when annoyed; made a cameo appearance in the film 'Who framed Roger Rabbit?'

Goofy: first called 'Dippy Dawg', it wasn't until his seventh outing that he finally became 'Goofy' – Walt Disney apparently hated the character.

Muttley: the self-centred dog with the unforgettable wheezy laugh.

Roobarb: lovable green dog with a wobbly look because of crude animation due to a tight budget – but which produced a distinctive look and became a cult classic.

 A dog is one of the remaining reasons why some people can be persuaded to go for a walk.
O A Battista

INDIANA HOUND

George Lucas' dog Indiana not only provided the inspiration for the name of Indiana Jones in the trilogy of films about the whip-cracking archaeologist, but also for the character of the hairy Wookie in his earlier triumph, Star Wars.

✿ ✿ THE CREATION OF DOGS AND CATS ✿ ✿

A newly discovered chapter in the Book off Genesis has provided the answer to the question 'Where do pets come from?'

Adam said, 'Lord, when I was in the garden, you walked with me every day. Now I do not see you any more. I am lonesome here and it is difficult for me to remember how much you love me.'

And God said 'No problem. I will create a companion for you that will be with you forever and who will be a reflection of my love for you so that you will love me even when you cannot see me. Regardless of how selfish or childish or unlovable you may be, this new companion will accept you as you are and will love you as I do in spite of yourself.

And God created a new animal to be a companion for Adam. And it was a good animal. And God was pleased. And the new animal was pleased to be with Adam and wagged its tail.

And Adam said, 'Lord, I have already named all the animals in the Kingdom and I cannot think of a name for this new animal.'

And God said, 'No problem. Because I have created this new animal to be a reflection of my love for you his name will be a reflection of my own name, and you will call him Dog.

And Dog lived with Adam and was a companion to him and loved him. And Adam was comforted. And God was pleased. And Dog was content and wagged his tail.

After a while, it came to pass that Adam's guardian angel came to the Lord and said, 'Lord, Adam has become filled with pride. He struts and preens like a peacock and he believes he is worthy of adoration. Dog has indeed taught him that he is loved, but perhaps too well.'

And God said, 'No problem. I will create for him a companion who will be with him forever and who will see him as he is. The companion will remind him of his limitations, so he will know that he is not always worthy of adoration.'

And God created Cat to be a companion to Adam. And Cat would not obey Adam. And when Adam gazed into Cat's eyes, he was reminded that he was not the Supreme Being. And Adam learned humility.

And God was pleased. And Adam was greatly improved. And Dog was happy and wagged his tail.

And Cat didn't care one way or another.

> *Today we are all thinking about what each of us can do towards making the world a better place for every man, woman and child to live in. We must not forget to include animals in our programme, they too must have a better world to live in.*
> Maria Dickin

❖ WESTMINSTER DOG OF THE YEAR ❖

This is a light-hearted competition, organised jointly by Dogs Trust and the Kennel Club, and which has been running since 1993. It's open to dogs from both Houses and all parties, with the title being judged on good deeds and personality rather than pawlitics. Aimed at promoting the special relationship between dogs and owners and to promote responsible ownership, previous winners have included a blind dog and one which raised the alarm when a fire started, probably saving lives in the process.

In recent years, the results have been

2006: Tag, a German Shepherd owned by Labour MP Eric Martlow
2005: Torres, a pug belonging to Conservative MP Tony Baldry
2004: Zack, a Bedlington Terrier owned by Labour MP Vera Baird
2003: Lulu, a Newfoundland belonging to Conservative MP Roger Gale
2002: Bippy, a Jack Russell owned by Lord Williams, leader of the House of Lords

❖ ISLAND OF DOGS ❖

The Canary Islands weren't named for the little yellow songbird, but after a breed of large dogs. The Latin name was Canariae Insulae, meaning 'Island of Dogs'.

10 WAYS TO SUPPORT A CANINE CHARITY

- *Make a money donation.*
- *Apply for a credit card – some animal charities operate credit card schemes with every transaction you make helping to generate funds.*
- *Sponsor a long term canine resident or a kennel at a shelter. This can also make a terrific gift for an animal loving friend who has everything.*
- *Volunteer your time as a walker, kennel hand, or fundraiser at a rescue centre. Or maybe you have a special skill you could offer for free and which would be helpful, such as website design?*
- *Recycle unwanted gifts by donating them as raffle prizes or for resale on stalls.*
- *Buy cards and gifts from charity catalogues.*
- *Buy an extra pack of dog food each week, fortnight or month, to give to a charity.*
- *Organise a sponsored 'something' to help raise funds.*
- *Items such as used postage stamps, foreign coins, old mobile phones, and even old printer cartridges are used by some charities to help raise revenue – find out what things are wanted, and encourage friends to help you collect them.*
- *Ask for a collecting box you can keep at home and put your loose change in it. The pennies will soon mount up, and every single one can help make a difference.*

SAND SOUNDS

Barking Sands is a beach on the island of Kauai in the Pacific Ocean, and currently used as a rocket launch site for the US Navy. Said to have been discovered in 1850 it gets its name from the white sand which when very dry, is supposed to make a noise similar to a dog barking when two handfuls are clapped together.

No matter how little money and how few possessions you own, having a dog makes you rich.
Louis Sabin

"GET A DOG..."

US President Harry Truman's advice to political hopefuls was that they should get a dog as it was likely that it would be their only friend in Washington.

WOOD GREEN ANIMAL SHELTER

Begun by Louisa Snow to help the plight of abandoned and injured animals on the streets of London following World War I, Wood Green has been rescuing and rehoming animals since 1924. In 1933 Dr Margaret Young became involved with the charity and before long the small London house where it had all started became too small and a farm purchased in Hertfordshire to accommodate the increasing numbers. A third site has since been added in Cambridgeshire; over 6,000 animals are taken in by the charity each year.

A minister was asked to dinner by one of his church members.
He knew she was a bad housekeeper but agreed.
When he sat down at the table, he noticed that the dishes were the dirtiest that he had ever seen in his life.
"Were these dishes ever washed?" he asked his hostess, running his fingers over the grit and grime.
She replied,"They're as clean as soap and water could get them".
He felt a bit uncomfortable, but blessed the food anyway and started eating. It was really delicious and he said so, despite the dirty dishes.
When dinner was over, the hostess took the dishes outside and yelled, "Here Soap! Here Water!"

MUSHING TERMS

Drivers of dog teams are often referred to as 'mushers' – the word probably derived from the word 'marche' (go, run) used by the early French explorers. Rather than shouting 'Mush!' to encourage their dogs onwards, modern drivers are more likely to use the following command words

Hike! – Go!

Gee – turn right

Haw – turn left

Easy – slow down

Whoa – stop

On by – keep going past another team, or other distraction

YEAR OF THE DOG

Each of the 12 years in the Chinese lunar calendar is named after an animal, including the Dog. According to legend, before departing from earth the Lord Buddha summoned all the animals. But only twelve came to bid him farewell, so as a reward he named a year after each one in the order they arrived. The Chinese believe that the animal which rules the year someone is born in has a profound influence on personality, saying 'This is the animal that hides in your heart'. Dog people are honest and faithful to those they love, but tend to worry overmuch and are prone to find fault with others. Career-wise they make ideal secret agents or business people. Recent Dog years are: 1934, 1946, 1958, 1970, 1982, 1994 and 2006

RECORD FENCE

The Dog (or Dingo) Fence in Australia is the longest fence in the world; started in 1880 and finished in 1885 it runs for 5,320 Km, is 6 ft (180cm) high, made of wire mesh and extends 1 ft (30cm) underground. Originally built to be a rabbit proof fence, in 1914 it was converted into dog-proof fence instead, in an attempt to protect sheep flocks by keeping dingoes out of the south-east part of the continent where they had already been largely exterminated. Ironically enough, it has been suggested that the large kangaroo population inside the fence which competes for food with the sheep is largely due to lack of dingo predation; consequently stocking rates are lower with the fence than they would be without it.

POINTY NAMES

Sighthounds are those members of the hound group who, as the name implies, hunt by sight rather than scent. Non-pedigree sighthounds include

LURCHERS:
crosses between a sighthound and any other non-sighthound; traditionally one which is a herding dog such as a collie

LONGDOGS:
crosses between two sighthounds

WHIRRIER:
a cross between a whippet and a terrier

These are all types, rather than breeds, and so are not recognized by the Kennel Club.

❉❉ WACKY DOGGY GADGETS 8 ❉❉

Patents exist for various gadgets including earrings for poodles (ear piercing required), a doggy dust cover, a talking dog collar, and an appliance for 'hygienic removal of dog excrement in order to prevent soiling of parks and play areas' – a plastic tube attached at one end to a suction device, and at the other to the dog's rear end.

He wandered a little round our legs,
neither wagging his tail nor licking at our hands;
then he looked up and my companion said:
He's an angel!
John Galsworthy

❉❉ DRINKING HOLES ❉❉

It was Richard II who decreed that all public houses must show a sign outside or else forfeit their ale, and ever since it has been traditional for each pub to display a pictorial interpretation as well as its name. In the days when most people were illiterate, this made it easy for everyone to identify different hostelries; over the years dogs were often a popular choice, reflecting their role in hunting, sporting and other country pursuits. The commonest doggy names are 'The Dog', 'Dog and Duck', 'Dog and Partridge' and 'Dog and Gun'. Unusual ones include 'Dog and Doublet', 'Dog and Dumplings', 'The Mad Dog at Odell', 'Dog and Trumpet' and 'Dog and Truck'

❉❉ COCKNEY RHYMING SLANG ❉❉

CHERRY HOGG:

dog

DOG AND BONE:

phone

DOG'S EYE:

meat pie

DOG'S KNOB:

job

DOG FOR PM

If you've ever thought that the country is going to the dogs you aren't alone; when UK owners were polled by a pet food company to discover which breed of dog they thought would make the best job of running things, the Labrador came out top, followed by the German Shepherd and Border Collie. When it came to finding the best canine leader of the Opposition, the Dobermann clinched the top spot, followed by the Bulldog and German Shepherd. Surprisingly, the list also included the Miniature Poodle and Yorkshire Terrier amongst its candidates.

> *If you pick up a starving dog and make him prosperous,*
> *he will not bite you; that is the principal difference*
> *between a dog and a man.*
> Mark Twain

POLITICAL PET

Canadian Prime Minister William Lyon MacKenzie King was said to have consulted his pet dog Pat for political advice

The following ad appeared in a newspaper:
SINGLE BLACK FEMALE
SBF Seeks Male companionship, ethnicity unimportant. I'm a svelte good looking girl who LOVES to play. I love: long walks in the woods, hunting, camping, riding in your pickup truck, fishing trips, cozy winter nights spent lying by the fire. Candlelight dinners will have me eating out of your hand. Rub me the right way and watch me respond. I'll be at the front door when you get home from work, wearing only what nature gave me. Kiss me and I'm yours.
Call 555-2121 and ask for Daisy.

(The phone number was the Humane Society and Daisy was an eight week old black Labrador Retriever.)

WINNIE'S POODLE

Sir Winston Churchill's poodle Rufus led a cherished and pampered life; at mealtimes he joined the rest of the family in the dining room. A cloth was ceremoniously spread for him on the Persian carpet next to his master's chair, and a butler served his meal.

One anecdote has it that whilst watching the film 'Oliver Twist' one evening at Chequers, Churchill reached across to cover Rufus' eyes at the point when Bill Sikes was about to try and drown his dog. "Don't look now, dear" he murmured, "I'll tell you about it after."

Both Rufus and his successor, Rufus II are buried at Churchill's residence at Chartwell, just beyond the croquet lawn, and marked by two flagstones.

RSPCA

Launched in 1824 with the humbler name of the 'Society for Prevention of Cruelty to Animals' one of the 22 founder members included 'Humanity Dick', the MP Richard Martin who had steered the first anti-cruelty bill through Parliament. The first national animal protection society in the world, it aims are to prevent cruelty, promote kindness and alleviate the suffering of animals. Initially it was a battle to change the general attitude towards animals, but by 1840 the Society was held in such high regard that Queen Victoria gave her permission to prefix its name with the word 'Royal'. By 1842 news of its work had spread outside London and in response to requests branches were gradually set up around the country; today there are 174 branches in England and Wales, plus 40 clinics and 36 animal centres.

❧ RSPCA FACTS ❧

- The charity's annual running costs are £82 million.
- There are 323 uniformed RSPCA inspectors and 146 Animal Collection Officers.
- Someone dials the RSPCA national cruelty and advice line for help every 25 seconds.
- In 2005 69,900 animals were rehomed , of which 19,000 were dogs.

❧ MILES OF SMILES ❧

When Jennifer Kirkwood's cherished Boxer was stolen, she wasn't prepared to sit around waiting and hoping that maybe she would either be returned or would escape to find her own way home. Together with her family, all Jennifer's spare time was spent searching the area around her home; finally after covering 5,000 miles during the two month search, she was reunited with her pet when she was spotted at a campsite.

❧ CEMETERY OF THE YEAR ❧

Along with nominations for human cemeteries, one for pets in Flintshire, UK was short listed for a Cemetery of the Year Award.

❧ PET PASSPORTS ❧

On Monday 28th February 2000, a five-year-old pug named Frodo Baggins made history by becoming the first dog to enter the UK under the 'Pet Passport' scheme, which allowed pets for the first time in nearly 100 years to travel from abroad (albeit only certain specified countries) without the need to undergo six months quarantine. He was accompanied by 15 other dogs, although not by Claude, the Basset Hound owned by Lady Fretwell and credited as being the inspiration who had led her to battle for the scheme to be introduced. Recovering from surgery after swallowing a lead, his long awaited place was taken instead by a Labrador belonging to his owner's daughter.

Although Frodo was officially the first dog allowed into the UK with a Pet Passport, he wasn't in fact the first to enter legally since 1901 when the quarantine laws were introduced to prevent the spread of rabies. That honour went to Casiss, a Pyrenean Mountain dog belonging to William Dowell; Prime Minister Tony Blair waived the quarantine laws to allow the pet to accompany her owner in 1999 on his return from France where he had been receiving cancer treatment and a kidney transplant.

❧ LONG HAUL CANINE ❧

The first long haul canine passenger on the Pet Travel scheme was Vickie, a Yorkie from Japan; the first dog on the scheme to die from a disease contracted abroad was an 11-year-old Westie called Bliss. Despite receiving tick treatment before re-entering the UK, Bliss died of Babesia canis, carried by ticks.

> *Sharing your home with a rescue dog has to be one of life's greatest gifts. They know you have helped them. And you know that they have helped you too.*
> Anthony Head

❧ FIRST FLIGHT ❧

Canine actor Rin Tin Tin's son, Rin Tin Tin jr was the first dog to make a commercial plane flight, in 1933.

❧ DOG RESCUES ❧

A survey carried out for the Dogs Trust revealed that of the 105,201 stray dogs rounded up in the UK by local authorities during 2005, nearly 8,000 were destroyed for want of a home. The final tally is actually likely to be far, far higher than this as 34 per cent of the authorities contacted failed to respond, and the figures don't include those put to sleep by vets and other animal welfare organisations which don't operate a 'no kill' policy.

❧ THE INCREDIBLE AUTHOR ❧

Inspired by stories of dogs travelling great distances to find their owners, Canadian author Sheila Burnford wrote one of the great classic animal stories of all time, 'The Incredible Journey' first published in 1961. Set in Ontario, it tells the story of how Luath, a young Labrador, Bodger an old English Bull Terrier, and Tao, a Siamese cat journey together across wild country, facing many perils together to eventually and unexpectedly be reunited with their family. A film version was released by Walt Disney in 1963, and remade in 1993 as Homeward Bound: The Incredible Journey, with a further sequel, Homeward Bound II: Lost in San Francisco appearing in 1996.

✤✤ WHO WROTE THAT? ✤✤

Gone to 'Rainbow Bridge' is a term often used by owners whose pets have died, after the title of a popular poem thought to have been written sometime between 1980 and 1992. It is probably one of the best known pieces of pet loss literature, having been reproduced countless times in books, greeting cards, posters, and on the Internet, and is generally attributed to 'Author unknown' or 'Anonymous'. Although the original authorship remains uncertain, there are in fact three main contenders who all claim to have written it, including grief counsellors Paul C Dahm and Dr Wallace Sife, and William N Britton, a co-founder of Companion Golden Retriever Rescue in Utah.

Whoever the author, it is nevertheless a sweet and touching tribute which rarely fails to touch the emotions

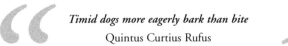

> *Timid dogs more eagerly bark than bite*
> Quintus Curtius Rufus

✤✤ RAINBOW BRIDGE ✤✤

Just this side of heaven is a place called Rainbow Bridge. When an animal dies that has been especially close to someone here, that pet goes to Rainbow Bridge. There are meadows and hills for all our special friends so they can run and play together. There is plenty of food, water and sunshine, and our friends are warm and comfortable.

All the animals who had been ill and old are restored to health and vigour. Those who were hurt or maimed are made whole and strong again, just as we remember them in our dreams of days and times gone by. The animals are happy and content, except for one small thing; they each miss someone very special to them, who had to be left behind.

They all run and play together, but the day comes when one suddenly stops and looks into the distance. His bright eyes are intent. His eager body quivers. Suddenly he begins to run from the group, flying over the green grass, his legs carrying him faster and faster.

You have been spotted, and when you and your special friend finally meet, you cling together in joyous reunion, never to be parted again. The happy kisses rain upon your face; your hands again caress the beloved head, and you look once more into the trusting eyes of your pet, so long gone from your life but never absent from your heart.

Then you cross Rainbow Bridge together ...

(Author unknown)

LEADING THE WAY

The only dogs allowed inside the Palace of Westminster are guide dogs and sniffer dogs who help with security sweeps. MP and ex-Cabinet Minister David Blunkett's guide dogs have of course, become a familiar sight by his side; his first dog Ruby was succeeded by Teddy who was the first dog to be allowed into the Chambers of the House of Commons. Following Teddy was Offa, a Golden Retriever/German Shepherd cross who unfortunately had to retire due to illness; Lucy stepped ably into his pawprints for the next ten years. Before handing over to her successor Sadie in 2003, Lucy had lead an exemplary life, only slipping up a couple of times, once when she vomited and on another occasion when during William Hague's final prime minister's questions, she got up, shook herself and walked out.

THE BEST PRESENT OF ALL

When Barry the German Shepherd grew too large for the flat where he lived in Italy, his owner regretfully sold him. A little while later the owner moved to West Germany and was astounded when on Christmas Eve one year and 1200 miles later, he found Barry whimpering on his doorstep.

The dog's kennel is no place to keep a sausage
Danish proverb

THE BLUE CROSS

Founded in 1897, the charity was originally called 'Our Dumb Friends League', and by 1898 had expanded amazingly to 22 branches in the UK, and by 1906 had opened it's first animal hospital offering care for animals whose owners couldn't afford veterinary attention. The charity's aims include ensuring the welfare of animals by providing practical care and promoting responsible ownership, doing so through education, rescuing and rehoming at the 11 adoption centres around the country, and treating pets of owners who cannot afford private veterinary care.

In conjunction with the Society for Companion Animal Studies (SCAS) the Blue Cross Pet Bereavement Support Service also offers support for bereaved owners via telephone or email.

BLUE CROSS FACTS

- In 1918 a quarantine kennel was set up for dogs brought back to the UK by members of the armed forces returning after being overseas during the First World War.
- The charity was the first to employ an animal behaviourist to assist owners with problem pets.
- There are four animal hospitals, three in London and one in Yorkshire.

ROVER'S RETURN

If you find a stray dog, by law you must either

- Return it to the owner, if known, or arrange for your local Council's Dog Welfare Officer to take charge of it, or take it to the nearest Police station if out of normal Council working hours.
- If, after 7 days, the owner of a stray dog has not come forward, ownership may be transferred to someone else, and the original owner's claim is likely to come to an end.
- If you find a stray dog and would like to keep it you must inform your local Council that you have found a dog and wish to keep it, providing a full description. In return you will be given a certificate to confirm that you have reported it; without this document you could be accused of dog theft.
- Return the dog to the owner if it is claimed within 30 days. You can ask the owner to reimburse you for any reasonable costs incurred for looking after it.

LAST RESTING PLACES

There are various places in which a dog may be buried. We are thinking now of a setter, whose coat was flame in the sunshine and who, so far as we are aware, never entertained a mean or unworthy thought.

This setter is buried beneath a cherry tree, under four feet of garden loam, and at it's proper season the cherry tree strews petals on the green lawn of his grave. Beneath a cherry tree, or an apple, or any flowering shrub of the garden, is an excellent place to bury a dog. Beneath such trees, such shrubs, he slept in the drowsy summer, or gnawed at a flavoured bone, or lifted his head to challenge some strange intruder.

These are good places, in life or in death. Yet it is a small matter, and it touches sentiment more than anything else. For if the dog be well remembered, if sometimes he leaps through your dreams actual as in life, eyes kindling, questing, asking, laughing, begging, it matters not at all where that dog sleeps and at last. On a hill where the wind is unrebuked, and the trees are roaring, or beside a stream he knew in puppyhood, or somewhere in the flatness of a pasture land, where most exhilarating cattle graze. It is all one to the dog, and all one to you, and nothing is gained, and nothing is lost – if memory lives.

But there is one best place to bury a dog. One place that is best of all. If you bury him in this spot, he will come to you when you call – come to you over the grim, dim frontier of death, and down the well-remembered path, and to your side again. And though you call a dozen living dogs to heel, they shall not growl at him, nor resent his coming, for he belongs there. People may scoff at you, who see no lightest blade of grass bent by his footfall, who hear no whimper, people who may never really have had a dog. Smile at them, for you shall know something that is hidden from them, and which is well worth the knowing.

The one best place to bury a good dog is in the heart of his master.

(Ben Hur Lampman)

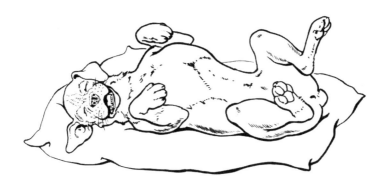

* INDEX *

A

accident prone dogs 103
advertisements 126, 217, 220
age in 'dog years' 31
ageing, signs of 88
agility 64-6
Agincourt, battle of (1415) 45
Ahern, Bertie 161
Alaskan Malamutes 22
Alden, Timothy 191
Alexander the Great 22
allergies 77
alternative medicine 105-7
amputee dogs 132 3
Amundsen, Roald 92-3, 213
anal sacs 92
Andrex puppies 220
Animals in War memorial 13
Anne, Princess 69
answering machine messages
 151
Antarctic programmes 14
antifreeze 90
Anubis, Egyptian god 198
April Fool's Day hoaxes 109-
 10
Argos, legendary dog 54
artificial respiration 9-10
Ashley Whippet Invitational
 40
assistance dogs 67, 129, 206,
 210
Association of Pet Dog
 Trainers 78
Australia, Dog (Dingo) Fence
 240
authors, dogs as 94-5

B

Baker, Matt 229

Bally Shannon (Irish
 Wolfhound) 51
Barbie and Tanner 157
barking 14, 214
Barking Sands 238
Barry, Dave 153
Barrymore, Drew 125
Barry (St Bernard) 210, 213
Battersea Dogs and Cats
 Home 35, 37, 44, 69
Battista, O.A. 235
Bedford, Duchess of 199
beds, dogs sharing with
 humans 175
Beecher, Henry Ward 35
behavioural problems 47
Benchley, Robert 77
Bergin, Bonnie 86
best friend, being your dog's
 161
the Bible 8
Bichon Frise 73
Billings, Josh 161, 190
birthday parties for dogs 154-5
black dogs 230
 phantom 59-60
Bloni (Hitler's dog) 108
bloodhounds 26, 68, 127,
 173, 192
blood transfusions 148-9
Blue Cross 247-8
Blue Peter dogs 13, 63, 87,
 109, 144, 186, 229
Blunkett, David 247
blushing 128
Boatswain (Lord Byron's dog)
 58
Bonaparte, Napoleon 49, 64
Bone, Alistair 43
books, dogs in 82-3

Bosch, Michael 209
Boucicault, Dion 222
Boye (dog of Prince Rupert)
 53-4
brainiest breeds 58
brain workouts 151
Braun, Eva 21, 194
breath freshening 157
breathing
 checking respiratory rate
 146
 signs of distress 49
breeds
 biggest 72
 crossbreeds 27
 facing extinction 50
 most popular 110
 named after people 22
 names of 523
 origin of 18, 100
 pedigrees 27
 smallest 83
 top 10 brainiest 58
 UK breed groups 46-7
Brillantini, Gianfranco 224-5
Brough, Edwin 68
Browning, Elizabeth Barrett
 86-7
Bullock, Sandra 82
Burden, Charles 218
Burnford, Sheila, '*The
 Incredible Journey*' 245
Burns, Robert 196
Burrell, Paul 69
burrs 49
Bush, George 95, 231
Bush, George W. 231
Buster (Paul O'Grady's dog)
 218
Butcher's Great North Dog

Walk 25
Butler, Samuel 27
Byron, Lord 58, 139

C

Caesar (Edward VII's dog) 180
Cambridge, Ada 68
Canary Islands 237
Canine Partners for
    Independence 67
cardio pulmonary resuscitation
    (CPRP) 10
Carnarvon, Lord 59
Carter, Howard 59
Carter, Jimmy 53
cartoon dogs 235
car travel 166
cats 26, 236-7
cattle, attacks by 112-13
Cavalier King Charles Spaniels
    62, 170
celebrities
    canine custody cases 156
    dog owners 22, 95, 99,
    218-19, 233
    singer's dogs 202
Celebrity Dog School 44
celebrity names for dogs 179
cemeteries for dogs 90, 94, 97,
    244
Cerberus, dog of the
    Underworld 198
Chanda Leah (world's smartest
    dog) 35
Chandler, Scott 28
charities, ways to support 238
Charles II, King 22, 112, 170
Charles I, King 152-3
Charles, Prince of Wales 94
Che Foo (dog of the Duchess
    of Bedford) 199
Cherokee legend 61

chewing 116
Chihuahuas 83, 219
China 64, 157
    law on dogs in 155
    Year of the Dog 240
Chips (US war dog) 207
chocolate poisoning 143
Churchill, Winston 33, 99,
    153, 213, 243
Chyna (German Shepherd) 62
Clary, Julian 44
clicker training 151
Clinton, Bill 23
cloning dogs 16
cocking legs 52
Cockney rhyming slang 241
Coco (Cavalier King Charles
    Spaniel) 62
collars 19, 130, 201
companion dog shows 28
computers 29
confirmation terms 141
Connolly, Billy 156
Coolidge, C.M. 145
Cooper, Jilly 153
Corbett, David 221
Corgis 68, 69, 115
Corinth 193
Coton de Tulear dogs 191
Cott, Gerry 207
Cracknell, James 221
creation of dogs 236-7
crossbreeds 27
Crufts Dog Show 30, 47, 48,
    64, 215, 226
Cuchalainn, Irish hero 63
Custer, George Armstrong 32
custody battles for dogs 156,
    177
cuts and grazes 49

D

Dachshunds 204, 226
dancing with dogs 164-5
dangerous dogs 188
Dash (Queen Victoria's dog)
    62
dating agencies 40
death 90, 94, 96, 97, 100
    dog cemeteries 90, 94, 97,
    244
    and howling dogs 58-9
    last resting places 248-9
    Rainbow Bridge 246
dehydration 136
designer dogs 27, 42
dewclaws 167
Diana, Princess 69, 94
diary of a dog 81
Dickens, Charles 35
Dickin, Maria 208, 233-4, 237
Dickinson, Emily 25
Disc Dogs 45
Discover Dogs exhibition 28
divorce and dog custody 156,
    177
Dobermann Pinschers 22
dock jumping 41
Dog Days 131
dog food 149, 185
    bodyweight and capacity
    for 60
    keeping your dog slim 226
    liver bread 203
    storing 180-1
    treats 74, 188, 201
    and World War II 50
Dogger Bank 230
dog licences 160-1
dog persons 16-17
Dogs Trust 50, 215, 216, 226,
    230, 237, 245
doorbell for dogs 34

drug seizures by dogs 85
Dulux dogs 217
Dyer, Walter A. 228

E
ears 80, 97, 101
     long 52, 127
     shapes and descriptions
       127
Edward VIII, King 180
Egyptians, ancient 59
Eisenhower, Dwight 73
Elgar, Edward 72
Eliot, T.S. 158
Elizabeth II, Queen 68, 69,
     115
Endal (assistance dog) 67
Ephron, Norah 130
Eustis, Dorothy 33-4
exercise tips 36
extreme sports 41
eyes 80, 149-50
     failing eyesight 118-19
     shapes 152

F
feisty, origins of the word 219
fights, breaking up 113
films, dogs in 43-4, 79, 112,
     158, 169, 175, 195, 207,
     221, 233, 245
fire investigation 8, 40, 68
fireworks 179
first aid kits 135
Fisher, John 78
Fisher, Sandra 216
fleas 48, 72, 76-7
Flush (Elizabeth Barrett
     Browning's dog) 86-7
flyball 181-2
food see dog food
food detectors 134

foster mothers, dogs as 200,
     201
Foster, Stephen Collins 234
Frankland, Musgrave 142
Frederick the Great 130, 183
friend to the end stories 224-5
Frisbees 39-40, 45

G
gadgets 114, 145, 190, 204,
     241
Galsworthy, John 78, 100,
     162, 241
Gandhi, Mahatma 144
Garfield, James 193
Garm, dog of the Underworld
     198
gas masks for dogs 231
Gaza, Theodorus 233
Gazenko, Oleg 13
Gelert, Prince Llewelyn's dog
     168
German Shepherd dogs 226
gifts
     for dogs 154
     wrapping 116, 121
Goldsmith, Annabel 95
Goldsmith, Oliver 54, 147
grass eating 102
Great Danes 72
greetings cards 78
Greyfriars Bobby 97-8, 207
greyhounds 8, 130, 195
Gromit 231
grooming equipment 178
guide dogs for the blind 11,
     29, 33-4, 86, 199
     allergy friendly coats 42
     David Blunkett's dogs 247
     fundraising for 229
Guinefort, dog saint 174
Gula, healing goddess 57

gundogs 46
Gurt Dog of Somerset 60

H
haikus 71
hair types/styles 131, 144
Hannibal 43
Harding, Warren 58
Hattersley, Roy 95
Head, Anthony 216, 245
health benefits of dog
     ownership 162
healthcheck, five minute 80-1
hearing 101, 206
Hearing Dogs 186
heart rates 145, 172
heaven 196-7, 246
Henry VIII, King 43, 137, 228
Hill, Gene 74
Hilton, Paris 95, 121, 219
hip dysplasia 174
Hitler, Adolf 108, 166-7
HMV label 194
Hoagland, Edward 156
Hockney, David 86, 174
Hogarth, William 159
Hohrl, Ottmar, 'Wagner's Dog'
     73
holidays 184-5, 186, 188
holistic therapies 140
hook and loop tape 12
hounds 46
Hound Tor, Dartmoor 232
household hazards 189
house rules 189
howling dogs 58-9
hunting 192
Hurricane Katrina 114
hush puppies 224
Huxley, Aldous 218

I

ice balls 49
Ichigo, Japanese emperor 111
India 62, 63
insect stings 117
insults, doggy 227
insurance 108, 121
internet canine radio station 42
intestines 60
Irish Wolfhounds 72, 169-70
Isle of Dogs 228

J

Jack the Ripper 68
Jack Russel terriers 22
James II, King 170
James I, King 168
Jefferson, Thomas 167
Jerome K Jerome 148, 193
jogging 36
Johnson, Lyndon B. 157
Johnson, Samuel 86
Jonson, Ben 120
Josephine, Empress 64

K

Kafka, Franz 57
Kennedy, John F. 25
Kennel Club
    Activity Register 25, 165
    breed registration 18, 47
    Companion Dog Club 25
    dancing with dogs 164, 165
    endangered breeds list 50
    Good Citizen Gold Award 186
    origins 47
    schemes for pet owners 24
    Scruffs show 28
    Westminster Dog of the

Year show 237
Kimba 21
King Charles Spaniels 22, 112, 170
king, legend of dog as 72
Kipling, Rudyard 18, 136
Kirkwood, Jennifer 244
Kubla Khan 43

L

Labradoodles 27, 42
Laika (Russian space dog) 13, 25
Lamartine, Alphonse de 31
Landseer, Sir Edwin 62, 84
Lascaux cave paintings 74
Lassie 79
law on dogs 32, 45, 149, 152
    China 155
    controlling 172
    dog licences 160-1
    fouling 158-9, 170
    stray dogs 248
    United States 104-5
leads, extending or retractable 211
learning from your dog 206
Legh, Sir Piers 45
Lewis, Captain Meriwether 191
licking 75
Lincoln, Abraham 139, 208, 217
liquid medication 56-7
Lissette (Peter the Great's dog) 23
livesaving for dogs 8-10
Llewelyn, Prince 168-9
London, Jack 82
Longanis, Greg 207
Lowry, L.S. 159
Luath (Robert Burns's dog)

196
Lucas, George 235
Lump (Picasso's dog) 75
lumps and bumps 80
Luther, Martin 97

M

McCartney, Paul 203
MacKenzie King, William Lyon 242
McKinlay, President William 60
Madagascar 191
Madame Tussauds 220
man bites dog 109
Marco Polo 43
Markham, Joe 41
marriage to dogs 62
Marston Moor, Battle of (1644) 54
Martin, Richard 243
Marx, Groucho 10
Mary Queen of Scots 143
mastiffs 43, 45
Mastral, George de 12
Mayhew Animal Home 182
medicine 55-7
mercy dogs 51
Mesopotamia 57
Milky Way 61
millionaire dog hoax 222
missing dogs 103, 104, 120, 121
    returning home 194, 232
    reunited with owners 234, 244, 247
mobility problems 49
mongrels 19-20, 27
More, Sir Thomas 196
Moustache (war dog) 198
Mugford, Roger 11
mushing terms 239

music
  dancing with dogs 164-5
  for dogs 32, 42
  Elgar's *Enigma Variations* 72
  songs featuring dogs 74, 161
muzzles, emergency 137
Myburgh, Diana 175

N
nail clipping 138
names
  of breeds 52-3
  celebrity names for dogs 179
  changes 226
  doggy place names 122, 230, 231, 232, 238
  dog plant names 134
  of dogs 77, 152, 153
  pub signs 241
Napoleonic wars 198
National Canine Defence League 50, 215, 226
neutering 120
Nevil, Thomas 192
Newfoundland dogs 161, 190, 191
New Orleans 114
Newton, Sir Isaac 176
Nietzsche, F.W. 133
Nipper (HMV label dog) 194
Nixon, Richard M. 39, 157
Noah's Ark 57
Noakes, John 87
Nome, Great Race of Mercy to 212-13
Northern Ireland 160
noses 80, 104, 129
  colours 171

O
obesity in dogs 171
objects eaten by dogs 70
Odysseus 54
O'Grady, Paul 218
old dogs 12, 88, 142
Old English Sheepdogs 217
oldest dogs 14
Olympic mascot 14
101 Dalmatians 96
overweight dogs 162, 171
  keeping your dog slim 226

P
Paddy (Harold Wilson's dog) 192
paintings of dogs 62, 84, 145, 159
'Palm Dog' Trophy 175
panting 70-1
Parton, Allen 67, 169
pastoral dogs 46
PAT (Pets as Therapy) 137
Pavlov, Ivan 187
PDSA 230, 233-4
  Gold Medal 111, 129
pedigree dogs 27
Pekingese dogs 64
Pepys, Samuel 170
Peritas (dog of Alexander the Great) 22
Persia 55
Peter the Great, Tsar 23
Pet Passports 244
Pet Travel scheme 245
phantom black dogs 59-60
phrases and proverbs
  common doggy sayings 219
  doggy insults 227
  dog in the manger 223
  dogsbody 223
  hair of the dog 234

let sleeping dogs lie 224
raining cats and dogs 226
seeing a man about a dog 222
top dog 184
underdog 184
you don't keep a dog and bark yourself 224
pica 202
Picasso 75
pills, giving to dogs 55-7
place names 122, 230, 231, 232, 238
Plato 208
Pliny the Elder 138
police dogs 68, 140, 202, 229
politics 242, 247
poodles 144
poo eating 202
poop scooping, law on 158-9, 170
Pope, Alexander 53, 57, 201
pregnancy 102
Presley, Elvis 159
Prime Minister, dog for 242
property laws of dogs 213
proverbs see phrases and proverbs
pub signs 241
pugs 144
pulse rates 172
puppies
  development and growth 123-4, 125
  largest litter 28
purebred pedigree dogs 27
Pyrenean Mountain Dogs 167, 168

Q
Quintus Curtius Rufus 246

R

rabies 127
Rainbow Bridge 246
Ray, Mary 164
reading 86
reasons to have a dog 147,
  158, 165
recycled dog waste 154
rescue dogs 186, 209, 245
  black dogs 230
  famous owners of 44, 82,
    125, 166, 216
  greyhounds 195
  RSPCA Dog of the Year
    competition 228
responsible ownership 163
rewards, timing of 77
Rice, Marion 11
Richard II, King 241
Richthofen, Baron von 125
Rin Tin Tin 195, 198, 245
Rivers, Joan 205
road accidents 152
Rochester, John Wilmot, Lord
  11
Rogers, Will 214
Romans and dogs 7, 43, 45
Roosevelt, Franklin D. 99,
  211
Rossini, G. 84
royal family 69
RSPCA 243-4
  Dog of the Year
    competition 228
Rufus (dog of Winston
  Churchill) 243
Rupert of the Rhine, Prince
  53-4
Russian space dogs 13, 25

S

Sabin, Louis 238

St Bernards 158, 162, 210,
  213, 215
Samoyeds 22
Sam Simon Foundation 186
Satie, Erik 82
Scilly, Isles of 192
Scott, Robert Falcon 92, 93
Scott, Sir Walter 42, 62, 93
Scruffs dog show 28
scuba diving dogs 109
Seaman (Newfoundland dog)
  191
search and rescue dogs 8, 40,
  68
Shackleton, Ernest 35
shaggy dog stories 223
Shakespeare, William 14, 45,
  176
Shep (shepherd's dog) 221-2
shooting accidents 101
sick dogs 137
sighthounds 240
'The Simpsons' 186
Simpson, Wallis 144
Sirius 131
Skinner, B.F. 187
skipping dogs 35
skydiving dogs 31
smallest breed 83
smartest dog 35
smells 30, 120, 157
sniffer dogs 68, 85, 206, 221
snow balls 49
Snow, Louisa 239
Snuppy 16
songs featuring dogs 74, 161
South Pole expedition 92 3
space dogs 13, 25, 146
spaying 120
Staffordshire pottery dogs 76
Stallone, Sylvester 43-4
star signs 61

Stein, Alex 39-40
Steinbeck, John 124
Stevenson, Robert Louis 101
stolen dogs 70, 104
strange dogs, greeting 214
stray dogs and the law 248
superstitions 176
surfing 28-9
Swift, Jonathan 28, 123, 201
swimming safety 183

T

tail docking 7
tail shapes and descriptions 217
tail wagging 20 1, 126, 134,
  205
Tanner (Barbie's dog) 157
tapeworms 89, 92
taste buds 160
Taylor, Elizabeth 23, 79
Tealby, Mary 35, 69
teeth 80, 101, 126, 207
  brushing 173
television programmes 44, 78
temperature 172
  taking 145-6
Tennyson, Alfred, Lord 55
terriers 46
Thatcher, Margaret 161, 203
theft, protection from 215
therapy, pets as 137
Theron, Charlize 158
Thomson, Joseph 190
Thoreau, Henry David 154
Three Dog Night 180
thunderstorms 179
Thurber, James 39
Tibetan Terriers 177
ticks 48
Timberlake, Justin 218
Tiny Tim (racehorse) 170
Titanic survivors 103, 177-8

top dog 184
toy dogs 47
toys 41-2, 52, 190
  unsuitable for dogs 34
training 142, 202, 204
  origins of modern methods
    187
  positive reinforcement 231
  trainers/classes 78, 190, 204
  treats 201
travelling dogs 195, 230, 245
'Troilus and Crisedye'
  (Chaucer) 224
Truman, Harry 238
Twain, Mark 18, 90

U
underdog 184
United States
  9/11 dogs 40
  hush puppies 224
  presidential dogs 39, 53,
    73, 99, 116-17, 139,
    157, 167, 193, 203, 217,
    231
  Sam Simon Foundation
    186
  War Dog Fund 210-11
  weird US dog laws 104-5
unluckiest dog 100
utility breeds 46

V
vaccination 91
verbal commands
  giving 200
  number of 197
Veronese 74
Vest, George Graham 218, 221
veterinary schools 174
veterinary surgeons 138
Victoria, Queen 35, 62, 64,

144, 243
Vietnam war 110
Voltaire 94
votes for dogs 89

W
Wag and Bone Show 199
Wagner, Richard 73
Wagometer 11
walks
  making more interesting
    32-3
  ten things to check after
    walking 48-9
  world's largest dog walk 25
war dogs 43, 45, 59
  Army War Dog School 55
  Dickin Medal for 208
  First World War 51, 59,
    63, 162-3, 234
  Napoleonic wars 198
  Second World War 50, 54
    5, 126, 140, 174, 193,
    207, 208, 231
  US War Dog Fund 210-11
  Vietnam War 110
Warhol, Andy 174
war memorials 13, 63
Warren, Sir Charles 68
Washington, George 116-17
water 85-6, 136, 151
Watson, Sir William 89, 108
Watts, Isaac 175
weighing a dog 173
Westminster Dog of the Year
  show 237
Wharton, Edith 70
White, E.B. 178, 204
William III and Queen Mary
  144
Williams, Stephen 18
wills, dogs as beneficiaries of

96, 97, 175
Wilson, Harold 192
Wilson, Woodrow 204
Winfrey, Oprah 201
wisdom, canine 225
The Wizard of Oz 79
Woburn Abbey, Bedfordshire
  199
wolf ancestors 7
Wood Green Animal Shelter
  239
Woodhouse, Barbara 118, 217
Wookey Hole Caves, teddy
  bear collection 23
Woolf, Virginia 87
working dogs 46
World Cup trophy, recovery of
  stolen 221
world records
  bathing dogs 159
  dog on 'Death Row' 113
  high jump 153
  largest dog walk 25
  largest litter 28
  largest sit in 199
  longest ears 52
  longest human dog tunnel
    185
  longest jump 189
  longest tongue 129
  smallest dog 133
  smartest dog 35
  strongest dog 31
  strongest dog team 130
  weird 39
worms 89, 92, 93, 96, 97

Year of the Dog 240
Yorkshire Terriers 83

Z
Zellweger, Renee 233